The Baul Tradition

Sahaj Vision East & West

The Baul Tradition

Sahaj Vision East & West

M. Young

Hohm Press
Chino Valley, AZ

Layout and design: Becky Fulker, Kubera Book Design
Cover design: Zachary Parker

Library of Congress Cataloging-in-Publication Data

Young, M. (Mary), author.
  The Baul tradition : sahaj vision East and West / M. Young ; Foreword by Parvathy Baul.
      pages cm
  Includes bibliographical references.
  ISBN 978-1-935387-83-1 (trade paper : alk. paper)
  1. Bauls. 2. Spiritual life. 3. Music--Religious aspects. 4. Lozowick, Lee, 1943-2010. I. Title.
  BL1284.84.Y66 2014
  294.5'512--dc23
                          2014012874

Hohm Press
P.O. Box 4410
Chino Valley, AZ 86323
800-381-2700
http://www.hohmpress.com

This book was printed in the U.S.A. on recycled, acid-free paper using soy ink.

PERMISSIONS

The publisher and the author acknowledge that efforts were made to obtain permissions for quoting Sri Anirvan, *Letters from a Baul,* and Swami Ramdas, *The Essential Ramdas,* even though "fair usage" would generally apply. Anyone knowing of the permission-granting agency for quotes used is invited to contact the publisher so that additional acknowledgement may be assigned in future printings. Thank you.

Quotations from Dr. Robert E. Svoboda are used with his kind permission.

Line drawings of Ganesha and Yogi Ramsuratkumar's bowl and fan are used with the permission of Nara Allsop.

PERMISSIONS FOR THE CD "SANGEETHA"

"Anonde Bawlo" was recorded at Jagabandhu Ashram in Bengal and is reproduced with the kind permission of Guru Sri Sanatan Das Thakur Baul. "Pare Loye Jao Amay" (Take Me Across) is reproduced with the kind permission of Parvathy Baul.

All other songs are courtesy of Hohm Sahaj Mandir archives and Bad Poet Productions.

To the Baul spirit,

wherever it lives

Table of Contents

Preface

THIS BOOK HAS BEEN INSPIRED BY MY TEACHER, AMERICAN BAUL KHEPA LEE LOZOWICK (1943–2010), who established a spiritual path in the West that blends lineage (*parampara*) and spiritual clan (*sampradaya)* in a way that is unique. It is my intention for this book to offer the reader an introduction to his legacy, which was developed over thirty-five years of his teaching work under the guidance and with the blessings of his master, Yogi Ramsuratkumar.

During Lee's lifetime, he encouraged his students to travel, as often as possible, to India with him to meet Yogi Ramsuratkumar, who Lee revered as the spiritual source of his work in the West. As his students, we were privileged to spend time with Lee in the intimate company of Yogi Ramsuratkumar, to receive his *darshan* and his blessings time and again, to be a part of his mandala and his play. It was Lee's often spoken and written wish that we would turn to Yogi Ramsuratkumar in the ultimate sense, as an embodiment of the Divine on earth. While Lee remained the true heart-son of his master, he also had a natural resonance with the Bauls of Bengal that, over the decades of his teaching, manifested in amazing ways that come to life in the pages that follow. Numerous books have been published about Lee's relationship with Yogi Ramsuratkumar—it is the Baul dimension of Lee's work that is the primary focus of this book.

Lee's unique contribution to the spiritual path in the West has multidimensional aspects. In the midst of the "wild heresies" that he lived (explored in these pages), Lee was paradoxically fond of saying, "I am very conservative. My path is a traditional path." A disciplined yogi, Lee established three ashrams that are dedicated to Yogi Ramsuratkumar as sanctuaries that serve as containers of lineage blessings and spiritual practice. This is the foundation of Lee's path, upon which he fashioned the amazing embellishments of his own earthy brand of Baul music and yoga.

Over time, study, and practice under Lee's guidance, I began to realize that it is not so easy to grasp the depth of the Baul path unless one has an understanding of the substratum, the ancient foundation, of Indian tradition upon which it rests. Like all spiritual sects of India, the Bauls cannot be separated from the milieu in which they arose; to understand them, we must at least glimpse the ground upon which they stand. For that reason, I have sketched a bigger picture in these pages, including some brief historical perspectives on relevant streams of the vast ocean of many currents, which is called "Hinduism"—the milieu of Lee's guru, Yogi Ramsuratkumar, and his guru, Swami Ramdas.

Lee's Baul path in the West, therefore, is also rooted in India, and I have chosen to honor that tradition by freely using Sanskrit words and terms in the text. There are many reasons to honor the Sanskrit tradition: primarily, the innate transformational and vibrational power of Sanskrit simply does not exist in English, although I have attempted to provide simple, succinct definitions for these terms. (Readers will also find it helpful to access the Glossary in the back of this book as you encounter Sanskrit terms.)

Furthermore, to cultivate a working knowledge of these terms is one important way that we can honor the Eastern traditions that are being brought into the West during our lifetime. By doing so, we shed light on and affirm our own experience as it stands upon the foundation of a wisdom tradition that is thousands of years old, which many believe is the origins of all spirituality on our planet. I hope that readers who are unfamiliar with Sanskrit will fall in love with its mystic beauty and grandeur, as I have. For the sake of simplicity and to ease the academic drift of this work, I have not used any diacritical marks.

Readers who are familiar with the Bauls of Bengal will find specific information about *kaya sadhana* (the alchemy of the body), tantric practices, and the infamous "four moons practice" of the Bauls noticeably missing in this book. While I address this subject in general principle, it is the Baul way (which is true of any living path) to pass esoteric aspects of practice from one initiated practitioner to another—that is, through an oral tradition of initiation. It suffices to say that the tantric yoga tradition in general has been well-plumbed by scholars of the East and West, and there is a great deal of information about it to be found in readily-available books and treatises. (There is a bibliography provided at the end of this book for suggested further study.) But, as any true Baul will tell you, there is no substitute for the direct experience of individual *sadhakas* and *sadhikas* whose hearts, minds, and bodies have been kindled through an ardent engagement with practice on the traditional path, practicing under the guidance of guru and lineage.

An introduction to the Western Bauls would not be complete without a direct experience of the *rasa* that lives in the music, which is so integral to the legacy of Khepa Lee. For that purpose I have included a companion CD titled "Sangeetha," a Sanskrit word that means "music." I encourage you to listen and imbibe fully, using the songs for study and deeper exploration, and—most of all—allowing them to touch your heart.

ACKNOWLEDGMENTS

It gives me great joy to acknowledge the many people who have contributed to this book, beginning with Khepa Lee Lozowick and Yogi Ramsuratkumar—the source and inspiration of the Baul Tradition in the West. Secondly, I thank my *gurubhais* Purna, who in his resonance with our guru provided the catalyst to make this project happen, and Lalitha, who gave her unconditional enthusiasm and helpful review of the text-in-progress. Lalitha's introduction is a joy to read; in it we catch a glimpse of the depth and richness of her spiritual journey on the Baul path under Lee's unerring guidance.

To the inner circle of Lee's mandala—my sister *sakhis* Mirabai, Rose, and Sharana—I offer love, *pranams*, and heartfelt gratitude for your blessing and your vivid, sometimes madcap embodiment of our guru's transmission.

To Lee's friend, the late ethnographer and lover of Baul, Deben Bhattacharya—wherever you are, thank you for many inspiring mornings, spicy lunches, and afternoon teas at your flat in Montmartre, where you also fed the fire of our passion for the Bauls as we sat listening, deep in the rhythm and flow of your amazing stories.

To all the readers of the manuscript-in-progress—Lalitha, Parvathy Baul, Sharana Lhaksam, Jim Capellini, Nachama Greenwald, and Paula Zuccarello: your contributions were invaluable. Thanks to copy editor PZ especially for helping me with "slash and burn" editing and to SL, who championed this project from start to finish and made many invaluable suggestions for the arrangement and flow of the text and chapters. Thanks to Joshua Leavitt of Sat Loka Ashram, whose succinct synopsis of specific readings and subsequent suggestions were plowed into the field.

Many thanks to Zac Parker for producing "Sangeetha," the companion CD of Lee's music for this book and for the compelling and beautiful cover design. To Becky Fulker, who worked tirelessly to hone the complex layout up to the last minute, I offer my deep appreciation.

I'd like to thank Judy Lief, *acharya* and long-time disciple of Chögyam Trungpa Rinpoche, for encouraging me to write a "small introductory book" about our path.

To Lee's dear friend, Dr. Robert Svoboda, thank you for so generously contributing to this book by giving readers the perfect, inspired context from which to embark.

And finally, heartfelt gratitude is due to the immense contributions of Parvathy Baul and her guru, Sanatan Baba, who continues to make offerings to the *murti* (photo) of Khepa Lee everyday on his ashram because "love never dies." To you, Parvarthy—great devotee, lover of *ektara*, mad singer of God, *khepi*, friend, cohort and inspiratrix on the path—I offer love, gratitude, and pranams.

May all beings be blessed by this endeavor.

M. Young
May 4, 2014
Triveni Ashram
Arizona

Proem

Dr. Robert Svoboda

Paramparaa, the Sanskrit word for "tradition," literally means "uninterrupted succession," suggests "focused on that which is beyond," and can even be interpreted to mean "that which is beyond the beyond." Of the world's many traditions ("beliefs or behaviors passed down within a group or society with symbolic meaning or special significance with origins in the past"), those that center on spirituality are literally "focused on that which is beyond," on that Reality which is Beyond all characteristics and conceptions.

Many are the traditions that have arisen and endured over the span of human history, for in the words of the Rg Veda, *ekam sat, vipraa bahudaa vadanti*: "Truth is One, but Those Who Are Inspired speak of it in various ways." Those Inspired Ones who conveyed their inspirations to students engendered beliefs and practices that have in some cases continued to inspire down to the present day.

The transitory nature of all manifestation generates over time the inevitable changes in human environment and culture that force traditions to evolve, and when difficulties arise during the transfer of a tradition from one generation to the next it is not uncommon for that tradition to cease to represent an "uninterrupted succession" of its founding principles. There is often great disagreement among a tradition's "hosts" about how traditions should or should not evolve, or whether they should evolve at all, if they are to continue to faithfully transfer revelations from the distant past into the distant future via the present.

This is particularly the case as ancient spiritual paths get transplanted into communities that are often far removed in space, time and cultural mechanics from the communities in which they originally arose, for geography and culture are now no barriers to a tradition that is bent on putting down roots in a foreign land. Under circumstances so alien to those in which the traditions actually grew, some succeed at retaining their external skin at the expense of their inner marrow, or *bhava* (state of being); others preserve the *bhava* but cannot retain its *rasa*, the flavor of Reality that is the intended fruit of the *bhava*. Few indeed are those in which the taste of the original juice actually continues to flow.

Mysterious are the workings of *bhava* and *rasa* as they wind through the alluvial fan of the ever-shrinking world, especially with regard to the much-misunderstood path followed by the Bauls of Bengal, and the extraordinary cross-fertilization that has occurred after the fantabulously eccentric Lee Lozowick set out with his students to locate and interact with a living Baul lineage. In *The Baul Tradition* M. Young has documented this quest, and the fruitful collaborations that have grown from it, enhancing the tale immeasurably by setting the Bauls and their teachings in an appropriate historical and cultural context. A worthy contribution to Baul literature, the book excels both as an admirable introduction to the mechanics of the paths of both the Eastern and Western Bauls, and as a description of the nectar that emerges through the alchemical blending of the juices of those lineages, refined in the fires of sadhana. *Rasikas* who read it will even be able to taste the splendid flavor of the transcendent living *rasa* thus engendered; a fine achievement indeed. May that *rasa* long flow! ✻

Foreword

Mari Young's book on Baul is going to make a huge contribution to the Baul practice, giving a proper glimpse into the Baul world through a practitioner's eyes. Mari has spent more than twenty-five years studying about and practicing as a Baul. It's a different perspective than other books available today. And her knowledge is not limited to only the Baul path. She also understands so much about all of the traditions in the world, from both an anthropological perspective and a practitioner perspective. Mari's personal experience—in combination with her sincere scholarship and familiarity with many places and cultures around the world—make her perfectly suited to put this book in a very modern context. I'm certain everyone will enjoy it!

Baul is a very old tradition, but there is not much in the way of written teaching that is available for aspiring practitioners. Over the centuries, there have been many small books written by Baul practitioners but they were mostly hand-printed in very limited quantities. Because of this, they remained only within the local community, never being reprinted after the masters left their bodies. These little books never gained popularity outside the Baul community and so the international class of people—the ones doing academic research into Baul—never gained access to them.

The majority of those early texts are now lost forever. What we have remaining today is mostly the songs, which, if you really follow them, give a little history, a little bit of how the evolution happened in the practice and how the masters and the lineages came about. But that is very different from a deeply personal account of a practitioner's sadhana; their life with the master and their insight into the meaning of these songs, how the songs are incorporated into the sadhaka's flesh and bones. There is one book written in recent times by a senior Baul practitioner, and that book is *Baul Premik*. It was written by my own master, Sanatan Baba. In that book, Sanatan Baba speaks directly about his sadhana. He speaks specifically about the songs and how the teachings are transmitted through the songs. He is very clear, but that book also has not been distributed in a very big way; only very few copies are in print and it is not published in English.

In the early twentieth century a group of books on Baul started appearing in English. They were published by university presses and other academicians, and so these books became the standard for Baul study. Anyone from anywhere in the world who wanted to study about Baul ended up finding and reading these books—but they were not written by Baul practitioners, not by the one who is seeing the Baul world in a spiritual sense, from the point of view of practice. They were written more as anthropological and cultural studies, tracing the history or sometimes just printing the poems and songs without any further explanation.

Seeing the Baul in the right context is very important. The researchers who write academic texts have specific formats that they have to follow; they don't have much space for personal experience. That approach doesn't serve the purpose of Baul and the Baul masters, but serves only the purpose of a particular study that is going to be archived in the libraries. In such studies it is easy for mistakes to be made and to get repeated because the writers are not practicing, and so they don't know. Their understanding remains superficial because they don't have the inner strength to pierce the deeper layers of meaning in Baul practice. Their misinterpretations get written in these books—and then repeated by others who believe these books are having authority—and in the end such mistakes become a history.

This book is a different way of looking at the Baul tradition altogether. It is both personal and scholarly, giving an international space for Baul as a practice, as a yoga in the world. Sometimes Sanatan Baba used to speak to me about how important it is for a practitioner to write their own books, insisting that I should write my own book. It is so important to have books written by the practitioners because their experience and understanding of this lineage will be totally different from someone who is just gathering information and writing it down.

We live in a very different world today than existed even fifty years ago. It is now a world of information where people are studying about almost anything you can think of. Baul is no longer strictly an oral tradition because nowadays nearly everyone can read and write. We can keep a clear account of our practice. When we only speak the teaching, it is easily forgotten. Writing down our personal experience of sadhana is a way of documenting our time.

Baul is very deep. We cannot define it, saying, "This is Baul or that's Baul." It would be like saying, "The sky is..." You can never really say what is the sky. Likewise, you can never really say what is Baul, but we can try to write our personal account, our understanding, our interpretation. And when it is positive, it's going to help. Mari's book is very positive. For those who are really interested in knowing Baul, this book is going to be one of the important, rich sources for understanding Baul in a clearer and more open light.

I have seen tremendous growth in the six years that I have known Mari and the Bauls of the West. Lee, their master, left his body only two years after I met him. When the master goes, there is no longer a single authority figure to look up to. Lee's departure meant that the students were left alone, perhaps a little confused, as they worked to understand their place and their responsibilities. I watched as this confusion melted and the students came to see that, yes, Lee is still there and is still the teacher, but his teachings and the path itself are now what is most important. He gave a different task to everyone, clues and keys to the particular lock that they were intended to open. That, I think, is the real work of the master—to find the right people for the right keys, to do the right thing.

Stepping back and holding to the path more than holding to the person of the guru is a really big change. That's why it is not just useful but also important that this book be written just now. The Bauls of Hohm Community are seeking to understand the roots from where they have come, trying to analyze through writing and meditating on the similarities and also the differences in the Baul traditions East and West. They are identifying themselves more with the work of Baul, with the lineage and the path, than with the particular master. Everyone in the community is finding their own individual way to continue with the practice. They know that Lee is one of the messengers, one of the people standing like milestones in the journey.

It is a very powerful time when the master leaves the body. Yes, you have to remember the great masters, like Lalon Fakir and Chaitanya and of course your own lineage of gurus, but it does not end there. The path itself will always remain. There will be great people coming… and going. That's the truth. You cannot hold on to someone. This book is about holding on to the path, and I think that's how it should be. Lee must be smiling from heaven!

Parvathy Baul
Kerala, India
March 25, 2014

Parvathy Baul at Lee's ashram in France, 2013.

Namaskhar!

My Namaskhar to the devotees of America!
The devotee and the deity are the same—thus spoke my Guru.
Of all God's plays, the very best is His taking human form.
He keeps playing this again and again,
Appearing as the human Avatar.
Khyapa says, Sanatan, listen, worship at the Guru's feet.
So I keep carrying this one-stringed ektara,
My friend for life.
It helps me cross the River of Sorrow.

> Guru Sri Sanatan Das Thakur Baul
> Composed in 1991
> during his visit with Khepa Lee

Introduction

I am no scholar. However, I would like to offer this introduction as an adventuress and practitioner of the Baul path for over thirty-three years. In reading this fabulous book by M. Young I am quickly drawn into its depths. Not only does the author demonstrate an impressive degree of scholarship but she is also uniquely positioned, as a peer adventuress and practitioner herself, to capture the thrilling sense of wonderment that we in the West have experienced as our deep resonance with the Baul path slowly revealed itself to us over time. I have read many books on Baul, and have traveled to meet Bauls East and West. I have participated enthusiastically and yet had never fully connected—to my satisfaction—the myriad clues and pieces into a detailed map of the Baul territory. I felt the solid ground beneath my feet, and yet had not truly grasped the great depth and breadth of the foundation upon which I stood. With this book we easily see the evolving picture of Baul—from ancient times to present day—as the author takes practitioner and scholar alike by the hand and aligns the many clues for us. Telling a captivating story along the way, Young skillfully blends both academic research and personal, intimate interviews with Baul masters, interviews that she herself conducted over many years.

I was on the scene in 1985 when my spiritual master, Lee Lozowick, first declared that we were Bauls. It was just after dinner at the ashram and about twenty of us were at the table conversing with Lee about our community and the roots of our school. Someone asked, "What should we tell people if they ask us what we are?" Without hesitation, Lee responded, "Tell them we're Bauls!" It was at that moment that we got our first conscious whiff of the synthesis that M. Young describes so eloquently in this book. Baul has a distinct fragrance. We all knew the scent, but had never had a name for it, had never known what to call this earthy, juicy, throbbing and heart-broken mood within which we conducted our lives of practice. Our sadhana in Lee's company was experienced as an immense Gift, and yet none of us knew from where it had come. Knowing that Lee was a fine scholar and uncompromising practitioner, it was obvious to me that this announcement heralded the beginning of a great new adventure for all of us. I determined that night to find these Bauls!

By early 1986 I found myself traveling to India with Lee and "gang." My personal instructions from Lee were to sleuth out if there were indeed any "real" Bauls left in Bengal and if so, who and where. Along with participating in our regular group activities I also took many enthusiastic side trips, looking for hints as to where we might find a genuine Baul. I was told by every so-called expert to give up the chase since the only Bauls alive were ragged street entertainers performing old Baul songs for money or drugs. They were perverts, thieves, desperate beggars and in general had no real spiritual practice. I was politely advised that, "Bauls were not the sort of people a nice lady from America would want to meet."

Weeks passed in this way and then, in the holy city of Varanasi on the banks of the Ganges, we had a breakthrough. At the famous Banaras Hindu University, my companion and I learned of a retired professor who had specialized all his life in Baul topics of various sorts. We were told, "If anyone knows how to help you, he does." So, we were off on the hunt. After getting completely drenched in heavy rain (we were traveling in an open rickshaw) we arrived at the professor's door in soggy saris with dripping hair and looking completely disheveled—not at all like respectable researchers on a quest. He sorted us out with dry clothes and hot cups of tea and then sat us down in his study, books scattered everywhere, to finally address our eager questions. To our shock, he proceeded to tell us the usual story of Baul "perverts" and that we should give up on this silly quest. We had endured enough of this and we decided to dig in our heels and make a stand. Surely this educated man could see that we

were not merely curious tourists. We were practitioners, serious and sincere in our task, capable of discerning the difference between a disciplined yogi and a wannabe rascal and pretender. We sought the company of a *practicing* Baul, a genuine Baul.

The professor finally softened, his eyes narrowing in respect and a smile curling the corners of his mouth. We had won his attention—as though we had passed some sort of test—and his mood entirely changed. Nodding thoughtfully, he proceeded to set us on the right track, saying there were very few genuine Baul masters left and that they lived in isolated areas. We should go to Shantiniketan, he insisted, if we were to have any luck at all. He mentioned the elder master Guru Sri Sanatan Das Thakur Baul at that time, but he didn't know if Sanatan Baba (as he is respectfully and more commonly known) was still alive. We had our first real lead, a huge breadcrumb that would eventually lead us straight to the door of a truly genuine and revered master of this amazing sect.

At this point Lee assigned a couple of the men to travel to the rugged areas outside of Shantiniketan in order to follow-up on the leads I had uncovered, which eventually led us to the ashram of Sanatan Baba. From that point on, my husband and I were given the wonderful opportunity to be Lee's personal representatives in many adventures that put us in the position of developing a long and enduring friendship with Sanatan Baba—who is now ninety-three years old— that continues to this day. As the deepening friendship between us evolved, we regularly discovered circumstances which further highlighted the many similarities between Baul sadhana in the East and West.

In 1991, early in Sanatan Baba's visit to Lee's ashram in the U.S. and before our subsequently taking him on tour in the Western States as a wandering Baul master-minstrel-beggar, Sanatan Baba was asked to perform at the posh private home of a wealthy music lover in a small and exclusive mountain town in Arizona. By word of mouth alone, the beautifully appointed home filled to overflowing with an excited audience. There were Baul and ethnic music enthusiasts, professors and spiritual practitioners. Everyone had gathered for the rare opportunity of spending time with an authentic Baul master. This ended up being my first experience of Baul begging, Sanatan Baba-style.

A group of about sixty people packed into the room and was swept away in the uplifting mood of the masterful spiritual teachings encoded in Sanatan Baba's Baul songs. Afterward, the space was buzzing and filled with animated discussions in every corner of the house and out into the cool night air. Sanatan Baba immediately knew what needed to happen. Baul performance is a reciprocal event, the flow of *prana*—life-force, breath and energy—completing a circuit from performer to audience and back again. Sanatan Baba took me aside and explained through his translator that after this offering of songs, Baul "madhukari with ananda" (loosely translated as

"begging with bliss") should be done—the traditional sacred begging bowl should be passed around. From his cloth bag he pulled a well-preserved, beautiful, canoe-shaped container about twelve inches long and five inches wide at the middle, described as the seed of some huge unusual fruit. He told me to take this much-used sacred vessel to beg on his behalf.

Catching the attention of the room, I explained what Sanatan Baba had requested. The bowl quickly overflowed with gifts of money, a few delicious candies and perhaps some tobacco (whereas in Bengal, as M. Young describes here, it would have overflowed with rice, vegetables, the Indian cigarettes called *bidis*, and rupees), and Sanatan Baba's face shone with brilliant satisfaction. As we walked to our car through the moonlight, Sanatan Baba was literally singing and skipping with joy, commenting on the spiritual synchronicity and obvious flow of grace in it all. For the rest of the tour I was the designated beggar, gathering *bhiksha* (alms) for him.

Along these same lines, a couple of years later (1993) I put together a team of four people to go to Bengal and visit Sanatan Baba's ashram for a month on Lee's behalf. Sanatan Baba took us with him as he wandered from village to village on his rounds of *madhukari*, wherein we witnessed the joy and appreciation of the people as he offered spiritual nourishment though his songs and they offered nourishment to him and his ashram through giving the resources they needed. We felt right at home, as we were all reminded of our ongoing Western-style Baul *madhukari* which Lee encouraged us to practice at home. My experience with Sanatan Baba was the perfect training ground and preparation for the countless times my husband and I "begged" in the years to come for various forms of goods and services on behalf of our ashram. This type of begging has such dignity and grace. It is a lawful exchange but it requires something very unusual on the part of the beggar. The Baul beggar must set aside the common man's pride and rest instead in the pride of the spirit—a priceless quality that M. Young writes more extensively about in her book.

I witnessed another striking parallel between the Eastern and Western Baul *sampradayas* at this private home as well. Sanatan Baba, just after his performance, was taking tea in a small side room with a few of his personal traveling group. Various members of the audience would peek in and say hello, clearly still being drawn by the magnetism initiated in the Baul performance. At one point a man walked in and sat down right in front of Sanatan Baba, obviously trying to get close and command attention. He introduced himself and started in with questions (thinly veiled demands, in my opinion) about Sanatan Baba's personal inner work, esoteric sexual practices, and whatever he thought might be "Baul secrets" for enhancing spiritual powers. Sanatan Baba pointedly did not speak. The visitor asked his questions a second time and the translator again translated. Sanatan Baba sat quietly and would not speak. The man became slightly aggressive in his questioning, leaning a little closer into Sanatan Baba's face and implying that Sanatan Baba simply did not understand his special questions. Still Sanatan Baba would not speak to him and, at this point, had turned his body slightly away from the man. The man finally left in an agitated mood.

Sanatan Baba then explained to us (I'm paraphrasing) that this man was trying to take teachings he had in no way earned and so did not deserve. I knew that on the Baul path the teacher-student relationship is paramount—it is the chalice in which teachings are earned and given. There was clearly no such relationship with this man, and Sanatan Baba did not even give him one word. I had observed this same scenario being handled in a similar way with Lee in our Western Baul *sampradaya* as well, and so I was delighted to see the calm steadiness of Sanatan Baba's refusal to be drawn in or to compromise.

Since 1985, when the fragrance of a connection between Bauls East and West was carried to us on a subtle breeze, this evolving cross-pollination—with visits back and forth in traditional Baul fashion—has continued to the present day. A significant example of this evolution involves Sanatan Baba's spiritual daughter and senior devotee-initiate-teacher, Parvathy Baul. Lee and Parvathy Baul first met in 2008 in Kolkata, at which time she served as translator at a potent meeting between Lee and Sanatan Baba, who had not seen one another since Sanatan Baba's U.S. tour in 1991. For this visit in 2008, Sanatan Baba's children and grandchildren—eleven people altogether—piled into an SUV built for seven to make the four-hour journey from their ashram in rural Bengal to Kolkata where Lee was engaged in a short tour with his blues band, Shri.

M. Young fills out the story for us in her book, but I will add a few remarks of my own, since this meeting with Parvathy Baul catalyzed a close friendship between us. We kept in close contact over the next year, during which time she visited and participated at the initiation ceremony of my small ashram in Washington State and we conversed by phone on a regular basis, ultimately arranging to meet again in India in early 2009. Only one year had passed since Parvathy and I had first met, and yet the feeling was one of deep familial connection. My husband and I and two of my students decided to make the journey to South India in January.

We visited Parvathy and her husband Ravi at their home in Kerala, and then traveled together to Anandashram, the ashram of Swami Papa Ramdas—a place that Parvathy had always wanted to see. After many adventures in the south, we prepared to head into the final and most important leg of our trip: Parvathy had made reservations for all of us to fly north to Bengal where she was expecting to receive the final, formal initiation—called Purna Vairagya—from her guru Sanatan Baba at his ashram.

I was one of the few present at Parvathy's Purna Vairagya initiation, in which Sanatan Baba gave her the responsibility and authority for initiating others, preserving and communicating his teaching and particular stream of the Baul path. During this initiation I officially accepted the life-time responsibility of being Bhiksha Ma for Parvathy. Parvathy explained that this is a "special type of spiritual mother" who advises and protects the initiate and particularly helps in her personal well-being. This was definitely a pivotal moment in which an even more substantial link was forged between our two streams of Baul—reminiscent of two strong families cementing ties through a welcomed and enduring marriage.

I have been both startled and pleased at some of the pieces of the Baul puzzle that M. Young has brought together in this unique volume. In my own studies, I always felt that information about the importance of women in Baul was oddly missing, with women only referenced in the form of poetic and generalized appreciation. Here in Chapter Three I learned—in the most precise presentation I had yet uncovered—of the detailed and significant importance among the Vaishnava Sahajiyas of a skilled and spiritually mature woman. I found my eyes reading and re-reading the author's description of the *Necklace of Immortality*—and yours likely will too! Next, what a surprise I had as I read in Chapter Four about the women of Nityananda's (the fierce tantric devotee of Chaitanya and famous spiritual giant in his

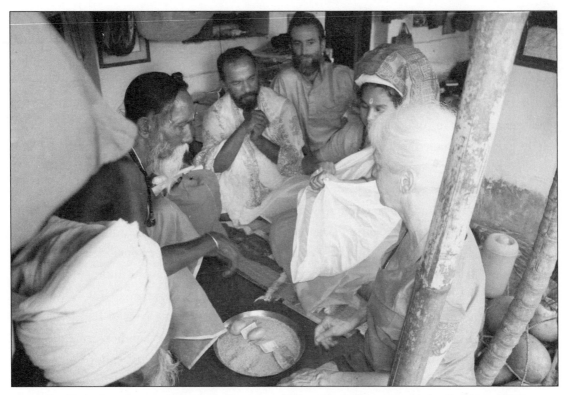

On Baba's ashram, from left: Sanatan Baba, Ravi Gopalan Nair, Jim Capellini, Parvathy Baul and Lalitha.

own right) household being some of the earliest Baul spiritual leaders. The author shows clearly how these women's spiritual maturity had evolved into the beginnings of Baul as distinct from either Nityananda's Nath Siddha background or Chaitanya's more austere Vaishnava path.

Added to these personal favorite facts about women practitioners are quite a few things I believe are fresh in M. Young's approach. These include her pulling together material showing precisely how the Baul path developed over thousands of years, rather than the commonly presented picture that Baul is only four hundred to five hundred years old, originating with Chaitanya. The reader feels carried along as she investigates, step by step, all the sources of this deeply human tradition. We learn of ancient songs from Buddhist roots, called *dohas*, which are still sung by Bauls today. I have personally witnessed this in the performances of Parvathy Baul, who is a talented Baul scholar in her own right, and whom M. Young interviews for this book.

Baul arising in the West? Now we come to something not written about before, which makes M. Young's material a must-read for Baul enthusiasts. As the author begins to weave the well-documented tale of the first organized Baul *sampradaya* in the West, the reader will likely find themselves wearing a big grin as they learn how Baul practice and teaching has manifested for the emerging "new kids on the block." Every element of traditional Baul culture has its counterpart in the West, and I was enchanted to rediscover—through the eyes and scholarship of M. Young—all the practices and forms I had become so familiar with: the music and dance, *bhavas* and *rasas*, lifestyle and dharma.

In the beginning of my thirty-three years on this path I was drawn to the rich mood of Baul as to a delicious and rare fruit, but I didn't really know anything about the tree from which it had come. Lee encouraged my friendship with Sanatan Baba, and in turn Sanatan Baba introduced me to the branches and trunk of this tree, giving me a glimpse into the bigger picture and exposing me to just how rare the fruit of it was. But more was still needed. What I was missing, without my really knowing it, was a key to the "link" between my Baul *sampradaya* and the living lineage (*parampara*) to which I belonged. How, exactly, do I reconcile my belonging to the *parampara* of Swami Papa Ramdas, Yogi Ramsuratkumar and Khepa Lee Lozowick with my

At Parvathy's Purna Vairagya initiation.

belonging to the spiritual clan of the Bauls? The missing link lay at the source, within the ancient roots that provide nourishment for the trees of both my lineage and my clan. With M. Young's current work I feel and experience even more deeply the magnificent scope and enduring nature of this unique tree that yields such ambrosial fruit.

Baul is not a religion—it is a direct relationship to Reality. Baul is alive and well and much older than many scholars have documented. It is a juicy story in the telling.

Thank you M. Young!

Lalitha Thomas
April 2014
Rasa Creek Sanctuary, B.C.

CHAPTER 1

Bauls East & West

Everything that exists, exists for the humor of God.
It just exists because God created the universe to enjoy.

Khepa Lee

TWENTY-FIVE YEARS AGO, when Khepa Lee first asked me to study the Bauls of Bengal, there were very few books on the subject. My source book was a weathered, hardcover copy of *Obscure Religious Cults*, written by Dr. Shashibhusan Das Gupta, published in 1946. A gift from my teacher, this seminal work (which includes fabulous chapters on the Sahajiyas and the Bauls) still resides in my library; its pages are yellowed and crumbling, and I handle it with the reverent care due to an artifact. Since that time many studies and research efforts on the enigmatic Bauls have been published—today, many of these sit on my bookshelves next to Das Gupta.

Who are the Bauls, and what is their teaching and spiritual culture about? Baul bards, minstrels, yogis, and mystics have wandered the dusty roads of Bengal for centuries, going from village to village to ply their spontaneous and simple art, singing songs and dancing with joy in the way of *sahaja*, uplifting the ordinary person with their poem-songs, transporting the listener above the daily grind for survival into a direct experience of the sublime. In more recent times, the Bauls have thrilled their audiences in both the East and West with their evocative songs, their symbolic garb, their enigmatic spirit and unique style. Their iconic image—head thrown back in ecstatic song, *ektara* held high—is unmistakable, but this is only the surface appearance of a profound way of life. Not all Bauls are singers and performers, not all wear a patchwork robe; some are renunciates, some are householders. But all true Bauls have one thing in common: they are serious practitioners of the spiritual path.

The Bauls are carriers of sacred secrets, and in order to make sense of what they do, or the symbolic language of their songs, one must dive into the rich matrix of Baul culture or *sadhana*. My initial forays into learning about the Bauls yielded the same facts that many scholars and ethnographers reiterate on four essential tenets of the Baul Way:

1) Radical reliance on the guru or spiritual preceptor.

2) Wandering and begging (*madhukari*) as a way of life.

3) Teachings encoded in song and dance (*Baul gan* and the all-important *bhava*).

4) Yogas of the body (*kaya sadhana*), including hatha yoga and yoga of sexuality and breath.

Living on Lee's ashrams and traveling in his company, I have had the opportunity to meet and get to know a number of Bengali Bauls as well as Lee's friend Deben Bhattacharya—the ethnographer and lover of the Bauls who first translated their songs into English. In the process of those meetings, evolving relationships, and my own years of *sadhana*, I found these four "tenets of the Bauls" to be a limited and superficial glance at a very deep and profound tradition. I began to develop a more complex and comprehensive view of what it means to be a Baul—East or West—which eventually catalyzed the writing of this introductory book.

Ideas and views of what it means to be Baul are as numerous as there are Bauls in the world. With that in mind, please read with the knowledge that the synthesis and distillation I have attempted in this book represents my own experience of and reflections on a vast and complex subject. Others may draw different conclusions or look through another window or lens.

Baul spiritual culture is essentially a *sahaja* path. On the Baul way, we embark upon a road that will, if followed diligently and with passion, reunite us with the inborn *sahaja* nature—the naturally ecstatic

primordial essence of being that is God's gift to His creatures. This innate blueprint is characterized by the love, beauty, bliss, wisdom, and dignity that underlies the dense blanket of personality and social conditioning under which every human being labors. From the Baul view, to rediscover *sahaja* is to realize one's unity with all of life, and further, from that unity, to discover the beauty and sweetness of loving God.

Those who make the journey cultivate a way of life that is defined by a sometimes confusing amalgam of simplicity and complexity. In attempting to distill that complexity for the sake of interested readers, the following principles of the Baul path are presented in Sanskrit terms with English translations. It is my fervent wish to honor the roots of the Baul tradition and to "connect the dots" between East and West, while describing or defining those terms in contemporary language.

Sahaja – a profound trust in the innate nature of the human being as divine; the essentially tantric view that all of life is sacred and interconnected.

Ishta Devata – a direct personal relationship with God through a personal deity or "man of the heart."

Guruvada or Guru Yoga – surrender to and reliance on the guru or spiritual guide, who may also be the doorway to the personal deity or Beloved.

Nama – the use of the divine name as mantra; the yoga of mantra and sound.

Bhava – the cultivation of divine mood (*bhava*) and *rasa* (taste, juice, divine elixir) as a means of communion with the personal Beloved.

Bhakti – worship, prayer, inner life based on devotion to a chosen deity.

Brahmacharya or renunciation – disidentification with social customs, psychological or mental forms, including caste (class) and gender differences, religious orthodoxy and dogma; spiritual disciplines and practices, or various forms of *tapasya* (austerity).

Madhukari or Beggary – among the Bauls of Bengal, this is literally begging for alms (*bhiksha*); in the West, the term Beggary refers to the foundational attitude of a life surrendered to the Will of God. To be a beggar is to rely on Divine Providence—to accept what is given. Cultivating humility and simplicity in one's daily life.

Baul gan or poetry and song – dharma or teachings expressed in music, poetry and art in all forms; aesthetic appreciation as an immediate, direct way of cultivating *bhava*.

Kaya Sadhana – spiritual practices based on the innate wisdom of the body, including yogas of the body, breath and sexuality.

Parampara – spiritual lineage; the divine light, blessing, *shakti*, or Grace that is passed down through a line of individual human beings of profound spiritual realization.

Sampradaya – spiritual clan, or the importance of spiritual community, school, or sangha.

We will return to these tenets again and again in the next chapters as we delve into the historical and philosophical roots of the Baul tradition in Bengal, which provide a groundwork for the chapters that explore the path of the Bauls in the West originated by Khepa Lee Lozowick.

Lee's story is unique in the history of Eastern teachings arising in the West. Ten years after a spiritual awakening in 1975 gave birth to his work with students, Lee recognized that his revelatory path and practices were extraordinarily similar to those of the Bauls of Bengal. This resonance was so powerful that in 1985, in answer to the question, "When people ask me what our tradition is, what should I say?", Lee said, "Tell them we are Bauls." This statement—part declaration, part prophecy—not only named but provided movement and fuel to the growing *sampradaya* of Bauls in the West, informally known as the Hohm Community.

As the years passed and the *sadhana* of Lee's students evolved, the resonance between Bauls of the East and West took a distinct shape in Lee's ardent devotion to his guru, the revered south Indian saint, Yogi Ramsuratkumar. Lee shared a life-long, intimate and loving relationship with Yogi Ramsuratkumar, who blessed and supported the teaching work of his American heart-son, including Lee's role as guru, his poetry, music, and rock & roll, and his informal affiliation with the Bauls of Bengal.

In the beginning, the connection between the Hohm Community and the Bauls of Bengal seemed esoteric and mysterious—after all, Lee's guru was not a Bengali Baul. In later years, Lee sometimes said that he believed his guru had had close contact with the Bauls during his years as a wandering beggar. In fact, Yogi Ramsuratkumar was born and raised near Varanasi and lived for years in Bihar where there are many Bauls. Still, Yogi Ramsuratkumar's guru was Swami Papa Ramdas of Kerala, whose line is strictly traditional and devotional, not overtly tantric, as are the Bauls.

However, Lee's connection with the Bauls soon became more apparent. After initial meetings with the Bauls during an India trip in 1986, Lee initiated one of many musical experiments—a rock band called liars, gods, & beggars, which played songs with Lee's lyrics and music that was composed by his students. LGB performed and toured for twelve years, establishing the foundation for many projects yet to come, including Lee's blues band, Shri; Attila the Hunza; the Denise Allen Band; and finally, the Lee Lozowick Project.

At Lee's invitation, in 1991 Guru Sri Sanatan Das Thakur Baul lived on the Arizona ashram for six weeks with his sons, Biswanath and Basudev, during which time they toured and performed in the American Southwest. It was the first mingling of the Bauls of the West and East, and both Lee and Sanatan Baba enjoyed each other's performances. It was then that Sanatan Baba declared Lee the "Baul guru of the West" and Yogi Ramsuratkumar a "Baul guru."

Lee's original lyrics, put to music composed by a number of his students, have been recorded in over forty CDs. Similar to traditional Baul songs, Lee's poetry and songs express the teaching in ordinary vernacular, the language common to all people. The live performance of these songs by Lee and his students has always carried a unique form of transmission that defies description—like the songs of the Bengali Bauls, in which the body is suffused with the magic of music, rhythm, melody mingled with the power of the word.

At the same time that there is a deep resonance in terms of music as vehicle of dharma, there is a depth of path and practice found in the basic weave of daily life that is consonant between the Bauls of the West and their Bengali cousins and elders. Today, the Western Bauls are a loosely organized *sampradaya* of practitioners who have dedicated their lives to the teachings and practices given by Khepa Lee in the lineage of Yogi Ramsuratkumar. Some live on ashrams established by Lee in Arizona, France, and India while many live as householders in areas as diverse as the United States, India, Canada, Australia, Mexico, and Europe.

Lee's mandala also includes the ashrams established by two of his students who carry on the teaching: Purna Steinitz of Sat Loka Ashram in Montana and Anjaneya Ashram in Germany, and Lalitha of Kripa Mandir, a sanctuary in British Columbia, Canada. At Lee's instruction, Lalitha has been closely involved with Sanatan Das Baul over the years; as Lee's emissary, she was pivotal in the ongoing development of the relationship between Eastern and Western Bauls.

Naturally, there are notable differences between the Bauls of the East and West in terms of how these essential teachings and practices are lived in the cultural milieus in which they exist. One of these differences is Lee's strong emphasis on the written dharma and the publication of books, which is rarely found among Eastern Bauls. Also, while the Bauls of Bengal tend to be sparing with formal ritual, the practices of the Western Bauls are closely guided and influenced by Lee's root guru, Yogi Ramsuratkumar, and therefore ritual practices (*puja*) are a part of daily worship on Lee's ashrams. Bauls on both sides of the world love the simple worship of a *dhuni* fire—an informal but powerful sacred fire that *tantrikas* of all paths hold in common.

Simultaneously, the thread of continuity is easily revealed in the shared emphasis on *guruvada* or guru yoga—radical reliance on the guru—which is inseparable from the worship of an *ishta devata* (chosen deity). Equally notable is the common use of mantra or *nama*, the repetition of the Name of God.

Amongst all Bauls, the cultivation of *bhava* is of crucial importance to the path as the means to communion with a personal Beloved, often expressed in the creation of art, song, and poetry. Sometimes referred to metaphorically as gathering honey for Lord Krishna, *bhava* is cultivated through numerous means that invoke *rasa*, or the many flavors and tastes of the Divine manifesting on Earth. For the Western Bauls, this includes all forms of traditional practice as well as music, dance, feasting, the intimate *sadhana* of committed, long-term relationships, communion experienced in friendships and the parent-child relationship, as well as creativity in general and all artistic endeavors, love of nature, aesthetic appreciation, spiritual disciplines, contemplation, meditation, and prayer.

The Baul Path is a tantric path in the broad sense, which means that no aspect of life is rejected but is used or entered into as a potential realm of experience from which spiritual value may be extracted. At the same time, Lee's teaching emphasizes that it is equally important for a *sadhaka* to make clear distinctions: there will inevitably be aspects of life experience that one wisely chooses not to engage—not out of rejection, fear, piousness, recoil, or judgment, but because it is simply not conducive to one's aim. This recognition that engagement with a particular experience or event will not be a positive influence for the fulfillment of one's individual *sadhana* could be called developing discrimination— or learning the wisdom of one's *svadharma* or personal dharma, which is always resonant with universal truth, or the *sanatana dharma*.

"They came, they sang and danced, and they disappeared into the mists," wrote one of many famous admirers of the Bauls. Perhaps it is the *sahaja* perception of the poetic interplay between beauty and impermanence that makes the elusive Bauls so compelling. Far from the clamor and complexity of today's Kolkata, with its fast-paced, thick amalgam of modern and ancient ways of life, the Bauls of Bengal have flourished despite calumny, criticism, poverty, and hardships of all kinds. Walking the razor's edge between joy and sorrow, love and loss, the Bauls have a way of life that carries a vital message—like a refreshing wind—that is needed in our current times, when the rediscovery of timeless truths is crucial to our survival.

"Baul" is simply a word—meaning "mad, madcap" or "taken by the wind"—used to describe the state of mind of one who walks a path that is rarely taken, and who has a vision of Reality so piercing and clear that they are often called "divinely mad." A true Baul is a spontaneous occurrence, an evolutionary pulse of Nature that may arise as the spirit of *sahaja* in all cultures, times, and places throughout history. The Baul spirit may be expressed by spiritual teachers, artists, healers, poets, musicians, geniuses, or leaders in any field; many of these great ones demonstrate within their chosen path the character of the iconoclast, the rebel, the lover, the mystic, the visionary, the radical prophet of searing insight.

Among the Bauls of East and West, the aim of the path is to gather honey for the love of the Lord. Along the way, we engage a conscious participation and inner work that hones and sculpts our awareness and capacity to serve Life. The purpose of this inner yoga is ultimately to forge a clear vessel for the sake of the enjoyment of the Supreme Being, as Khepa Lee hinted at in the quote at the beginning of this introduction.

The Baul path, in both the East and the West, could be called a journey from *rupa* to *svarupa*. *Rupa* means "form," and *svarupa* refers to the essential blueprint or prior reality that exists as a subtle substratum to the world of concrete forms. In the doctrine of *rupa* and *svarupa*, it is understood that the human being is essentially divine, and this divinity may be discovered through the life and activity of the body. As we grow into a conscious awareness of the *svarupa* underlying our identification with the human form and its personality, we encounter more subtle dimensions of being that are capable of knowing truth, wisdom, and objective feeling or divine mood in relationship to the Supreme Reality.

The concept of *rupa* and *svarupa* is of vital importance among Bauls, because it leads to their great distinguishing mark—direct experience with the Divine that may lead to loving God in personal terms. On a path in which the personal Beloved is a vivid and real relationship, what "feeds" or attracts the Supreme Being is of supreme importance. As Lee wrote, God would like to enjoy His or Her creation—it could be said that God has a sweet tooth! Like a bee is drawn to the sweet nectar of the flower, the Divine has a craving for the many tastes of *rasa* to be revealed in the nuances of devotion, harmony, peace, kindness, love, gratitude, and praise.

And so, the Baul message has meaning and utility for everyone, regardless of spiritual path or preference; it contains a greatly needed medicine for the growing maladies of our contemporary world. The Baul way of life is earthy and connected to the cosmos; it embraces the sweet along with the bitter; it seeks harmony in relationships of all kinds; it draws us into a life of natural simplicity and yet there is great enjoyment and pleasure to be savored. The Baul way of life is a dance of *bhoga* (enjoyment) and *yoga* (discipline), a natural wisdom that springs from ancient sources that are rooted in the fertile spiritual soil of Mother India. ✿

> Oh Father, Yogi Ramsuratkumar
> 	the Bauls of Bengal are known as a Heretic sect,
> 		a sect of madmen and sinners.
> Oh Father, Yogi Ramsuratkumar,
> 	when a Baul is considered to have really found
> the fruits of Sadhana,
> 	sometimes a word is added after his name.
> Oh Father, Yogi Ramsuratkumar,
> 	this word, meaning mad, is Khepa.
> Oh Father, Yogi Ramsuratkumar,
> 	to Your son You are always Yogi Ramsuratkumar,
> yet in some ways lee feels
> 	You are also his Khepa Baba
> (though lee would not be so brash
> 	as to call You that,
> nor would lee cease to be Blessed by the constant ringing
> 	of Yogi Ramsuratkumar in his body).
> Oh Father, Yogi Ramsuratkumar,
> 	Your son longs for You always.[1]
>
> — Lee Lozowick

---

[1]   Lee Lozowick, *Death of a Dishonest Man*, March 2, 1991, p. 397.

CHAPTER 2

Roots

AT THE ROOT OF THE ROOTS OF THE BAULS, we find the concept of *sahaja*, which is older than its origins in the Sanskrit language. In the time before there was written language and recorded history, *sahaja* existed as the objective nature of Creation, Nature, Prakriti, or Shakti, perceived as a goddess fully alive and imbuing every thing and every being with divinity. If we consider the possibility that mankind's evolution is not linear, it seems probable that great knowledge was accessible to conscious awareness in the misty stretches of remote time. That knowledge sprang from *sahaja*, the innate wisdom of being, revealed through the human body itself, in tune with the natural world and the cosmos beyond.

Over the span of time, those currents of wisdom have become distinct streams of accumulated, revelatory knowledge that flow within the vast ocean of existence. To enter such a stream of the path (and there are many, for God is very generous) is to receive its wisdom, so that the individual *jiva* (soul) travels with greater speed and efficiency toward its destination. At some point, the wisdom of a particular stream may be encapsulated in scriptures, systems, and schools or *sampradayas*—platforms from which individual seekers may dive into the river in a powerful and transformative way; we can enter such a stream and be swept along in its power and grandeur as we make our way home. Diverse streams of knowledge are often labeled by religious scholars in terms such as Advaita Vedanta, Bhakti, Siddha, Tantra, Sahajiya, Baul—and yet, once one enters the *sahaj* vision, these terms may be understood simply as our attempts to describe the wish of the Supreme Reality to reveal Itself in benevolent patterns and currents arising in the evolution of consciousness.

This chapter explores the emergence and intermingling of specific streams that form the matrix underlying the Baul path today. These have endured over time, evolving as they flowed into new time periods or cultural milieus in human history to inform and guide seekers of God. The ancient wisdom of the Vedas and Upanishads are found underlying Indian and Hindu spiritual philosophy and practice in general, and so it is there that we must begin.

THE VEDIC TRADITION

The Vedas are the oldest known records of human thought, predating even the Sumerian myths and stories written in cuneiform in the early civilization of the Fertile Crescent—formerly known as Persia and now as Iran and Iraq. Most scholars agree that the sage Vyasa "arranged," collected, or wrote down the four Vedas—Rig Veda, Sama Veda, Yajur Veda, and Atharva Veda—in Sanskrit (the oldest of the Indo-European languages) somewhere around 1500 BCE, but the Vedas existed as an oral tradition as early as 4000 BCE and probably much earlier. Whether the Vedas were received and passed down before or after this time period cannot be proven, but this date carries the authority of the astronomical data that is given in the Rig Veda ("Knowledge of Praise"), the oldest and most often quoted of the four Vedas.

The Vedas are collections of poems, hymns, and inspired insights into the nature of Reality, which were radically apprehended by the ancient *rishis*, seers, poets (*kavis*), or children of light. The *rishis* "saw" the truth of existence that lies hidden behind the veils of maya. The great seers perceived, with their inner eye, the subtle wisdom that is inherent in the created world, from remote cosmos to immediate terrestrial life, and they communicated this truth in *sandhya bhasa*—the "twilight language" of symbol, myth, and poetic metaphor.

The renowned Indian scholar Surendranath Dasgupta called the Vedic religion a "sacrificial mysticism," in which highly ritualized fire sacrifice lay at the heart of religious practice in the civilization of the Indus and Sarasvati Rivers. The central significance of fire sacrifice was intended to revivify or rejuvenate the cosmic order; to appease and please the deities with praise and oblations (offerings); and to fructify and harmonize the tribe, clan, or village. The fire itself was understood as the god Agni, who took the prayers and praise of the ritual's participants to heaven. While the primary offering into the fire was milk mixed with water, other precious substances—including honey, flowers, herbs, or blood—were included as well.

The Vedas dealt not only with sacrifice and mysticism but also with practical and cultural aspects of existence, including the four estates or castes and their specific roles and tasks, as well as humankind's communication with the Divine and the multiple strata of Creation. There were two types of fire ceremonies prescribed by the Vedas: domestic and public. Every Brahmana (priesthood), Kshatriya (warrior) or Vaishya (merchants, farmers, and artisans) family was obliged to perform fire sacrifice (*homa*) over a single fire every day at sunrise and sunset. The fourth caste, Shudras, or servants, were left to the mercy of public rituals officiated by priests; these gatherings required three fires, several priests who intoned the sacred mantras while officiating over the fires and offerings, and crowds of participants who watched in silence. It is likely that these rites were performed outdoors, under the trees or in the center of a village, in a highly charged atmosphere of mystery and meaning. They were not only seeking to please their favorite god or goddess, but to invoke the sacred presence of the deity—or to merge with the Supreme Being, which is not limited to form.

Vedic ritual is characterized by Agni, the holy essence and divine light behind the fire, and Soma, the god of ambrosia and immortality. While fire ritual was the central aspect of Vedic religion, the message of the Vedas included a powerful emphasis on asceticism, sacrifice, meditation and mantra.

Around 800 BCE the Upanishads began to appear in a written form, expressing the evolution of Vedic philosophy over time. These inspired writings focused on Brahman, the unitive Supreme Reality from which all existence has come. The wisdom of the Vedas and Upanishads became established as the substratum of Indian spirituality—a fertile ground that mingled with pre-existing tribal traditions and, over vast reaches of time, formed the roots and trunk of a venerable and vastly overarching tree of many branches.

These and other Vedic teachings may be discovered in virtually every path of the Indian traditions. If we look closely, the Vedas contain the archaic seeds of yoga, devotion, nonduality, and tantra, all of which are central to the Baul tradition. These wisdom streams co-existed and flourished, synthesizing and evolving together even while there were major differences in theory or practice found in *advaita* (nondual) or *dvaita* (dual), *bhakti* (devotional), tantric, or strictly Vedic pathways.

The Vedic Seers

The world of Vedic India was a sacred one in which every action was understood as part of the cosmic order. The ancient sages saw the Universe as an eternal ritual of sacrifice. It is the self-sacrifice of the Absolute which gives birth to the relative, and the very nature of life is one of transformation of energies. Every aspect of creation, divine or human, reflects this transformation. We cannot live without taking part in this cosmic ritual, both as instrument and as victims, and it is through this conscious participation in the sacrificial ritual that cosmic order is maintained.

The seers taught that the Universe is maintained by a hierarchy of energies known as devas (literally, "the shining ones"). These are the causal energies from which the subtle and gross worlds evolve, and are personified as the numerous divine beings of Vedic mythology. The devas, although diverse and often of opposing natures, are just the different aspects and subdivisions of the one absolute causal energy. The whole of manifestation is a chain of subtle correspondences, and it is through ritual, correctly performed, that these subtle correspondences can be enlivened and the human linked with the divine.[1]

— Alistair Shearer

---

[1]   *The Upanishads*, translation and commentary by Alistair Shearer et al, pp. 43–44.

Each stream emerged and evolved to provide spiritual influence or super fuel to get the seeker up the mountain. And, there are many paths up the mountain that lead to the same peak.

TANTRA

Tantra is far more ancient than its emergence in written scriptures around 300 CE. From as early as twenty thousand years ago (and some scholars speculate that it was far earlier), people of antiquity worshipped local deities, usually a mother goddess, to insure the ongoing fertility and well-being of the tribe. Tantric perspectives are easily traced in the Vedas and Upanishads, but these are recent appearances when compared to the actual evolution of humankind. From the timeless *sahaja* perspective, there is no question that, since the archaic dawn of humanity, there have been women and men who intuitively discovered the interlinking secrets and transformative subtle powers of the body, ritual magic, yogic practice, and consciousness.

Imagine the yogis and yoginis of ancient times living—in solitude or in tribal enclaves—in the pristine beauty of the remote, primordial world and, through their inward journey, discovering the secrets that lie sleeping within the human body. Slowly, over thousands of years of human experience, evolving from inchoate tribal and shamanic magic to specific means and methods, it became known that an individual could cultivate intense bliss in the worship of an *ishta devata* and reach a supreme state of consciousness through ritual, discipline, and the interplay of flesh-and-blood partners in sexual union.

In this way, specific knowledge was revealed to individual practitioners, then refined and passed down from guru to practitioner along lineage streams through oral tradition to be written down eventually in the form of scripture. However, to assume that tantric knowledge did not exist before it was written down—like the Vedas—is a small view of spiritual evolution in humankind; in fact, this is a limited way of thinking that comes out of the Western dependence on rational, empiric, linear thought. A parallel example of this evolutionary process occurring over time is found in the system of *asana* and yogic practice described in Patanjali's *Yoga Sutras* (150–200 CE). The wisdom of the body known as *asanas*, or the postures that have been developed and passed down through the systems of hatha yoga, were surely known and practiced by the yogis of antiquity long before Patanjali existed.

Such accumulated bodies of living knowledge occurred not only in the East but also around the world, among the Egyptians, Mayans, Celts, many indigenous tribal peoples, and (in more recent centuries) in the European occult alchemical tradition, to name a few. Much of this knowledge lives on today in the underground or esoteric streams of the major religious traditions of the West. In the Indian tradition, these bodies of knowledge are called *vidyas* and worshipped as living deities.

Hindu Tantra is essentially the worship of the feminine principle, or Shakti, as the primal active energy of the Absolute, depicted as Shiva. The ancient Sanskrit word "tantra" is sometimes translated as "loom"—perhaps an interpretation of its more literal meaning of the root "tan," which means to stretch or extend. An ancient tantric Buddhist text states, "tantra is continuity."[2] This literal definition deepens the metaphor of a loom, in which threads are stretched, extended, and then interconnected through a process of complex weaving to create a whole fabric. This is poetic language for the basic tantric philosophy that the individual *jiva* or soul can realize its innate divinity or *atman* without renouncing the enjoyment that is native to life and embodiment—family, relationships, creativity, children, food, drink, music, dance, artistic endeavor, and so on.

Although tantric practice may predominantly involve the ritual worship of the goddess as *ishta devata*, the tradition cannot be confined to the worship of the feminine principle. Tantra is fluid by definition; its tapestry is inclusive, woven of many different threads that naturally weave together Shiva and Shakti, as they are the inseparable Mother/Father of Creation. In practice, the lines between the worship of Shakti and Shiva are extremely blurred—many tantric sects actively worship both. Shiva and Shakti are not only conjoined and interdependent—as

in the symbolism of the *lingam* and *yoni*—but ultimately the same. This means that, according to tantric philosophy, the manifest worlds are not merely an illusion—they are the very real manifestation of the Divine Absolute. In this view of Reality, tantra elevates all of Creation. David Gordon White's "working definition" of tantra resounds with the view of *sahaja*:

Tantra is the Asian body of beliefs and practices which, working from the principle that the universe we experience is nothing other than the concrete manifestation of the divine energy of the godhead that creates and maintains the universe, seeks to ritually appropriate and channel that energy, within the human microcosm, in creative and emancipatory ways.[3]

As a spiritual symbol, Shiva represents the Absolute, formless, unborn, undying Purusha, or pure consciousness. Shakti represents the vast Creation, Nature, or Prakriti—the universe of worlds within worlds of form, from subtle to gross. It is the cosmic play between these two polarities that engenders Creation. Shiva, as consciousness, cannot "do" anything such as create, play, evolve, or participate; he exists as the prior condition of consciousness or abstract Reality. It is only through Shakti—his active energy, which is the creative, playful, evolutionary,

---

[2]   The *Guhya-Samaja-Tantra*.
[3]   David Gordon White, "Introduction," *Tantra in Practice*, p. 9.

participatory expression of Shiva—that the manifest worlds come into being. Therefore, from the tantric view, if one wishes to engage the evolutionary journey that leads home, one worships the goddess. If one worships the goddess, then one is firmly planted in the body, in nature, and in the rich cornucopia of life; it is here, in the fullness of life, that we discover the truth of our existence.

While the Vedic and Upanishadic tradition teaches that realization or spiritual evolution is accomplished through sacrifice, renunciation or extreme asceticism, in which one abandons all identifications with worldly life, the senses, and the body, Tantra takes a revolutionary position, posing the essential question: If we are given innate divinity as our birthright—the *atman* or the Self— then why do we have to struggle so hard to "attain" what is already present within us? Why do we have to renounce pleasure in order to realize bliss?

David Gordon White writes that the purpose of tantric practice—either through ritual or through yoga—is to uncover and make manifest this true nature. The body becomes the necessary organic matrix in which this occurs. He concludes, "Rather than being impediments, the world and the human body become channels to salvation."[4] This view dovetails with the concept of *sahaja* as the inherent "already present enlightenment" that is the primordial condition of beings, which permeates both Buddhist and Hindu tantric traditions. Life is simply what it is, and it is obvious in its divine nature. The diverse created elements of life arise from and as *sahaja*, the primordial essence of being.

In this view of life, Creation is not separate from its Creator. All of Creation is fundamentally *sahaja*, or the primordial spiritual essence, which Lee described as "Organic Innocence" imbued with "the Primacy of Natural Ecstasy." *Sahaja* is naturally ecstatic, which means that Creation is essentially pure and blissful in its innate recognition of interrelatedness between all that exists. It is this vision of oneness and unity that imbues the diversity of life with beauty and relationships between human beings and all of nature with nobility and wisdom.

The *sahaja* path is the spontaneous, natural, innate, easy way of realization because one's true nature is pre-existing and already present. This "easy" aspect of *sahaja* does not mean that one does not need discipline. In order to realize one's innate nature without rigorous extremes of ascetic practice, Tantrism developed mantras, rituals, and *sadhanas* in which the pursuit of ultimate realization is the context of activity in all aspects of daily life, ritual, and worship.

The spirit of *sahaja* is captured in the simplicity and universality of the sacred *dhuni* fire, which has been passed down from time immemorial to *tantrikas* and *sadhus* of all paths who tend the fire as the focus of

---

4   Ibid, pp. 9–10.

their meditation, prayer, or austerity. The *dhuni* is shaped like a *yoni* and is considered to be an embodiment and invocation of the goddess. Unlike the traditional Vedic fire rituals, worship at a *dhuni* fire is accessible to all people, all sexes, from all castes and walks of life, which is a large part of its appeal to practitioners.

Because *tantrikas* practice in all aspects of life, sexuality is included as a dimension of experience that may be approached as a form of yoga. The idea of sacred sex as a form of *sadhana* is considered profane by orthodox paths that teach the renunciation of desire in all forms. Today, Tantra is a commonly misunderstood and even abused concept, largely because of the psychological obsession with sex and sexuality that is so prevalent in the West. Too many Westerners interpret the practice of sexual yoga as a means for self-gratification, for greater sensual pleasure, or simply for entertainment or fun. In fact, such a practice is marked by a demand to greater clarity, the relinquishing of personal identity and attachment, and freedom from sentimentality and egoic desires. The actual practice of Tantra burns away the desire for personal gratification and, sooner or later, impels a direct confrontation with impermanence and emptiness.

The World is Real

The key to understanding Tantric practice is the mandala, the energy grid that represents the constant flow of divine and demonic, human and animal impulses in the universe, as they interact in both constructive and destructive patterns. Like the Vedic sacrificial altar of which it is a streamlined form, the mandala is a mesocosm, mediating between the great and small (the universal macrocosm and the individual microcosm), as well as between the mundane and the sublime . . . . This grid is three-dimensional, in the sense that it locates the supreme deity . . . . the source of that energy and ground of the grid itself, at the center and apex of a hierarchized cosmos. All other beings, including the practitioner, will be situated at lower levels of energy/consciousness/being, radiating downward and outward from the mandala's elevated center point.

Because the deity is both transcendent and immanent, all of the beings located at the various energy levels on the grid participate in the outward flow of the godhead, and are in some way emanations or hypostases of the deity himself (or herself). For Hindu Tantra, this means that the world is real and not an illusion; this is an important distinguishing feature of Hindu Tantric doctrine. Rather than attempting to see through or transcend the world, the practitioner comes to recognize "that" (the world) as "I" (the supreme egoity of the godhead): in other words, s/he gains a "god's eye view" of the universe, and recognizes it to be nothing other than herself-himself . . . . [T]his means that buddhahood is virtual within all creatures. In the words of the Heyvajra Tantra (2.4.70, 75), "All beings are buddhas" and "there is no being that is not enlightened, if it but knows its own true nature." [5]

— David Gordon White

---

[5]   Ibid, p. 9.

In traditional tantric practice, sexuality is not denied, but used when and where it is appropriate to the individual's unique circumstance, under the guidance of a qualified, trustworthy teacher or guru. Many tantric practitioners do not advise walking the razor's edge of sexual yoga, and only in very rare instances are sexual practices found in writings—the Sahajiya texts being an exception. In many paths, sexual yoga is intended to be engaged for an intentional period of time, then transcended or sublimated in the alchemical sense.

Many serious tantric practitioners choose to focus on ritual and yogic aspects of the path, remaining *brahmacharya* or celibate: as one Baul practitioner cautioned, "Better not to go there!" Sexual practice is considered dangerous because it unleashes a tremendous amount of psychosexual energy that can be difficult to channel or assimilate in useful and creative ways. An unstable character or weak ego can be overwhelmed and/or shattered by the power of transformational forces. In some cases, the sexual aspect of Tantra can unearth latent psychosis in the practitioner, including inflation of

Tantra

Tantra was never intended to serve as a starting point on a spiritual journey. Its description as being fast and terrifying (ugra) implies that anyone who seeks to follow the Tantric trail ought first to be thoroughly prepared for it, minimizing physiological weaknesses by using Ayurveda to balance the doshas and rejuvenate the tissues, and employing Yoga to purify the nadis (ethereal nerves), circulate prana, and initiate the process of Kundalini awakening. Only after the organism has become comfortable with Kundalini can one afford to consider the actual practice of Tantra.

Just as it takes at least ten thousand hours of work to master any craft (three hours daily for ten years, on average), one must experiment with one's practice for thousands of hours before awareness becomes effectively rewired. Good gurus specialize in discouraging students from confusing exciting incidents with tangible progress, downplaying the importance of those profound spiritual experiences that can seduce us into believing that we have achieved something of note.

Tantric transformation rarely transpires suddenly and irrevocably; it is usually a matter of punctuated evolution, of (sometimes tedious) reiterations of the same practices day in and day out until a particular pattern is worn away and a persona's pieces suddenly rearrange into a new configuration. Though Tantra offers the tools, it cannot operate them for you; but lift them and use them wisely, and you will see the results. If you will begin by addressing your long-set patterns, your habitual ways of looking at yourself and at the world, you will soon find yourself embarked on your own personal search for samarasa.[6]

— Dr. Robert Svoboda

---

[6]   Dr. Robert E. Svoboda, "Searching for Samarasa," drsvoboda.com.

the ego and highly charged grandiosity or self-obsession.

Even in traditional tantric paths, sexual union between partners as a yogic process is not always the wisest choice—it may be more productive to practice "right hand" tantra, which is largely a process of visualization, mantra, and ritual. The mature perspective is to understand the dangers and pitfalls and remember that we do not want to engage sexual yoga without a qualified guide. It is not necessary to grasp at the glittering bauble of so-called tantric sex on the way; the spiritual path has many efficacious means to achieve its ends. Indeed, Tantra seems mysterious and alluring, and yet the essence of tantra is found in every aspect of our lives. Tantric practice occurs within a huge arena in which we may work toward a spiritual transformation that rekindles our cellular memory of connection to the Earth, the Cosmos, and the Beyond.

Tantra emerged out of evolving oral teachings imbibed by the disciple directly from the master, a self-sustaining process that is saturated in the wisdom traditions of India over hundreds and even thousands of years. Traditional Tantra has a monastic or renunciate dimension with a solid foundation in the realization of nonduality and the way of *tapasya* (austerity). It also has a strong devotional dimension, and in this way it engenders *bhakti* and resonates with Vaishnava practice. It is grounded in ancient tribal worship of the Mother Goddess, and in this way it is practical and accessible to everyone.

It has informed countless other traditions, which have adopted many of its yogas and techniques of worship.

While a superficial look at the many sects that exist within what is called Hindu Tantra may yield useful definitions such as Baul, Sahajiya, Nath Siddhas, Aghora, Shaivite, Shakta, and so on, this distinction begins to vanish the further one progresses in practice. A practitioner comes to realize the universal connections between diverse paths and knows from the depths of his or her own experience that there is ultimately no difference between *tantrika*, the nondualist, the Baul, or the *bhakti*—all are inspired by the intermingling joy of truth, beauty, bliss, and love, found in great abundance in the dance of Life. It does not matter whether one worships Brahman, Ram, Krishna, Shiva, Kali, Durga, Jesus, Buddha, Allah, or simply *sahaja*—all lead to the same *eka*—the same oneness.

BUDDHIST SAHAJIYA

The connecting links between Tantra and the way of *sahaja* are found deeply imbedded in the *sahajiya* cults that gave rise to the Bauls. Long before the Bauls, tantric practice and *sahaja* teachings found a receptive home in the uprising cult of Buddhism in India.

By the fourth century of the current era, the reformist religious movement initiated by Siddhartha Gautama Buddha (563–483 BCE) was in full flower in India. Buddhism brought with it a fresh wind of simplicity and nondual teaching that did not require the intervention of Vedic priests and their complicated rituals, endless sacrifices to garrulous gods and goddesses, and restrictions based on caste and sex. (For example, even today women or individuals of lower caste status in India are not allowed to enter certain temples to worship. Rituals conducted by priests to deities are expensive and involve money up front or in the form of payment to the priest himself.)

For the next six hundred years Buddhism spread easily among the populace, converting many Hindus with its simplicity and direct access to realization. In this way, Buddhism and the ideals of *sahaja* were a perfect complement. In the long run, this important event in history resulted in a fertile cross-pollination of philosophy and spiritual practice between Hindus and Buddhists. As Buddhism grew, so did systems of tantric yoga, and these were adopted by both Hindu and Buddhist sects. While tantric sects proliferated all over India, in Bengal it was the merging of these with *sahaja* and the teachings of Lord Buddha that produced the early Sahajiyas of northeastern India and Bengal in particular.

The Buddhist Sahajiyas wrote down their revelations in *caryapadas*, or verses on practice, carried along in the tantric songs or *dohas* that went with them. Using poetic terms, the Sahajiya Buddhists captured their philosophy, *sadhana*, and dharma. Kanha, one Buddhist Sahajiya poet, wrote:

My citta (mind) is perfect vacuity.
Don't be sorry at the disappearance
of the skandhas or the five elements.
How can it be that Kanha is no more,
for he is throbbing,
forever pervading the whole universe!
Only foolish people are sad
at the sight of the decay
of the perceivable.
Can the flow of waves
dry up the whole sea?
Foolish people do not see those
who exist in their subtle sahaja form,
as they do not find the cream
that remains, pervading the milk.
Here, in this world, entities neither come
   nor go,
Yogin Kanha revels in these thoughts.

In this *caryapada*, Kanha reflects upon death with strong undertones of the Mahayana Buddhist doctrine of *sunyata*, or emptiness, which is clearly blended with the *sahaj* vision and the Vedic and Upanishadic teachings of Hinduism; such was the creative interplay of dharma and practice that existed for centuries between Hindu and Buddhist tantric cults. In fact, Das Gupta writes that the Buddhist Sahajiya cult was an amalgam, a creative synthesis, of Buddhism, Vedanta, Tantra, and Yoga.[7]

Whether Buddhist or Hindu sects were dominant in Bengali culture at any given

---

[7]   Das Gupta, *Obscure Religious Cults*, p. 35.

After the Gupta period most of Bengal contin-ued to be ruled by Hindu kings until the middle of the eighth century, when the country came under the powerful Buddhist Pala kings. The majority of the population, particularly those who were socially humble, adopted the rulers' religion and Bengal became one of the most important grounds for the dissemination of the Buddhist ideals. The Palas ruled till the middle of the twelfth century when they were replaced by the Sens, the Vaishnava Hindus from the south, whose reign lasted for a little over a hundred years.[8]

— Deben Bhattacharya

time seems to have been, to a great degree, determined by the ruling dynasty of the era. During the reign of the Hindu Vaishnava Gupta kings (320–550 CE), the arts and sciences flourished. The Guptas were known for their religious tolerance, which made it possible for Buddhism to continue to thrive in Bengal. During the rule of the Buddhist Palas (eighth through twelfth centuries CE), Buddhism was the popular religion; when the Hindu Sens ruled (twelfth through four-teenth centuries CE), religious sects took on a Hindu slant and Buddhism waned. A strong Muslim influence came into play during the Moghal Empires (fourteenth century CE), with their dynasties and shahs and nawabs.

Even with the flux of the political cli-mate and religious tolerance or intolerance in Bengal over hundreds of years, with diverse rulers and sweeping popular move-ments, the foundation of Bengali religious practice and mood was and remains to this day largely Hindu, based upon the ancient Vedas and later teachings of the Upani-shads, *puranas* (collections of ancient oral traditions of mythological legends and sto-ries about the Hindu gods and goddesses), and the great epics, the *Ramayana* and the *Mahabharata*.

While many sources claim that the Sah-ajiyas took a devotional Hindu Vaishnava turn due to complex political factors such as the onset of a new ruling dynasty (the Hindu Sens of the eleventh and twelfth centuries), it is more likely that it arose in the fertile, widespread *bhakti* renaissance of medieval times, liberally figured as beginning around 500 CE and extending to 1500 CE, which we will return to shortly. However, of equally powerful influence during this time was the great nondual visionary, Shankara.

ADI SHANKARA AND ADVAITA VEDANTA

From the vantage point of time, the pre-dominance of Buddhism that swept through India as a reformation of Vedic religion seemed to foreshadow the coming of Adi Shankara (788–820 CE), whose teaching rivaled and surpassed Buddhism, return-ing popular religious sentiment in general back toward Hindu traditions. While the

---

8   Deben Bhattacharya, *Songs of the Bards of Bengal*, p. 26.

Buddhist Sahajiyas

We don't have the Buddhist Sahajiyas any-more in Bengal, because most of them were destroyed, either by Hindu kings or the Islamic rulers, but there were masters who wrote down their songs. All these traditions were oral. They were mendicants who would never settle anyplace. They carried the coco-nut shell (in the old time it was not coconut shell, it was another fruit) and they carried ektara with them—one string—and it was a meditation of walking, singing, and chanting. They would walk mile after mile, go to differ-ent villages and beg, and people supported them by giving food.

We can only trace the history of that time through the songs. We have forty or forty-two songs, because most of these masters were burned to death. In all the scriptures they tell everything was broken, and they were put to fire. Two of the disciples of these masters received the death sentence, and they made two of the disciples run away to Nepal with only one palm leaf with these forty songs. This palm leaf was discovered much, much later, because we thought we didn't have any Bengali literature, we had only San-skrit. It is mostly written in the old Pali and Bengali mixed language. There was a scholar who found these songs in the library of a Nep-alese king, because these two disciples went there and gave it to the king to protect. [9]

— Parvathy Baul

Buddhist Sahajiyas were developing in Bengal, southern India was a hotbed of creativity and spiritual revolution that yielded the brilliance of Adi Shankara, the founder of Advaita Vedanta who was born in Kerala and traveled all over the subconti-nent expounding the all-pervading spirit of the Absolute as the ground of being called Brahman—the seamless ground of divin-ity that is underlying all appearances. With his early beginning in a more devotional approach (captured in his beautiful *sutra* to the goddess appropriately titled "Waves of Bliss"), Shankara left his roots in south India to wander and establish his teach-ings of pure nonduality in many important *pithas* or seats where Advaita could be learned. He ended his life in the far north at the source of the Ganges at the age of thirty-two, where he is said to have disap-peared into the Himalayas.

An extraordinary visionary, Shankara left an enduring legacy that became fully integrated into the spiritual landscape of India. The nondual Supreme Reality is the central theme of Shankara's teachings, which built upon Vedic and Upanishadic teachings of old—"Vedanta" meaning "Veda's end," [10] and "advaita" meaning "not two," or nondual. The unitive Brahman is *nirguna*—nondual or without attributes or qualities; it exists without any subject/object

---

[9] Interview by the author with Parvathy Baul, August 2013, Ferme de Jutreau, France.
[10] Georg Feuerstein, *The Yoga Tradition*, p. 569.

relationship, polarities, or pairs of opposites. One of Shankara's famous teaching statements is: "Brahman alone is real, the world is appearance, *atman* (the self) is nothing but Brahman."

According to Vedanta, in order that Brahman may become known, it manifests itself with qualities, although these exist only within Brahman. Duality does exist, as we find ourselves existing in it and relating with it; therefore, from Nirguna Brahman comes Saguna Brahman, or Brahman with qualities, and from this comes the possibility of a personal creator God, or Isvara, and by application, an *ishta devata*.

Isvara as a Godhead with qualities is symbolically depicted as a trinity called the Trimurti. Each of the three images or "faces" of the Trimurti signifies or symbolizes an essential quality of the Divine. Brahma is the creator; Vishnu is the preserver; Shiva is the destroyer. However, the mere mention of Isvara provokes a devotional mood, leading back to the *bhakti* aspect of the path. This trinity pervades the vast iconography, philosophy, and spiritual mythology of Hinduism, but among the *bhakti* traditions of Hinduism, it is Vishnu and Shiva who reign supreme among these three and are often worshipped as the Godhead itself. Among Vaishnava sects, the primary worship is dedicated to one of Vishnu's *avataras*, Lord Krishna.

Vishnu as Narayana

The form Narayana first imagines through maya is Vasudeva-with-Lakshmi in a realm called Vaikuntha composed of a supremely pure mode of matter (suddha-sattva) beyond our reckoning. The non-dual Vaikuntha is changeless, transcendent to sun, moon, and fire, and any who reach it do not return to space and time. Vasudeva-with-Lakshmi is the primordial "Father-Mother," the highest mode of Narayana that beings can worship. Through maya, Vasudeva-with-Lakshmi makes formations (vyuhas) of himself to produce the cosmos and us, and differing forms (murtis) to act for us and to be served by us. Notable among these are three goddesses (devis) called Sri (kingship), Bhumi (the material realm), and Candika-Durga (victorious conquest); three gods (devas) called Visnu (pervading sustenance), Siva (destruction), and Brahma (emanation); and two humans called Balarama and Krshna . . . . [11]

— Dennis Hudson

THE BHAGAVATAS OF SOUTH INDIA

While Advaita Vedanta and tantric sects like the Buddhist Sahajiyas were on the rise, the devotional Vaishnava cult of the

---

[11]   D. Dennis Hudson, "Tantric Rites in Andal's Poetry, *Tantra in Practice*, edited by David Gordon White, p. 207.

Bhagavatas was simultaneously developing in south India, planting the seeds of the massive *bhakti* renaissance that was coming. The Bhagavatas were inspired by the twelve Alvar poet-saints, the most famous of which were Namm Alvar and the great poetess Andal. The Alvars (the "deep-diving ones") lived during the eighth and ninth centuries and created a body of inspired devotional poetry to Vishnu (known as Hari and Narayana, the personal aspect of Brahman) specifically in his incarnation as Lord Krishna. They left a legacy of passionate yearning for God as a personal deity, with an emphasis on the beauty, charm, grace, and transcendental grandeur and magnificence of God's play on earth and in the cosmos.

By the tenth century of the current era, the *Bhagavata Purana*, or *Srimad Bhagavatam* had taken form as a collection of the mythic stories and themes centered around Lord Vishnu and especially his *avatara*, Krishna. These stories were based on a rich oral tradition that dates back to at least the fourth century of the current era. The Bhagavatas lived by the wisdom of this great *purana*, and it is here that we find, written down for the first time, the story of the *ras lila*, or Krishna's play with the *gopis* (milkmaids) who lived in the idyllic forest village of Vraja.

It was this rich and ripe milieu of wisdom and knowledge that gave rise to the rituals, myths, practices, and complex

> **The Ras Lila**
>
> *Later commentators noted that the cowherdesses....do not go off alone for solitary union with Krshna, but remain together; they unite with him collectively, as if bathing together in the cool waters of his stunningly beautiful presence. Here erotic imagery depicts communal experience as it does in the famous "Dance of Delight" (ras lila) described in the Bhagavata Purana 10.29-33. Dancing in a circle in Vrndavana forest, Krshna appeared to each cowherdess as if he were with her alone, and yet they were all there together, united in their focus on him. Shared love of the Supreme Male is the basis of human community, Bhagavatas believe, for all souls in relation to God are like dependent females: their own fulfillment comes from giving God pleasure in the way servants give to a master, or polygamous wives give to a shared husband.*[12]
>
> — Dennis Hudson

philosophy and theology of the Bhagavatas. The *Bhagavata Purana* existed as an oral tradition for hundreds of years until it was collected and written down by Bhagavatas during the time of and after the lives of Andal and the Alvars.

As the maintainer and preserver of life and cosmos, Vishnu is the very aspect of God

---

[12]   Ibid, p. 213.

Absolute that dreams multiple universes simultaneously. Mythologically imaged as a beautiful, blue-skinned, four-armed divinity who sleeps upon Anantanaga, his serpent with many heads, Vishnu dreams the dream of the cosmos and the myriad arisings and subsidings of life at all levels in all dimensions, terrestrial and celestial. As the preserver of life, Vishnu takes incarnations in the human realm whenever the balance of opposites has become disturbed to re-establish order, peace, harmony, love; when darkness has taken over the world, Lord Vishnu comes to earth as Rama, Krishna, or one of his other forms specifically to kill the "demons" that are running rampant and upsetting the cosmic balance.

The mythic legends and activities of Vishnu are symbolic stories that inform us of the process of the individual soul in relationship to the Divine. The Bhagavatas believed that Narayana is the unchanging, endless Supreme Person, a boundless mass of scintillating light throwing off sparks that engender creation. Narayana then transforms himself, with the help of his Shakti, into space/time and manifests in the next formation as Vasudeva, which evolves into the next formation, called Bhagavan (Lord), who becomes Vishnu and is known in the intimate form as Hari, who then takes incarnation on Earth as Krishna.[13]

My full and swelling breasts
meant for the Supreme Being
whose body bears the Wheel and the Conch
are like the food set aside by brahmans
in the fire sacrifice
for the gods dwelling in heaven—
So if you say they are meant for a man,
that would be like a fox that wanders in a forest
who enters, licks, smells,
and picks over the food,
And I won't go on living,
don't you see, Manmatha?

With my body tarnished,
my hair disheveled,
my lips colorless,
and eating only once,
O splendid and able God of Desire,
Don't you notice the vow I endure?
Don't you see my lord,
only one thing is left to say:
Be gracious in a way that crowns my womanhood
and grant me this boon,
"She will seize the feet of Keshava the Beloved."

Worshipping three times a day,
venerating your feet,
tossing pure flowers in worship,
I sing your praise,
yet flawlessly I serve him alone,

---

[13]   D. Dennis Hudson, *The Body of God*, pp. 31–36.

He whose color is the sea that surrounds the
    earth—
and if I don't receive true life,
I shall run wild
and weep
and wail
and cry out, "Mother!"
And that will disgrace you entirely,
don't you see,
just as if you had yoked an ox to the plow
and worked it
but never gave it food.

By venerating the two feet of Lord Kama
whose bow is sugarcane
and whose arrows are flowers
and by saying,
"The one there who ripped off the tusk
of the incomparable roaring elephant
and split the mouth of the bird,
he the color of blue gem,
set me aside for him."
Goda, daughter of Visnucitta....
composed this garland of Tamil with desiring
    love,
and those adept in the reciting of it will
without a doubt,
reach the feet of the King
of those dwelling in Visnu's realm.[16]

— Andal

According to the Bhagavatas, pure wisdom and absolute knowledge of the self is accessible only in Vaikuntha—Vishnu's heaven realm—and is given only to those who have undefiled consciousness. This means that in the Kali Yuga—the current times, when suffering and passions are the most overwhelming—very few will escape the swamp of illusion and reclaim the knowledge of their true identity as a spark from Narayana's generative, original light. This suffering of the illusion of separation from Narayana creates great anxiety, which causes beings to cling to false security of all kinds, giving rise to ceaseless grasping in endless rounds of desire, anger, and greed. Although this is true, the Bhagavatas found hope in the incarnation of Bhagavan as Krishna, savior and redeemer of the lost and hopeless. For this purpose, the Bhagavatas turned to the practice of repeating or chanting the sacred eight-syllable mantra, *Om Namo Narayanaya*.[14]

The revered poetess of the Bhagavatas, Andal, was a historical person whose life as recounted in her poetry has been passed down through the centuries. According to scholar Dennis Hudson, Andal's poems contain not only a biographical description of her *sadhana* but also of tantric rites held during the month of Margali that ends with the winter solstice, with which Krishna associates himself in the *Bhagavad Gita*.[15] At some point during this

---

[14]   Dennis Hudson, *Body of God*, p. 172.
[15]   Ibid, pp. 434–436.
[16]   Ibid, pp. 436–439.

month, the girls of Andal's village arose in the chilly predawn, gathered a drum and other ritual implements, then walked to the river together to bathe and then fashion an image of the goddess from sand. They worshipped this goddess to gain her blessings for the benefits of all during the year beginning with the winter solstice: for the sake of the people, they prayed for rain, and for themselves, they prayed for a husband.[17] Hudson comments on the "genius" of Andal, a spiritual visionary who took the temple rites of the Bhagavatas and visually projected onto them the bathing rites and vows of the village girls in their prayers to the goddess:

....she then visualized the actors of that vow, herself included, as cowherdesses living in Krsna's village of Gokula, far to the north, in a previous age. Out of that complex perceptual patterning she spoke a poem believed by [Vaishnavas] to contain the essence of the Upanishads.[18]

Andal went on to blend and evolve these rites so that the male and female Bhagavatas rose in the dark before dawn as cowherdesses and gathered at the river to worship the goddess in the imagined Yamuna River. Andal visualized them as standing at the door of Krishna's bedroom, where they sing to him and beg him to open the door so that they might ask him for the drum that they need in order to worship the goddess.[19]

Andal's poetry contains a mysterious hint about the convergence between tantric practices and the devotional sect of the Bhagavatas, which preceeded the later synthesis that occurred between the tantric Sahajiyas and Vaishnava sects of Bengal. It is another example of how the lines and boundaries between practitioners and paths are often blurred in a way that gives rise to great creativity and spiritual growth, even while the integrity of the tradition remains intact.

The Bhagavatas worshipped Krishna as the personal beloved as well as the Godhead, or Divine Absolute; their era predates and finally dovetails with the early developments of the medieval *bhakti* renaissance. Their philosophy and teachings, and most of all their relationship to Krishna, are echoed in powerful ways among the Sahajiyas and the Bauls. Although we cannot trace a direct historical connection between the two sects, the Bhagavatas were the precursors of the *bhakti* renaissance that played a major part in the arising of the Baul spirit in Bengal many years later—and the resonance between them is unmistakable.

THE BHAKTI RENAISSANCE

The *bhakti* renaissance erupted in medieval India, bringing the sweet water of devotion,

---

[17]   D. Dennis Hudson, "Tantric Rites in Andal's Poetry, *Tantra in Practice*, edited by David Gordon White, p. 212.

[18]   Ibid.

[19]   Ibid, p. 213.

rasa, and divine mood to a rather dry, ascetic religious climate. In an inspired return to the ancient spiritual epics of India—the *Ramayana* (the story of Lord Rama) and *Mahabharata* (the story of Lord Krishna) with its central song, the *Bhagavad Gita*, in which Krishna expounds the yoga of devotion—the re-emergence of *bhakti* gave rise to a widespread development of philosophy and spiritual practice. These were further fueled by recently collected stories of the *Bhagavata Purnana* and the vision of God-intoxicated souls who perceived the possibility to go beyond nondual realization and into an awakened awareness of the essential realness of the world of form—Creation itself.

The passionate, far-flung resurgence of the *bhakti* tradition that took place in medieval India over several hundred years changed the face of spiritual understanding and practice for millions of people—just as the powerful reformist teachings of Buddha and Shankara had changed culture and consciousness in their times. Shankara's profound elucidation of nondual realization provided the fertile field, the necessary foundation, in which the *bhakti* renaissance could flower and bear fruit. From the view of the big picture, we see that with each new phase of development, human consciousness in relationship to the Divine was further evolved.

Beginning with Ramanuja, there were five great *bhakti* voices that emerged during this time of renaissance, each of whom founded one of the five major *sampradayas* of contemporary Vaishnava Hinduism. These schools still thrive today, not only in India but among Hindus worldwide.[20] As we will see in later chapters, the great *bhakti* visionaries tilled the soil and prepared the garden in which Jayadeva, Chandidas, and Chaitanya—as patron saints of the Bauls and their forerunners, the Vaisnava Sahajiyas—could plant seeds that would spontaneously flower, giving rise to tantric devotional streams of practice, *sadhana*, and lifestyle.

THE MERGING OF TANTRA AND DEVOTIONAL LOVE

The *bhakti* renaissance of medieval India gave a new shape to the inhabitants of the Bengali world in the emergence of a Hindu Sahajiya sect that grew from and co-existed with the older sect of the Buddhist Sahajiyas. The major differences between the Buddhist and Hindu Sahajiyas was that the latter sought a direct experience of living relationship with the Supreme Being, and toward this aim they emphasized the cultivation of intense feelings of love, while the Buddhist Sajajiyas were rooted in a non-theistic approach centered around the nondual teachings of *shunyata*, or emptiness. Nonetheless, they shared *sahaja* philosophy and yogic practices at the roots of the same tree: Hindu Tantra. On this subject, the respected Bengali professor, S. Das

---

[20] The five preceptors of the major bhakti sampradayas of India today were: Ramanuja (1017–1137), Nimbarka (1139–1200), Madhva (1238–1317), Vallachabharya (1479–1531) and Chaitanya (1485–1533).

Gupta, wrote extensively on this subject over seventy years ago.

Both Buddhist and Hindu Sahajiyas place the supreme importance, ultimately, on *sahaja*. In an interview conducted during a visit at Lee's ashram in France during the summer of 2013, Parvathy Baul, the spiritual daughter of Sanatan Das Baul, explained the Baul perspective:

> The Sahajiya is what I find very interesting. When we sing so much of Gaur Gauranga (Chaitanya) and we chant the Shikshashtakum and we wear saffron, it's often mistaken as a [purely] Vaishnava tradition. Many scholars write that Baul started from the fifteenth century after the bhakti movement by Chaitanya, but Sahajiya existed even before, and it had connection to the Buddhist practitioners. We have pure evidence only from the seventh century, but such a profound knowledge and practice cannot come in one day. It must have started a long, long time ago and then slowly matured into Baul.[21]

Buddhist and Hindu Sahajiyas shared the creative melting pot of the *sahaj* path, which yielded a great love for producing dharma art in the form of poems and songs. Song writers par excellence, they engaged in a rich exchange between small groups and lineages. While the Buddhist Sahajiyas wrote of *bodhichitta* and *sunyata*, the Hindu Sahajiyas wrote about ecstatic devotion to God—and about the esoteric yoga they practiced in order to realize Radha and Krishna within. ✵

The Evolution of Centuries

It will be incorrect to say, as has been said by some scholars, that the Vaisnava Sahajiya movement of Bengal is a purely post-Chaitanya movement having no relation whatsoever with the earlier Buddhist Sahajiyas, and that the two cults are fundamentally distinct. A close study of the literature of the Vaisnava Sahajiyas will leave no room for doubting the clear fact that it records nothing but the spirit and practices of the earlier Buddhist and Hindu Tantric cults, of course in a distinctly transformed form, wrought through the evolution of centuries in different religious and cultural environments.

The psycho-physiological yogic processes—frequently referred to in the lyrical songs of the Vaisnava Sahajiyas and also in their innumerable short and long texts—embodying the doctrines of the cult, are fundamentally the same as are found in the Hindu Tantras as well as in the Buddhist Tantras and the Buddhist songs and dohas.[22]

— Das Gupta

---

[21] Interview by the author with Parvathy Baul, August 2013, Ferme de Jutreau, France.
[22] Das Gupta, *Obscure Religious Cults*, pp. 115–116.

CHAPTER 3

Sahajiya

*The whole world is of the nature of sahaja—for sahaja is the
quintessence of all (svarupa); this quintessence is nirvana for
those who possess the perfectly pure mind (citta).*

The Hevajra Tantra

ALTHOUGH THEY CO-EXISTED FOR SOME PERIOD OF TIME in the rich cultural seedbed of
Bengal, the Vaishnava Sahajiyas evolved in a different direction than their cousins, the
Buddhist Sahajiyas. While the Hindu Sahajiyas incorporated the Buddhist tantric practice
merged with mahayana teachings on the nature of *shunyata* (emptiness), they were even more
significantly influenced by the religion of love found in Bengali Vaishnavism as it developed
from the great visionary Mahaprabhu Chaitanya.

The dominant feeling tone or *bhava* of love in all its nuances and subtle flavors was essential to the way of the Vaishnava Sahajiyas, and the cultivation of love, beauty, and joy became
a fundamental dimension of the path, with love, or *prema*, being the supreme of these. While
rubbing elbows with their Buddhist friends, the Vaishnava Sahajiyas took on a deep understanding of *sunyata,* and perhaps the complex, beautiful *yidam* practices of Tibetan Buddhism
were influenced by their Hindu Sahajiya brothers and sisters.

Like the Buddhists who wrote many *caryapadas*, the Vaishnava Sahajiyas were greatly
concerned with writing down their teachings. There is a significant body of literature that
expounds their *sahaja sadhana*—as many as two hundred-and-fifty manuscripts of small
texts, mostly written in the Bengali vernacular, contain their doctrines and practices. Perhaps more importantly, there are many poem-songs (*padavalis*) that have been preserved and
are still sung today, notably those of Chandidas, who is considered the greatest love poet of
Bengal and a patron saint of the Bauls. Lyrics as well as scriptural texts that belong to the
Vaisnava Sahajiya school are usually ascribed to Chandidas, as well as to other poets like
Vidyapati, Rupa, Sanatana, Vrndavana Dasa, Krishnadasa, Kaviraja, Narahari, Mukunda-
dasa and others.

All of the great poets, including the much earlier Jayadeva, and the great Vaisnava apostles—Rupa, Sanatana, Svarupa, Damodara, Jiva Gosvami and others—were considered to be practitioners of the *sahaja sadhana*. It is even said that Chaitanya himself (the revered ecstatic mystic who realized Radha and Krishna within his own body and founded the existing *sampradaya* of Gaudiya Vaishnavism) was considered by the Sahajiyas to have attained his realization, in part, through practice with female companions. This heretical view of the radical, noncomformist Sahajiyas extended to Buddha as well, who they say practiced *sahaj sadhana* with his consort Gopa.

THE DIVINITY IN HUMANKIND

The Vaishnava Sahajiyas were a sect of Hindu tantrikas who lived in northeastern India, especially in the region of greater Bengal (Bengal, Bihar, Orissa, Assam). They placed supreme importance on the *sahaja* ideal that human beings are microcosms of the macrocosm. In every way, the human man or woman is a personification of the Supreme Being, or Supreme Soul, and our divine inheritance is innate from birth, echoing the great maxim of the Upanishads, *Tat tvam asi*, or "You are That"—*atman* (the self) is none other than *brahman* (the Supreme Reality). There is no separation between the human being and the Divine; our bodies, minds, and souls exist as individual manifestations of

the Supreme Being, and yet, by the force of maya, we forget our noble heritage and must arouse the divine nature and innate connection with God. How that can be accomplished is the aim of *sahaja sadhana*.

Many philosophical schools commonly teach that human beings are born with the spark of God but have forgotten its origins due to illusion, attachment, and desire. These offer "systems"—technical, codified, and often linear in progression—by which human beings can be released from the illusion of existence and delivered into *moksha*, or liberation from the cycles of rebirth on Earth.

The Sahajiyas, on the other hand, take the natural, innate *sahaja* road in this regard. The Supreme Being has many qualities—mercy, beauty, splendor, truth, bliss, severity, magnificence, compassion—that fuel the cycles of creation, preservation, and destruction; these are the underlying propelling forces of the Great Process of Divine Evolution, a teaching term given by Khepa Lee. For the Sahajiyas, the greatest of these divine qualities is love. According to Sahajiya doctrine, it is the natural impulse of the soul to love; to be a vessel of pure love (*prema*) for the Divine is the highest possibility of a human life. The Sahajiyas created a spiritual culture that supported the awakening, flowering, and realization of innate love. And so, to the nondual statement *Tat tvam asi*—which is *sahaja*—the Sahajiyas added the dualistic, devotional fervor of bhakti: "I am Thine."

GOD'S DELIGHT

The love and joy of the *sahajiya* man is of a universal or cosmic character, though it easily pervades the most ordinary events of daily life. Such divine love permeates the whole world and does not exclude even the smallest insect of creation. The *Rasaratnasara* says:

God sports with love in the whole universe, even the Primeval Nature is going mad after this love. The movements of the planets and the stars proclaim this love, and the oceans and waves bear testimony to it. The play of Divine Love is visible everywhere and in every household. It can be felt as much in enjoyment as in austerities and ailments. The fact that God is love is proclaimed by every object of creation.[2]

While love and joy are considered the premiere qualities of God, they lead inevitably to beauty—as love, joy, and beauty go together. To know God's beauty depends upon the knowledge that God is in every aspect of Creation. God is the life of all; God is both *prema* (love) and *kama* (passion, lust), both the body and its shadow. He manifests as maya for the sake of Creation; he creates, preserves, and destroys. He is earth,

---

[1]   Bose, *The Post-Chaitanya Sahajiya Cult of Bengal*, pp. 213–14.
[2]   Ibid, p. 222.

water, air, fire. He is heaven and earth. He is present in movable and immovable forms and in formlessness. He is hunger and thirst in the body, as well as heat, cold, grief, greed, and illusion. God resides in whatever is born, and He is present as well in that which dies. He is the snake that bites and the physician who cures. He is illness and He is health. This is the mysterious nature of God; in all these, the marvelous beauty of the Supreme Being is made manifest.

He is ever full of love and joy, and His beauty pervades the Universe. The Sahajiyas place a particular emphasis on these three qualities, basing their teachings altogether on the culture of love, beauty, and bliss. The idea that the individual soul innately contains these characteristics presents us with the possibility to actively develop these innate qualities. In the symbolism of Radha and Krishna and their play in the enchanted realm of Vrindavana, the Vaishnava Sahajiyas found the perfect images to represent and embody an eternal state of being.

By entering into the feeling states associated with the residents of the mythical forests of Vraja—the primeval place of love play between Krishna and the *gopis*—one may attain Krishna, or God Himself. Freely using the *sandhya bhasa* or twilight language of myth, the Sahajiyas conceived of the Purusha and Prakriti of Samkhya as Krishna and Radha (objective or ultimate consciousness and nature or the manifest worlds, Shakti). The interplay of the cosmic Masculine and Feminine principles are described or mythologized in symbolic language in spiritual systems of all traditions; they are richly discovered in the many great philosophical schools of India, including in the *Pancaratra Samhitas*, the *Srimad Bhagavatam*, the *Bhagavad Gita*, the *puranas*, and in the works of great Vaishnava realizers such as Ramanuja, Nimbarka, and Vallabha.

In Samkhya, the relationship between Purusha and Prakriti is like a woman who is seated on the shoulders of a man, who must therefore do as she wishes, but for the Sahajiyas of Bengal, Prakriti (Radha) is united with Purusha (Krishna) in the intimate embrace of love as it exists between a lover and beloved. Their movements are a function of mutual pleasure, rapport, enjoyment, communion.

The Krishna of the Sahajiyas is not a historical person who takes birth and death in this world; he is a Supreme Being who exists in the sublime mystic reality—a personal Beloved of the soul. He exists in the mythical land of Vrindavana or Vraja, or in the subtle dimension of Vishnu's heaven, Vaikuntha; he has no physical existence, but he is so omnipotent that he can attract the heart of the whole world. To experience his *bhava*, his divine blessing, his love embrace, he must be worshipped with the mystic formula of passion-lust-pleasure. However, of essential importance is the *sahaja* aspect of this: Krishna as pervasive Supreme Being does not live "out there" somewhere, but in the body-mind-soul of every individual human being.

All the senses are engaged in realizing the mysteries of Krishna's love. In order

> ### Radha
>
> *Radha is not only the manifestation of the faculty of joy embodied in Krishna, but she represents his full potentiality, and in union is attached to him like musk and its scent, or fire and its heat. The idea of such inseparable union in the romantic sphere of love is the keystone of the modern Vaisnavism of Bengal, which has also been adopted by the Sahajiyas in developing their mystic cult.[3]*
>
> — M.M. Bose

to have the immediate, personal experience of the love of Krishna and Radha, the Sahajiyas turn primarily to the relationship between woman and man. Through sexual yoga, or union with a partner, one becomes a connoisseur of enjoyment in the *rasas* of love. The *sadhaka* and *sadhika* invoke and experience *rasa*, joy, bliss for the enjoyment of RadhaKrishna—the interplay of divine Masculine and Feminine as the Supreme Reality residing in the human being. This is our birthright. This is our possibility.

RADHA AND KRISHNA

For the Vaisnava Sahajiyas—and later for the Bauls—it is the feminine principle in the image of Radha, the divine consort, that rises up through the spine to unite with Krishna in the yogic process. This is an essential tenet of the Baul way, which develops the understanding that every human being is feminine in relationship to the Divine. One must cultivate the greatest qualities of the feminine dimension of life in order to realize the true love relationship with Krishna. In his book, *The Divine Player—A Study of the Krishna Lila*, contemporary Western author David Kinsley describes the relationship between the Vaishnava and Buddhist Sahajiyas in ways that are very similar to Das Gupta: "Like the orthodox Bengal Vaisnavas, the Sahajiyas believe that the love sport of Radha and Krishna takes place eternally."[4] It is the eternal play of Krishna and Radha, revealed in the *inner culture* of the individual, which the Vaisnava Sahajiya and the Bauls seek to discover.

In very general terms, the tantric perspective is one of continuity, of non-rejection of those aspects of human life—birth, death, sex, and the life of the body with all its messy organic processes—that are so often denied, dismissed, or repressed by conservative organized religions. In truth, these dimensions of human life carry the most intensely concentrated power to fuel the process of transformation, and therefore are of great interest to the serious practitioner.

At the same time, the sexual yogas are only one aspect of tantric practice, which may be engaged for a specific period of time

---

[3]   Bose, M.M., PCSCB, p. 235.
[4]   David Kinsley, *The Divine Player*, p. 174.

and commitment to *guruvada*, or guru yoga, being central to the path. David Kinsely writes about the process of yoga among the Vaishnava Sahajiyas:

[T]he kundalini (the female force in Hindu Tantrism pictured as a coiled serpent located beneath the genitals) is identified with Radha. When the sadhaka succeeds in arousing the kundalini in traditional Hindu Tantrism, it is believed to rise to the head and unite with Siva or a corresponding male principle.[6]

When considering the sexual yoga engaged between partners, there is an important distinction that is made in Krishna *bhakti* between *aiswarya* (majestic), and *madhura* (sweet) or *sringara* (erotic); for the Vaishnava Sahajiyas, erotic or sweet *bhakti* is considered a superior quality of worship—Krishna as lover. For the Sahajiyas, the union of woman and man recapitulates the divine union of Radha and Krishna and provides the fuel for the sweet, passionate *rasa* that pleases the Lord. The purpose of ritual sex among the Sahajiyas is to transform *kama* (desire) into *prema* (pure love) for the enjoyment of the Lord. Eventually the sexual mandala of two bodies joined together ceases to be necessary and may fall away; the individual *rasika* (enjoyer of *rasa*) has fallen into the state of love and remains in love with the Beloved.

of *sadhana*. For some practitioners sexual *sadhana* with a partner may not arise at all within a lifetime on the path; instead the yoga is engaged strictly internally, and many other aspects of yoga take the forefront of *sadhana*, with the worship of an *ishta devata*

---

[5] Kinsley, David, *The Divine Player*, p. 173.

[6] Ibid, pp. 173–4.

THE NECKLACE OF IMMORTALITY

In his extraordinary essay on the Vaishnava Sahajiyas and what is perhaps their greatest preserved written work, *The Necklace of Immortality*, Glen Hayes echoes the important distinction of the Vaishnava Sahajiyas and the Bauls of today: the practitioner does not seek to experience Krishna and Radha as divinities living outside themselves, but to make the tantric journey from *rupa* to *svarupa*, in which one realizes one's innate being as identical to and continuous with Radha and Krishna.

Hayes points out that this path was highly controversial in its time, and certainly it carries a shadowy element. A primary instruction to male practitioners was to engage a *parakiya* lover—a woman married to another man. Furthermore, the question of the consumption and use of the ambrosial essences of a woman's body exclusively for the male partner's transformation or enlightenment begs a discerning inquiry and is worthy of deeper reflection. Even though there was the historical reality of serious inequity between women and men (based on the religious and cultural milieu) among the Sahajiyas, nonetheless, the text of *The Necklace of Immortality* clearly holds the female partner in the highest regard and of the utmost importance; in fact, transformation is not possible without the help of a female adept.

> ### Rupa and Svarupa
>
> *According to Sahajiyas, every man has within himself his "true form" (svarupa) as Krsna, the divine masculine principle, and every woman has within herself her divine feminine principle as Radha. And rather than trying to visualize and then participate in the lovemaking of a god and his consort in heaven, Sahajiyas call upon all men and women to make love themselves in order to unify their essences and get to heaven. In doing so, Sahajiyas are using the physical world and their human bodies as platforms and tools for their experiments with the sacred.*[7]
>
> — Glen Hayes

Written in 1650 CE, *The Necklace of Immortality* was composed by Mukunda-dasa, one of many Sahajiya gurus who "attempted to blend the complex worlds of Tantric yoga and bhakti devotionalism, offering both men and women a powerful means of liberation from the apparent limitations of the ordinary world and their bodies."[8] As Hayes points out, it is a path that is quite offensive to orthodox streams, and yet it is a path with obvious appeal to the Western sensibility and idealism. The following excerpts of verses offer a glimpse into the teachings of this powerful text, which begins with invocations to the guru lineages beginning with Chaitanya and

---

[7] Glen Hayes, "The Necklace of Immortality: A Seventeenth Century Vaisnava Sahajiya Text," *Tantra in Practice*, edited by David Gordon White, pp. 310-11.

[8] Ibid, p. 315

the *ishta devata*, Krishna. After establishing the basic concepts of practice, lineage, and *sampradaya*, the text continues:

13) *Divine Love for Krishna is always pure, it is never stained. Get rid of the Vedas and never perform any Vedic rituals!*

14) *The first step on the path is to seek refuge at the place of the mantra guru. Ordinary physical birth is from a womb, but this only results in old age and hell!*

15) *When you are accepted by the guru you will be sheltered by the power of the mantra. Keep the instructions of the guru close to your heart!*

16) *With great care, the guru who has initiated you with the mantra will guide your practices. You must continue to follow these instructions for as long as you practice!*

17) *One of those commands is that you associate with a special community of practitioners. Through following such instructions, you will reach the state of consciousness of the Divine Existence.*

Mukunda goes on to speak to the transformations of the body that are possible through the *sadhana* that is required for a shared sexual yoga between men and women:

27) *A Divine Body (devadeha) must be born within the physical body. So how many men and women come to know that they possess a Divine Body?*

28) *With effort, you will discover the Divine Body within the physical body....*

29) *By performing ritual practices with a woman, the Divine Body will be discovered within the physical body. A woman who has realized her divine inner nature should serve as the passionate Female Partner.*

34) *The blessed Inner Damsel Body leads the adept to the Vraja heaven. With her body of eternity, she helps the adept to master the passions.*

35) *Without her, you'll never taste the passion-filled Cosmic Substances of the Vraja heaven. For adepts seeking Vraja, she is the very essence of the way of passion.*

37) *The Female Partner who is imbued with Divine Love shimmers with erotic energies, and is herself a well of Divine Essence. Having a splendid body like Radha, she is the well of both Divine Essence and Cosmic Substance.*[9]

The Vaishnava Sahajiyas were keepers of the esoteric knowledge that a woman's body contains a spiritual secret; through the yogic practices of taking sexual fluids (both semen and the precious female substances referred to in *The Necklace*) up through the urethra and into the spinal cord to flow upward to the brain, the man builds his

---

[9] "The Necklace of Immortality," pp. 319-320.

Divine Body to realize the innate *svarupa*, or the RadhaKrishna within. However, as one Baul practitioner told this writer, in the shadow side of tantric traditions, many yogis have used women for this purpose (too often female partners are "sucked dry," then discarded for another "juicier" partner); relationships of grave inequity or abuse have been the result. When studying tantric practices involving sexual yogas, there are many questions that should be asked, including issues of gender and power, and answered in a way that is equitable and liberating for both partners. The Western Baul view is that transformational substances are equally shared by both partners (a hint of the secret practice).

In a brilliant natural synthesis occurring over stretches of time and changes in political climates, the Sahajiyas of Bengal blended the orthodox worship of Lord Vishnu in the form of Krishna with Hindu Tantrism in rich, complex practices and teachings that were further fueled by the *bhakti* renaissance of medieval times.

Quite literally, the Vaishnava Sahajiyas carried the cellular knowledge of inherited ancient wisdom, passed down through generations, in the blood and bones of their organic beings, and with this as their ground, they became the pioneers and radicals of their place and time, who forged new paths toward eternal potentials of human transformation. It was this inheritance that was taken up by the even more radical Bauls. ✳

CHAPTER 4

Singers of God

*Everyone speaks of Sahajiya, but alas! Who knows its
real meaning? One who has crossed the region of
darkness can alone have the light of Sahajiya.*

Chandidas

THE ESSENCE OF THE SAHAJ WAY is communicated in the spontaneous praise of the Supreme Reality that takes creative flight in poems, songs, and *sankirtana*—chanting the Name of God. As the Bauls began to evolve, they took their greatest inspiration from poet-seers: Jayadeva, the twelfth-century wandering poet who wrote the *Gita Govinda;* the fourteenth-century radical Sahajiya poet, Chandidas; and a century later, Mahaprabhu Sri Chaitanya, the renowned mystic who was deified during his lifetime as an incarnation of both Krishna and Radha.

All three were singers of God: Jayadeva and Chandidas were *mahakavis*, great poets who wrote poem-songs or *padavalis* that have withstood the test of time, enduring over centuries to inspire seekers on the way. Sri Chaitanya, who is considered the root guru of the Baul lineages, made *sankirtan* his great song. He was inspired by his predecessors, Jayadeva and Chandidas, whose love songs he was known to sing, as recorded in his biographies. Exploring these three seminal influences on today's Bauls from a historical perspective sheds light on how this unique path emerged from the creative synthesis of its origins.

JAYADEVA AND PADMAVATI

During the time of medieval India, in which the *bhakti* path, or yoga of devotion, surged to the forefront of spirituality among the people in a vast, sweeping movement, creativity flourished among the wandering poets. It is at the first stirrings of this movement that we discover the Vaishnava poet, Jayadeva (AD 1200), whose passionate words of love and beauty have endured across the centuries to speak to the human heart. All of the great *bhakti* streams that came after Jayadeva owe much of their religious mythology to his rendering of

From the *Gita Govinda*, the "Song of the Lord"

Jayadeva, wandering king of bards
who sings at Padmavati's lotus feet,
was obsessed in his heart
by rhythms of the goddess of speech,
and he made this lyrical poem
from tales of the passionate play
when Krishna loved Sri.

If remembering Hari enriches your heart,
if his arts of seduction arouse you,
listen to Jayadeva's speech
in these sweet soft lyrical songs....

You rest on the circle of Sri's breast,
wearing your earrings,
fondling wanton forest garlands;
   Triumph, God of Triumph, Hari!

The sun's jewel light encircles you
as you break through the bond of existence—
a wild Himalayan goose on lakes in minds of holy men.
   Triumph, God of Triumph, Hari!

You defeat the venomous serpent Kaliya,
exciting your Yadu kinsmen
like sunlight inciting lotuses to bloom.
   Triumph, God of Triumph, Hari!

You ride your fierce eagle Garuda
to battle demons Madhu and Mura and Naraka,

leaving the other gods free to play.
   Triumph, God of Triumph, Hari!

Watching with long omniscient lotus-petal eyes,
you free us from bonds of existence,
preserving life in the world's three realms.
   Triumph, God of Triumph, Hari!

Janaka's daughter Sita adorns you.
You conquer demon Dusana.
You kill ten-headed Ravana in battle.
   Triumph, God of Triumph, Hari!

Your beauty is fresh as rain clouds.
You hold the mountain to churn elixir from the sea.
Your eyes are night birds drinking from Sri's moon face.
   Triumph, God of Triumph, Hari!

Poet Jayadeva joyously sings
this song of invocation
in an auspicious prayer.
   Triumph, God of Triumph, Hari!

As he rests in Sri's embrace,
on the soft slope of her breast,
the saffroned chest of Madhu's killer
is stained with red marks of passion
and sweat from fatigue of tumultuous loving.
May his broad chest bring you pleasure too![1]

            — Jayadeva

---

[1]   Barbara Stoler Miller, *The Gita Govinda of Jayadeva,*

the mythic story of Krishna and Radha into classical Sanskrit poetry.

The *Gita Govinda* is a celebrated achievement that stands out in the genre of sacred erotic literature in the world. Springing out of a vast transformational process that was occurring at this time, Jayadeva succeeded in bringing the reality of the mystical realm back to the marketplace of human need.

The cultural and religious milieu of the times created a fertile ground for this breakthrough of transcendent creativity. Buddhism was not the only contender for religious supremacy in India—Vedic traditions had been equally, although more politically, vanquished by adherents of Islam. The ancient framework of Hindu culture in north India had been decimated by repeated Muslim invasions from the eleventh to thirteenth centuries. There was much plundering and razing of hallowed temples and seats of learning; ancient texts and sculptures were destroyed, and Hindu culture was rocked to its foundations.

Many Hindu monarchs, who had served the culture as patrons of the arts, disappeared into the south at this time, while poets, craftsmen, painters and musicians moved to the safety of the mountains and forests of rural areas. Artists who had been trained in classical traditions discovered themselves almost in exile, in a new world among tribal people who "lived close to nature and expressed their innermost feelings in a language of refreshing simplicity."[2] This sweeping cultural upheaval had a far-reaching effect on the arts. Poetry was transformed from strict classical forms to a free-flowing vernacular style that was more connected to the earth and took on a new depth of unfettered, uncensored feeling.

Jayadeva came out of this creative outpouring. Like the Bauls of later times, he was born in the Birbhum district of Bengal. In his early life, Jayadeva wandered the roads of northern India, visiting the towns of Mathura and Brindavan, where he was deeply influenced by the enchanting scenery, the wandering *sadhus* and their tales of Krishna. A fervent Vaishnava, he went to the Jagannath temple in Puri, where he camped under a tree near the shrine. There his life was changed forever when he met a Brahmin who lived at the temple. After many childless years, this man had been graced by the Lord Jagannath (a form of Krishna) with the birth of a female child. She had grown into a beautiful, youthful girl who was given to the Jagannath temple as a dancer. Her father had a dream in which Jagannath instructed him to give the child to Jayadeva. Despite Jayadeva's reluctance, the old man left the child with him and, as the story goes, disappeared. The child became Jayadeva's famous dancing consort, Padmavati, with whom he lived happily for the rest of his life.

Over time Jayadeva grew into the visionary wordsmith who placed Radha in the

---

[2]   Amit Ambalal, *Krishna as Srinathji*, p. 12.

central role as the archetypal *gopi*—lover of Krishna—and Divine Feminine. Although the *bhakti* renaissance teacher Nimbarka also focused on Radha, Jayadeva forged ahead in boldly presenting an earthy, fresh, erotic Radha, clearly inspired by his relationship with Padmavati. Radha was a human person who became divinized, and everyone could relate with her. This metaphor of Radha's role in the loveplay with Krishna was one of the primary spiritual inventions of Jayadeva's *Gita Govinda*, which also objectified the role of the body in the mystical events of the soul.

Parvathy's duggi (drum).

Jayadeva and Padmavati found their way to the court of Lakshmanasena, the Vaidya king of Bengal, where they were renowed as poet and dancer. In India, poetry is always put to music, and when Jayadeva sang his poems, Padmavati danced. We can only imagine the soul-stirring moods these great artists inspired in their audiences. Jayadeva's poetry spread like wildfire and became so popular that "poetry began to be written in the local languages based on the *Gita Govinda*, using the same symbolism and extolling love in all its varying moods."[3] The poetic metaphors and imagery of the *Gita Govinda* were reproduced in many different art forms: paintings, songs, sculpture, rural ballads—all of which reflected this important evolution. Jayadeva's tiny, carved terracotta temple of Radha and Krishna at Joydeb-Kenduli in Bengal is the site of a contemporary Baul *mela* held annually. Performed as a lyrical drama, the *Gita Govinda* is an eight-hundred-year-old masterpiece that is considered the earliest example of the type of primitive dramatic play that still survives in Bengal.[4] To this day, the *Gita Govinda* is performed daily before the deity at the Jagannath temple in Puri.

---

[3]   Georg Feuerstein, *The Yoga Tradition*, p. 388.
[4]   Ibid, pp. 337–338.

Like frozen lightning, her fair face
I saw at the river bank
Hair plaited as a coiled snake,
dressed with jasmine lace
her darting glance and gentle smile
made me eager!
Throwing and catching a ball of flowers,
she revealed in full her youthful form.
As her breasts rebelled against her dress,
her face was bright with mischievous smiles,
and feet adorned with ankle bells
were painted red

Passion opened as a water lily
where the heart's idol dwelt
A washer maid
fell in love
with a high-caste priest,
words then crawled
from ear to ear,
and the whole world knew
of a secret love.
In the village where they lived,
they were afloat
on a sea of blame...

Like the rise of the new sun
through water-laden clouds,
the red mark of cinnabar
shines on her hair.
Her fair face, glowing
as a lotus of gold,
shamed the moon
and made him run away,
two million miles...

— Chandidas

CHANDIDAS AND RAMI

In the fourteenth century, Bengal produced the great poet Chandidas (1339–1399), who is still considered to be the father of Bengali poetry. The love songs of Chandidas, which loosely follow the style of Jayadeva, feature Radha and Krishna and are still sung by minstrels throughout contemporary Bengal.

Although very little is known about this compelling historical figure, the legendary story of Chandidas has endured and been passed down through the oral traditions of northern India for hundreds of years. His story is a timeless spiritual romance in which Chandidas, a young high-caste Brahmin, renounced his caste privilege to wander the dusty roads with his lifelong lover and mate, a low-caste washerwoman named Rami. Chandidas was the musician and poet, and Rami sang with a voice that inspired the gods and goddesses themselves. They lived in the remote villages of Rarh, or what is now Birbhum in Bengal, in a time when the love that is unique to one man and one woman was rarely experienced, much less fulfilled, within the strict definitions and ironclad rules of religious injunctions. Basic freedoms of the individuals that are taken for granted today in the West simply did not exist in their world. Chandidas, Rami, and the many who took the same path were revolutionaries and visionaries in their time and beyond—their story touches us all.

The poem-songs of Chandidas now grace the books of ethnographers and musicologists who have been deeply touched by his story; more vividly, his songs continue to be sung by the Bauls of Bengal. The *sadhana* and teachings of Chandidas and Rami—found in the poems—are rightfully considered a collaboration between the two. Their love remains a powerful symbol of the freedom to worship with joy and without the brutal constraints and repressive creeds of caste and rank, arranged marriage, and the formalized and stultifying dogmas that effectively created a religious prison for the masses of low- and mid-caste Hindus.

During their lifetime, the historical lines between the era of the Buddhist and Vaishnava Sahajiyas and the evolution of the Bauls blurred—they became one and the same. Although Chandidas lived in the milieu of the Sahajiyas, he is revered by Bauls as one of the primary originators of the Baul path. Heretical and revolutionary, Chandidas is often considered a Baul simply because of the themes in his poetry and the fact that he rejected caste and rank to spend his life with Rami. Unlike Jayadeva, who wrote in Sanskrit, Chandidas wrote in the vernacular Bengali language; this break from tradition was another aspect of his unique place as an iconoclastic visionary.

Chandidas' poetic voice was powerful enough to speak about the discovery of the Divine in and through the human body and in human relationships; his frank engagement with tantric practices placed him directly in the stream of the Vaishnava Sahajiya path.

With Jayadeva and Chandidas, the worship of Krishna became an increasingly intimate experience of a personal Beloved—a living God with whom the human person could have an immediate, direct relationship of many moods and textures that included a mysterious element of erotic sensuality. Chandidas wove his direct experience of divinity in the human body into a body of *padavalis* that continue to inspire, teach, initiate, delight, and mystify generations of seekers and practitioners.

CHAITANYA

Visvambhara Misra was born in a Brahmin family in a small village of West Bengal on February 27, 1486. His father, Jagannatha Misra, was a lover of Vishnu in the small community of Navadvipa. Visvambhara was an only child and grew to be a scholar and school teacher. After the death of his father, he married Lakshmi and became a householder, but his happiness was soon shattered when, while he was away teaching, his wife died.

He was very close to his mother, and to please her, he married a woman named Vishnupriya, but she could not fill the emptiness in his heart made by the death of Lakshmi. First he sought refuge in the teachings of Shankara and took initiation to become a Vedantin, and through a series of events he was convinced to renounce householder life and begin an ascetic life. After consulting a Vedic astrologer, he determined an auspicious time to take initiation (*diksha*) from Kesava Bharati of the Shankara tradition in which he was given the new name of Sri

Sri Chaitanya's Ashtakam (Eight Verses)

Ceto-darpana-marjanam bhava-maha-davagni nirvapanam
Sreyah-kairava-candrika-vitaranama vidya-vadhu-jivanam
Anand'ambudhi-vardhanam pratipadam purn'amrtasvadanam
Sarvatma-snapanam param vijayate Sri Krishna-sankirtanam

Hail unto the hymning of Krishna's holy Name—
that cleanses the mirror of our minds,
a downpour that totally extinguishes the forest fire of worldly woes,
a beneficence spreading the moonlight that brings to bloom
the lily of supreme good,
the life-breath that sustains the Bride of Enlightenment,
the high tide that swells the level of the sea of bliss,
a veritable nectar flowing from every syllable,
a bath that cools every fibre of our being.

Namnam akari bahudha nija-sarva-saktis
Tatr'arpita niyamitah smarane na kalah
Etadrsi tava krpa bhagavan mam'api
Durdaivam idrsam ih'ajani n'anuragah

Thou, with numerous names, hast infused all Thy divine power into them,
and Thou has put no restrictions on the time for their chanting.
But, O Lord, even when so abundant is Thy grace, no taste I find in me for them,
the luckless creature that I am.

Trnad api sunicena, taror api sahisnuna
Amanina manadena, kirtaniyah sada Harih

Hari, the Supreme Lord, becomes the object of remembrance to him
who feels himself humbler than a blade of grass,
who remains more patient than a tree in weathering all the storms of life,
and who honors all beings without any feeling of self-importance.

Na dhanam na janam na sundarim
Kavitam va jagadisa kamaye
Mama janmani janman isvare
Bhavatad bhaktir ahaituki tvayi

I seek not wealth, nor fame, nor pleasure, no literary greatness;
what I pray for is that in life after life I may have devotion to Thee
with no extraneous motive behind.

Ayi nanda-tanuja kinkaram
Patitam mam visame bhav'ambudhau
Krpaya tava pada pankaja
Sthita-dhuli-sadrsam vicintaya

O Son of Nanda! I, Thy servant, am drowning in the treacherous sea of transmigration.
May Thou have mercy to make me adhere to Thy lotus feet like a speck of dust.

Nayanam galad-asru-dharaya
Vadanam gadgada-ruddhaya gira
Pulakair nicitam vapuh kada
Tava nama-grahane bhavisyati

When shall that state come on me—the state in which at the very utterance of
Thy name, the eyes become flooded with flowing tears, the speech arrested by
choked-up voice, and the body is motionless and covered with horripilation!

Yugayitam nimesena
Caksusa pravrsayitam
Sunyaitam jagat sarvam
Govinda-virahena me

Separation [viraha] from Govinda makes for me a moment as endless as an age;
it makes my eyes shed tears as clouds in rainy seasons, and the whole world
appears to me as a dreary void.

Aslisya va padaratam pinastu man
Adarsanat marma hatam karotu va
Yatha tatha va vidadhatu lampato
Mat-prana-nathas tu sa eva n'aparah

Whether He embraces me or tramples on me who clings to His Feet,
in whatever way the fickle and frivolous one may torment me,
He alone is the Lord of my heart.

Taken from *Sri Chaitanya Mahaprabhu: His Life, Religion & Philosophy*, by Svami Tapasyananda,
Sri Ramakrishna Math, Chennai.

Krishna Chaitanya. However, he never took the final vows of that order, as his destiny called him in another direction.

He soon found sanctuary and inspiration with a local sage, Isvara Puri, and they were often in deep conversation about the Supreme Reality as Krishna. Through these discussions, Chaitanya's view began to evolve beyond the strictly nondual teachings of Shankara. Toward the end of the year 1508, when he was twenty-two years old, he went to Gaya to make oblations for the soul of his departed father. Isvara Puri was there, and they resumed their passionate discussions about Krishna, which deeply impressed the young Chaitanya. He then received a mantra from Isvara Puri to worship Krishna as Gopala. When he returned to Navadvipa, he was a changed man.

Back at home, he continued to teach school for four more months, but he had lost all interest in his vocation. He immersed himself in mantra and chanting the name of Krishna, until one day he shocked everyone in his class by falling spontaneously to the ground where he raved, shouted, and rolled around in ecstasy, which culminated in a period of rigid stiffness of his body.

Around that time Chaitanya began to spend time in the company of a group of Vaishnavas devotees named Advaita, Murari, Gadadhar, and Srivas. He quickly became known among the various local tantric sects and cults as an ecstatic Godman at Navadvipa in Bengal, and soon more devotees began to appear.

Before long, a man named Nityananda wandered into town. A Brahmin by birth, Nityananda was wandering in the area as an *avadhuta* of the Nath Siddhas, a radical tantric sect. He wore dreadlocks, smoked *ganja* (marijuana) and wore a loin cloth, and as he entered the village of Navadvipa, he yelled out, "Where is Chaitanya?" His big earrings, bone and *rudraksh malas*, and long, matted hair scared the villagers of Navadvipa; even so, Chaitanya was touched by this man, who became his foremost devotee.

As the states of divine madness grew stronger in Chaitanaya, he decided to go on pilgrimage to south India with Nityananda and a few other devotees. Nityananda, who was ten years older than Chaitanya, had already wandered extensively and knew the way to Puri in Orissa, south of Bengal. At the age of twenty-four, Chaitanya made his way to Puri with his small group, dancing passionately and chanting the name of Krishna along the way.[5]

At some point, Chaitanya left his Vedantin's monastic staff with Nityananda, who broke it into pieces and threw it in the river. When Chaitanya heard what his chief disciple had done, he was angry. He went alone to the Jagannath temple in Puri, forbidding his companions to accompany him—most likely as a punishment for Nityananda's behavior.[6]

---

5   Prabhat Mukerjee, *History of the Chaitanya Faith in Orissa*, pp. 23–24.
6   Ibid, pp. 25–26.

When he reached the temple, he rushed forward in a devotional frenzy to embrace the deity, but he was forcibly restrained by the doorkeepers, who thought he was a demented monk and wanted to keep him out. Overcome with emotion, Chaitanya fell down in an unconscious swoon and was carried outside.

After staying near Puri for some time, he continued on his pilgrimage as far south as Trivandrum and Kanyakumari, then eventually headed west toward Gujarat, where he bathed in the holy rivers and sang the name of Krishna. In 1512 Chaitanya arrived back in Puri, on fire with longing for Krishna. Nityananda, who had originally accompanied him to Puri, had been waiting for him there for two years. Chaitanya decided to settle in Puri, and he charged Nityananda with going back to Bengal to teach the path of *prema bhakti* (devotion based on love).

Surrounded by a growing group of followers in Puri, Chaitanya began to live a more ascetic life, eating little and often spending the night in meditation. The intense love that gripped him caused strange physical manifestations in which his body became distorted, stretched or compressed; sweat and blood oozed from the pores of his skin and he literally foamed at the mouth. At times he was lost in ecstatic trance, half conscious, and at other times he was in a normal state of consciousness. He soon became famous in the region for his ecstasies, which were not necessarily peaceful. He was tossed and turned by a passionate ebb and flow between human and divine states of being. Often he felt he was in Vrindaban, and he would sing *sankirtana* and dance wildly, then faint.[7]

The *bhavas* and fits of divine madness that came upon Chaitanya left him crying, laughing, trembling, and often dancing and singing. He could be insulting, provocative, irreverent or sarcastic. The worse his outer state—which sometimes looked as if he was suffering from poisoning—the more ecstatic and divine the internal *bhava*; on the inside, he was in bliss. He rolled on the ground, hair disheveled, sometimes burning with fever, sometimes emitting deep, haunting sighs, sometimes sulking or laughing uproariously, in deep enjoyment, for hours at a time.[8]

Mahaprabhu Sri Krishna Chaitanya became the most outstanding ecstatic visionary in the *sampradaya* of Gaudiya Vaishnavism. He is considered to have been an incarnation of both Radha and Krishna, the divine couple representing both masculine and feminine poles of God. Throughout his life, he frequently exhibited *mahabhavas* of ecstatic trance states and fits of divine candor. His legend and ongoing transmission inspired the burgeoning *bhakti* movement and specifically the singing of the name of God in ecstatic songs. Many

---

[7] June McDaniel, *The Madness of the Saints: Ecstatic Religion in Bengal*, pp 35–36.

[8] Ibid, pp. 36–37.

consider Chaitanya to be the originator of *sankirtana*, or the singing and chanting of *bhajans*—songs in praise of God.

Chaitanya died very mysteriously. Some say he walked into the ocean in an ecstatic state of longing for Krishna; some say he was murdered in the Jagannath temple in Puri and his body disposed of in an unknown way. Most biographers agree that he died in the temple, and that the matter of where his body is remains a mystery. Regardless of what the facts may be, his death has been widely mythologized: Chaitanya was "absorbed" into the Jagannath deity. If he was murdered, it might indicate that Chaitanya was more radical and even heretical, particularly in relationship to caste laws and the tantric side of the path, than his biographers and followers both believe and propagate even today.

Despite the unanswered questions surrounding his death, the legacy of Chaitanaya endures today in many different streams of the path, including the formal *samprayada* of Gaudiya Vaishnavism, ISKCON (The International Society of Krishna Consciousness), and radical bhakti sects like the Bauls of Bengal.

NITYANANDA

Chaitanya had many devotees, the foremost of which were Nityananda and Advaita. Chaitanya was a vowed celibate whose practice was not tantric but traditional Vaishnava,

> ### The Influence of Love Lyrics
>
> *The indebtedness of Sri Chaitanya to the love lyrics of Jayadeva, Vidyapati, and Chandidasa is well-known through the Chaitanya Charitamrita (biography of Chaitanya) and the songs of other poets; the inspiration derived from these songs was not negligible in molding Chaitanya's ideal of divine love. Apart from the controversy over the religious viewpoint of Chandidas and its influence on Chaitanya's ideal of love, it may be held that the general history of the Vaisnava Sahajiya movement, with its stress on Parakiya love, was closely related to the general devotional movement of Bengal.[9]*
>
> — Das Gupta

which encouraged austerity and adhered to Vedic caste rules. Chaitanya was a married Brahmin householder at the time of his awakening, which propelled him into the strict *brahmacharya* of a renunciate celibate. As was the custom for celibates, Chaitanya observed caste rules and avoided women during his years as an ecstatic guru. He was known to demand that women stand at some distance when receiving his *darshan*. On the other hand, when he took Nityananda as a devotee, Chaitanya instructed him to marry.

After Chaitanya became permanently established in Puri, he instructed

---

[9]   Das Gupta, *Obscure Religious Cults*, p. 114.

Nityananda to return to Bengal to teach the new faith, chanting the name of Hari or Krishna. As his own work evolved, Nityananda did not observe caste rules and gave a much higher status to women than his teacher.[10] After several visits over the years, Chaitanya told Nityananda not to come back to Puri.

Many biographers have questioned why Chaitanya instructed Nityananda to stay away from Puri. Certainly the teachings and transmission of Chaityana's new faith—which was growing in Bengal as a result of Nityananda's "ministery"—would not have suffered if Nityananda was away for a few months. Many biographers have pointed out that Chaitanya knew very well that Nityananda's life and practice was unconventional and would have been misunderstood and frowned upon in the temple city of Puri. In his wisdom, Chaitanya kept him away and busy at work, spreading the teachings of his master in Bengal.

From the beginning of their relationship, Nityananda had a more liberal outlook than Chaitanya. Nityananda was a *tantrika* at heart before he joined the Vaishnava sect of Chaitanya, with all of its caste regulations. After his return to Bengal, he spread the faith by giving initiation to people from all castes, while Chaitanya continued to

> ### Nitāi
>
> nitāi-pada-kamala, koti-candra-suśītala
> je chāyāy jagata jurāy
> heno nitāi bine bhāi, rādhā-krṣṇa pāite nāi
> dṛḍha kori' dharo nitāir pāy
>
> Take shelter at lotus feet of Lord Nityananda, where you will find the soothing moonlight of a million moons!
> If the world wants peace, it should take shelter of Lord Nityananda.
> To enter the dance party of Radha-Krsna, you must firmly catch hold of the lotus feet of Lord Nityananda.
> — A Baul song

observe the existing social order of caste rules.[11] After Chaitanya instructed him to marry, Nityananda complied by simultaneously marrying two women—the nieces of one of his close associates. Complaints were lodged against Nityananda and his conduct in Bengal, which reached Chaitanya's ears: "Instead of the robes of a mendicant, Nityananda is wearing silk garments, sandal garlands and living in luxury!"[12]

After Nityananda's death, one of his wives, his daughter, and his daughter-in-law—Jahnavi, Ganga, and Narayani—became spiritual leaders in their own right and took male devotees. Sita, the wife

---

[10]   Prabhat Mukerjee, *History of the Chaitanya Faith in Orissa*, p. 46.
[11]   Ibid, pp. 46–47.
[12]   Ibid.

of Advaita, became the head of his group after his death; she advocated "sakhi bhava," which engenders the mood of the friends of Radha and was resonant with worship of the feminine principle as Devi in her many forms.[13] According to oral tradition, it is in Nityananda's line that the early beginning of today's Bauls of Bengal are found.

Nityananda's unique contribution, which flowed effortlessly into the Sahajiya stream, fused the profound *prema bhakti* of Chaitanya's Vaishnava faith with strong tantric elements, including a natural inclusion of the feminine, both as human woman and as deity, to flow into the Baul lineages, where his spirit remains strong today. The legacy of Chaitanya, Nityananda (who is affectionately referred to as Nitai), and the singers of God live on in the passionate poem-songs of the Bauls. ✤

---

[13]   Ibid, p. 47.

CHAPTER 5

The Bauls of Bengal

We dance and sing to become egoless. We dance and jump to lose
our egos. Hari flows downwards; Radha flows upwards. That's
why we leap with joy, because it's the upward flow of Radha.

Sanatan Das Baul

HISTORICALLY, BENGAL HAS BEEN A FERTILE GROUND for spiritual, intellectual, and artistic creativity—a seedbed in which a commingling of spiritual traditions including Hindu, Buddhist, Muslim and tribal occurred over centuries of time. During the medieval era in India, Bengal was unique as a melting pot in which tantric and *bhakti* traditions merged. Around the time of the sixteenth century, the Bauls of Bengal began to emerge out of the popular and pervasive Vaishnava Sahajiya cults of northern India and Bengal in particular. Over the centuries, the Bauls evolved as a recondite, eclectic, unorganized group of mystics and *tantrikas*—wandering minstrels whose practices seemed hidden and obscure, although their poem-songs were "written" in the vernacular and sung in a colloquial style that touched the hearts of everyday village people. Some Bauls came from the upper echelons of Bengal—like radical Chandidas—who were inspired to enter into a revolutionary way of life. In this and many other ways, the Bauls transcended caste, sex, and religion and remained open to synthesizing wisdom from all aspects of life, partaking of whatever was useful around them.

Wandering the villages of rural Bengal and Bihar, the Bauls have brought inspiration and joy to the often besieged lives of common people through their ecstatic song and dance. The word "Baul" has been said to derive from the Sanskrit, *vatula*, meaning mad, affected by the wind, which is sometimes associated with yogic taming of the inner "winds" of the body. The depth to which Bauls engage life in the raw, free from the veils of conditioned social proprieties, yields a state of divine madness; one who has attained this coveted madness is called *khepa*.

The Bauls are synthesizers par excellence. They have a connection with the Sufi fakirs of West Bengal, particularly in their search for the Beloved, which the Baul poets often refer to as "the man of the heart," or "the unknown bird," or simply as Lord Krishna, who is sometimes poetically depicted as the full moon. More to the point, Bauls are unwilling to be limited; they remain free to use the imagery of Krishna, Radha, Kali, Shiva and any other iconography that catalyzes the poetic flight of their imaginations. While the imagery of Radha and Krishna remains dominant in their iconography, the Bauls are not constrained: for example, Sanatan Baba has often said, "Shiva was the first Baul!"

(From left) Sanatan Baba and his sons Basudev and Biswanath at Khepa Lee's Arizona ashram, 1991.

Looking back over the centuries, there is a long time in which it is difficult to tell the Vaishnava Sahajiyas and the emerging Bauls apart. Both paths are syncretistic, relying on *sahaja sadhana*, poetry and song, including tantric yogas of the body. Even so, there are differences between them, and one defining characteristic of the Bauls is their very earthy brand of mysticism and the revolutionary spirit that takes rebellion against orthodox religion to the limit. Unlike the Vaishnava Sahajiyas, who wrote numerous texts on their view of the spiritual path, the Bauls rarely wrote anything down.

THE MYSTERIOUS BAULS

In recent decades the Bauls of Bengal, with their colorful patchwork garb (*alkhalla*) and handmade musical instruments (*ektaras*,

anandalaharis and *duggis*), their long hair tied up in topknots and wrapped, turban-style, have sparked popular imagination in both the East and the West. The trend that lifted them out of obscurity and into the limelight by public acclaim began in the early part of the twentieth century, when the Nobel prize-winning poet Rabindranath Tagore sang their praises and referred to himself as a Baul. While the Bengali gentry and intelligentsia became enamored with their native sons and daughters—the very ones who were castigated and shunned for their radical counterculture ways in centuries past—the Bauls also began to draw the attention of musicologists and ethnographers as well.

In the late sixties, Albert and Sally Grossman introduced Purna Das Baul to the West, where he met Bob Dylan and appeared on the cover of the album, *John*

Wesley Harding. This turning point marked the beginning of numerous Bauls performing before audiences in America and Europe. Purna Das Baul (the son of Naboni Das, a renowned Baul yogi of the last century) and the madcap Gour Khepa were sought out by rock and roll luminaries like Dylan, Mick Jagger, and Allen Ginsberg. Together they traveled to the West in the 1970s, as did others, like Sanatan Das Baul, to perform for audiences in Europe and the U.S.

Known as the wise elder "Baul Samraj," Purna Das is an inspired singer whose voice has thrilled audiences all over the world with his extraordinary ability to invoke the Divine through music and presence. Gour Khepa, who died in 2013, was known for his wild divine madness, the raw and authentic charisma of his personality and his passionate playing of the *anandalahari*. The exemplary yogi Sanatan Das Baul traveled and performed with his sons in Europe and later in the United States, hosted by Lee Lozowick and the Hohm Community, as was Purna Das in later years.

All of these inspiring men are some of the many bright lights of an elder generation of Bauls, whose lives inspire seekers on the path today. Current times are producing a new generation of ambitious entertainers who don the costume of the Bauls but do not practice the strict *sadhana*, which is why Khepa Lee emphasized during his 2008 sojourn in Kolkata, "No yoga, no Baul."

Like their predecessors, the Bauls took naturally and easily to the *ulta* path, going in the opposite direction of conventional society and defying categorization. Taking Chandidas and Rami as their inspiration, the Bauls abandoned rigid religious, cultural, and social forms, which they call *anuman*—gossip, or secondhand knowledge. Instead, seeking a spontaneous, direct, personal experience of the Divine, which they call *bartaman*, they took to the open road to live freely, wander, sing, and dance.

From the Baul view, the Vedic caste-ruled priesthood—which mediates between God and man—is a symbol of separation. With a great emphasis on the sanctity of the human being, the Bauls seek to rediscover and empower the inborn divinity of each individual—and in their efforts toward this aim, they often travel down roads that are wildly unconventional, including their legendary love of *ganja* (marijuana or hashish).

It's no surprise, then, that the Bauls were sought out and befriended by kindred spirits such as revolutionary rockers Dylan and Jagger. The Baul *sahaja* mystique is undeniable; it speaks to the heart of the free spirit, and yet beneath the appearance of things, there is more going on than colorful costumes, anarchy, sexual freedom, abandon in

> The road to you is blocked
> By temples and mosques
> I hear your call, my lord,
> But I cannot advance—
> prophets and teachers
> bar my way…
>
> — Madan

Sanatan Baba singing at Lee's Arizona ashram, 1991.

The essence of love
Lies in carnal lust
Bearing a deep secret.
Only lovers can unravel it.

— Chandidas Gosain

Only a connoisseur
Of the flavours of love
Can comprehend
The language of a lover's heart,
Others have no clue.

The taste of lime
Rests in the core of the fruit,
And even experts know
Of no easy way
To reach it.

Honey is hidden
Within the lotus bloom—
But the bee knows it.
Dung beetles nestle in dung,
Discounting honey.

The forest of Brinda
Guards the essence of love—
Radha and Krishna,
With cowherds ruling the land.

Submission is the secret of knowledge.

— Anon.

debauchery (of which they are accused), or great music—in fact, to focus on these is a common error of the Western predilection for superficialities.

As Chandidas wrote, "Every one speaks of Sahajiya, but alas! Who knows its real meaning? One who has crossed the region of darkness can alone have the light of Sahajiya." His words hint at the deep waters of a transformational path that reveals the dark and light, the bitter and sweet. On this path, one must honestly face the raw reality of the emotional obsession and turmoil that drives the human dilemma, wreaking havoc in countless spinning displays of maya. In the process of this transformation, the *sadhaka* is utterly changed and left to abide in the searing light of *sahaja*—the pristine, primordial essence of being.

For this to actually occur, one must willingly leave behind everything known—all the safe harbors of one's childhood and education in the ways of the world, family, caste (or class status), all the wiles and ways of survival that have been branded into our very cells from babyhood to form the false personality that we assume ourselves to be. It is this armor of mind and body, with which we approach all of life, that must be deconstructed, disintegrated, dissolved or at the very least softened, so that the essential being might begin to peek out at the world. Recognizing the prisons in which we live— emotionally, mentally, psychologically, and spiritually—and the suffering (*duhkha)* of delusion *(moha)* with which we are burdened fuels the journey. But as Bauls, it is the *sahaja* vision of the human possibility, the vision of the Supreme Reality manifested in human life, which inspires the heart and leads us on, even when the way gets rough.

KAYA SADHANA

The Bauls left behind the Sahajiya concept of the *parakiya*—a female consort who is married to another man—and took the *sahaja* aim to new heights of spontaneity in their songs, their wandering, and their insistence on *bartaman*, or direct personal experience, rather than *anuman*, or secondhand "hearsay." Instead of *parakiya*, the Baul *sadhakas* are known to call their female consorts *deva dasis*, or female servants of God. When a woman *sadhika* attains a degree of respect for the fruition of *sadhana*, she is sometimes called by the affectionate honorific *khepi*, signifying a state of divine madness.

On the other hand, like the Vaishnava Sahajiyas, the Bauls practice tantric yogas of breath and sex, and in the sexual union between man and woman they find the living symbol of the love between human and Divine, or Radha and Krishna. Uplifting human relationship to the level of a profound spiritual practice, even a *tapasya* (spiritual discipline), the Bauls enter into an alchemy or *kaya sadhana* that may catalyze the awakening of kundalini—the Divine

Arizona 1991, Sanatan Baba and sons with Khepa Lee.

Feminine as Radha—to flow upward in the body toward union with Krishna as the Supreme Reality.

In this search for the Supreme Reality, they do not reject historically repressed and denied aspects of life, but embrace it all. From the Baul point of view, *what is, is*: we are incarnated in bodies that eat, digest, defecate, have sex, move, sing, dance, give birth, die, experience fear, sorrow, loss and love. Therefore it is practical and useful and to our advantage to include all of this in our efforts toward spiritual transformation, and especially those dimensions that carry the most primal intensity and sheer energetic power—sex and sexuality.

Because of their freedom-loving humanitarian idealism, music, dance, and use of intoxicants, Bauls have been called the "hippies" of West Bengal by some. This is little

Baul Akhras and Ashrams

There is the Baul akhra, and there is also Baul ashram—like Sanatan Baba's place, which is called Jagabandhu Ashram. He doesn't call his place an akhra because they have a daily routine. An ashram has a disciplined practice—a daily routine—and it is also very sattvic in its nature. There is a daily routine of meditation at a certain time, then you have meals, there are certain things happening through the day, and in the evening there is satsang. These are all the ashram activities that happen in the right time and everyone is oriented in one direction.

Akhra is not that way. Akhras are much smaller and there may not be many people, but there will be a teacher, a sadhaka. An akhra does not follow any timetable or routine. They eat anytime, sleep anytime, they don't shower. They drink and make the dhuni fire. Akhra is a place where there is more tantric practice. And if you dare behave so precisely and normally—get up in the morning and sit for meditation—they would say, "What? Is something wrong with you?" So, akhra and ashram are different.

Baul akhras are everywhere in Bengal and Bangladesh. These akhras are mostly not in the locality of a village. An ashram can be inside the village because they have a daily routine, so they have some contact with the daily life with other people, but akhras are mostly a little bit away from the social habitat because they are not following the daily life routine. The akhra will be much poorer and will be not visited by so many people from the village. They keep it like that so they can practice what they want without any interference, so the sadhaka is totally free from all responsibility, and he can do his sadhana. Only serious practitioners live there.

Akhras do not belong to anyone. There are akhras which are very old, more than five hundred years, and you can go there and even find many, many samadhis of different sadhus that lived there—different teachers that lived there. Usually very few people can do this kind of extreme practice, so a teacher sometimes will have one or two students; sometimes they will not have anybody, they just do their sadhana and go. If the teacher didn't have a disciple, the akhra will be handed down to another sadhaka, any other sadhu who wants it. They do live long term: once a sadhu starts living there, he can live there for years. All his life in that akhra, but it doesn't belong to him.

Usually Baul ashrams are also not big, they are kept small—the masters don't accept many students because the master has to work person-to-person. That's why he cannot accommodate many people, because it's a knowledge that has to be passed down.[1]

— Parvathy Baul

---

[1] Interview with Parvathy Baul, August 2013, France.

more than a modern variation on the critical view of conventional Hindus over the centuries. The Sahajiyas and Bauls have often been misunderstood and loathed, considered degraded and profane, or misguided at best; at worst, they have been harshly condemned as heretics, rascals, fools, pretenders, and generally the abominable among humankind. Such words as *durmada* or "wrongly directed" and *nirrti* or "sinful activity" are flung at them, largely because they walk the razor's edge of a tantric path that exalts the transformational potentials of the human body. But the fact that caste and class prejudice has played a significant role in such criticism cannot be overlooked.

For example, the arcane practice of the ritual use of bodily fluids—the "four moons"—is viewed by Bauls as an alchemical practice. For the *tantrika*, these substances (menstrual blood, semen, urine, and feces) carry potentials for a profound transubstantiation when used in ritual contexts; they are considered to have sacred potentials by virtue of the fact that the human body is sacred. Although these and many other elements of Baul *sadhana* may appear to be anarchic, or heretical or blasphemous in comparison to conventional mores and norms, the *sadhana* itself requires strict discipline and commitment to the principles of yoga.

VAISHNAVA BAULS AND TANTRIKA BAULS

There are some researchers, such as Jeanne Openshaw, who reject the idea of Baul as a *sampradaya*—those who are "Baul" are far too unorganized and anarchic to endure the kind of discipline and restraint that is necessary to participate in a formal "school," with protocols, scripture, and hierarchies. At the same time, there are some Bauls who insist that "Baul" is without question a *sampradaya* of a unique kind.

Taking the view that the Bauls are a *samapradaya* or spiritual sect must be qualified with an appreciation that Bauls tend to be extremely heterodox, disorganized, haphazard, and unlikely to agree upon various aspects of the path. Those practitioners who are identified as "Baul" share a specific stream of practices and philosophy, and yet as individuals they are multifaceted and eclectic, which creates some important distinctions among general groupings of Bauls as a whole.

Some Bauls are clearly more disciplined and conservative in their pursuit of a *sattvic* (harmonious, pure) lifestyle. Working within a radical form of Vaishnavism, they practice yoga, live on ashrams, serve their local villages and communities through begging (then sharing the food in communal feasts or *mohatsabs*), music, and by maintaining ashrams where people may come to *satsang* and *sankirtana*. Many of these Bauls seriously commit to traditional Vaishnava practices such as vegetarianism and abstinence from alcohol; however, like most Bengali Bauls, they may smoke *ganja*.

On the other hand, some Bauls are more anarchic and radically tantric in their approach. They tend to live on *akhras* rather than ashrams; these are more informal, less organized, more undisciplined, and often not as accessible to villagers and visitors. Their lifestyle usually includes the use of alcohol, meat, *ganja*, and less formal sexual liaisons.

Both ashrams and *akhras* are managed through the time-honored tradition of begging or *bhiksha*—which is often referred to as *madhukari*. The *akhras* have a harder time interfacing with local society and may be very poor, because people are put off by the unorthodox nature of the activities that are engaged there. The *sadhakas* who are drawn to live in *akhras* take their tantric practices to the extreme, while the Vaishnava Bauls walk a fine line, living in such a way that allows them to mingle with society more easily. Because of a variance of emphasis on Vaishnava (devotional) or Tantra among individual Bauls or on an *akhra* or ashram, definitions or degrees of *kaya sadhana* change and morph based on the circumstance, the guru or teacher, and the practitioner.

Bauls are known to refer to themselves as Vaishnava Bauls or Hindu Bauls (as different than their cousins, the Muslim Auls), a distinction that has been well documented by researchers over the years. However, the Bauls are natural synthesizers who have taken aspects of many different paths and made them their own without compromising the essential tenets of their *sadhana*. It is difficult indeed to blend traditions without destroying the integrity of any given stream of the path, and for centuries the Bauls have excelled in accomplishing this creative marriage of elements. Many serious Baul practitioners remain elusive, mysterious, and impossible to pigeonhole or define, even while the integrity of their path remains intact.

RUPA AND SVARUPA

Radical transformation reveals the indwelling *svarupa* within *rupa*, the familiar forms of daily life. *Svarupa* and *rupa* are important teaching concepts of the Baul path which

---

Rupa and Svarupa

The manifested existence is the rupa *and the metaphysical existence is the* svarupa. *One is outer view and the other is related to the internal perspective. The physical form and beauty of men and women is known as* rupa, *and the spiritual form and sublime activities are called* svarupa. . . . *The divine Self is manifested in the human self, and in order to understand the true nature of Divine Self the* sadhaka *must proceed through the human self. Likewise* svarupa *is manifested in* rupa, *and* svarupa *can only be understood through the keen analysis of* rupa. Svarupa *can only be realized in the midst of* rupa, *through purified love and sincere devotion.*[2]

— R. M. Sarkar

---

[2] Sarkar, *The Bauls of Bengal*, p. 37.

articulate a pair of opposites found in the gross existence of form, *rupa*, and the divine existence of *svarupa*, which is sheltered or contained within *rupa*. Through the illumination of the inner potentials of *rupa*, *svarupa* is revealed.

Rupa is the form we see and experience, while *svarupa* is the underlying archetype that informs its appearance. The spiritual nature of the being dwells within the physical form and is revealed by and through that physical form— the body. Understanding and unveiling the essential spiritual nature of *rupa* as *svarupa* forms the core of Baul *sadhana*, making the practices of yoga, song, or sexuality key arenas in which *rupa* is actively engaged with the intention of revealing the indwelling *svarupa*. The creative acts of our lives bring the human body to life in ways that were previously unimaginable, opening the doors to realms of experience and transformation sought by men and women of God for thousands of years.

IN SEARCH OF BARTAMAN

The Baul message of the divinity within the human being—*manur manush* or the non-dual "man of the heart" revealed within the *sahaj manush*, or natural man—has brought inspiration and a healing balm to ordinary people who face a mighty struggle in life's

Biswanath in Arizona, 1991.

many hardships. The Baul path offers a way of spiritual development and sanctuary that is accessible to the many who feel the weight of dogmatic creeds, which are called *anuman*, "hearsay," "hypothesis" or "second-hand gossip." The Bauls are seeking *bartaman*—a direct experience of the divinity that resides within the human body. *Bartaman* or direct experience intricately links us to the *sahaj manush*, or natural man; in this way, the *sadhaka* realizes his or her innate capacity to experience God, both formless and in form.

Although *bartaman* is sought after and *anuman* is avoided, this context is not allowed to devolve into yet another restrictive creed. For example, while "playing with dolls" is a criticism of deity worship in conventional *bhakti* traditions, Bauls engage in an intimate interplay with the sacred images of Krishna and Radha in the inner culture. In this way *bartaman* is freely courted, but however much they may be revered, the deities are considered images that arise out of the innate being of every individual. The difference is the fluid context in which these traditional spiritual methods are engaged. This fluidity is also found in the domain of ritual; while conventional Vedic rituals are not typically part of the Baul path, there are many simple rituals that are performed on Baul ashrams, where the *samadhis* (sacred burial sites) of Baul saints and masters are tended daily with flame, flowers, and other offerings.

BAUL WRITERS

While Bauls are generally known to avoid putting their teachings down in written forms, over the generations there have been some Bauls who did write about their experience. Raj Krishna (1869–1946) was a Vaishnava Brahmin who left behind family, home, and caste to become widely known as a Baul guru.[3] Also known as Raj Khyapa, his legacy includes a written autobiography that recounts the major events of his life, including a scandalous relationship with a married woman, Rajesvar, with whom he eloped (she was married to another man and had a six-month-old daughter at the time). They spent the rest of their lives together, although based on his poem-songs, things deteriorated after some years.[4] Raj Krishna was a doctor, and he wrote down many of his remedies. He also encouraged his disciples to write poems, such as:

> My guru goes by the name
> Raj Krishna Paramahansa
> A perfect Baul, he is God to me
> I have realized these truths
> through his grace
> Hridananda says, I shall become Baul
> and go with him...[5]

Sri Anirvan, who called himself a Baul, both taught and wrote about Baul practices and philosophy in his books, including *Inner Yoga, Letters from a Baul,* and *To Live Within.* Interestingly, it was Sri Anirvan who linked the practices and inner yoga of the Bauls of Bengal with "the Work," as it was taught by Russian mystic G.I. Gurdjieff, practiced today by seekers the world over and called the Fourth Way.

Rabindranath Tagore, literary genius and winner of the Nobel Prize for literature, considered himself to be a Baul. In a famous statement made in his Hibbert Lecture at Oxford in 1930, Tagore said:

That is why, brother, I became a madcap Baul... I revel only in the gladness of my own welling love. In love there is no separation, but commingling always. So I rejoice in song and dance with each and all.

It was the infamous and renowned Vaishnava Baul Naboni Das who became Tagore's great inspiration. Legend has it that Tagore built Naboni Das a place in which to do his *sadhana,* personally photographed him, and spent hours with him exploring poetry.

There are those who do not agree that Sri Anirvan and Tagore are Bauls, simply because they wrote prolifically about the teaching and the practice.

---

[3]   Jeanne Openshaw, *Writing the Self,* p. xiii.
[4]   Ibid, pp. 28–29.
[5]   Ibid, p. xiii.

Such a criticism should inspire caution and inquiry into the tendency to become orthodox even about the unorthodox—it is important to recognize that one can become a fundamentalist even about radical Baul philosophy.

Baul Culture

Baul culture is not the songs, but there are certain poems, like verses, that talk about the inner practice. These are passed on from master to student. It's never published, and a Baul practitioner would never reveal the inner culture. It belongs in the practice, because for a practitioner, a sadhaka, *preserving the tradition happens through the body.*

When you go to a sadhaka, *you can get attracted to what he has, to the things he has. You can get all these things from him or her, but you will never get what he is. You have to work for that inside yourself. That is why the preservation of Baul* sadhana *always happens, because Bauls have survived every situation.*

Now the Bauls have become a big fashion in India. People say, "Oh, you know, I went to the Sufi festival and I heard the Baul songs. They're moving around and singing about the freedom that I feel." There are many, many books nowadays that people read, "Oh, Bauls!" They are just babbling. It all goes around and round and round, nobody goes deep into the work. There are many books already published, and they are still publishing books and poetry, but the Baul teachers don't write any books. When Sanatan Baba wrote a book, "The Baul Lover," it was this much. [She gestures how small it is.] He put all his life practice in it! Chaitanya took only eight verses to put everything in!

Books will not preserve the tradition. To preserve the tradition, as far as my understanding, we need to work with the next generation. We need to transmit this knowledge, whatever my master has given me, give it and build up a generation.

When we use the word sampradaya, *it means it's a specific knowledge. It's a lineage that is passed down, like Vedanta, like Tantra. And so Baul is the lineage, it's the lineage word, it's the* sampradaya. *So the preservation can happen only by transmitting the knowledge to the next generation. And not many people want to do that work; they cannot do it because you need extraordinary strength and understanding about this tradition, and you really have to practice to build up another person. And after all this you might fail because this person might just walk out. And they'll say, "I don't feel it anymore!" So it's a risk, but it's a service.*[6]

— Parvathy Baul

---

6   Interview by the author with Parvathy Baul, August 2013, Ferme de Jutreau, France.

Perhaps because of that, Bauls are known to disagree with each other on fine points of dharma, and they are not easily yoked by the word of a spiritual authority. Everything must be investigated and proven to be true by individual experience, which makes the common pitfall of the spiritual path—blind following—less likely for the Baul who has a "taste" for authenticity.

The question of whether it is ultimately useful to have a written scripture, documentation, or inquiry into the path is an interesting point of difference between Bauls East and West. In line with the Vaishnava Sahajiya way, Baul Khepa Lee placed a premium importance on the power of the written word, both as a transformational and alchemical process for the writer, and as a way to preserve and potentially transmit the teaching in the Western milieu.

At the same time, he understood that the only sure way to preserve and transmit the teaching and way of the spiritual path is to immerse one's self in living it fully. Finally, it is the inner life of the practitioner that preserves the path for future generations. However, Lee did not make a separation between the different modes of communicating dharmic truths; he understood the limitations and potentials of each—whether it is written down or sung and passed on orally, it must be lived fully— even as he utilized and enjoyed the unique dimensions of each mode.

For Bauls both East and West, the vital question of transmission of a living tradition depends upon the authenticity of individual

Sanatan Baba in California, 1991.

practitioners, which Parvathy referred to as "the Baul culture." As she points out, the true preservation of a lineage and teaching happens when the next generation has the opportunity to rub up against, so to speak, those initiated practitioners who are living the path and are immersed in the deeper practice of that path. This is at the core of the mystery of *bartaman*, or direct experience. That which leads to a direct experience of the Divine for one person may be very different for another. One person revels in the song, the poem that is sung, while another is more deeply moved by reading that same poem silently to himself or herself. Similarly, for one person the *sadhana* focuses on music and poetry while for another the *sadhana* may focus on yogic disciplines; one Baul may be a singer while another is the ashram cook. At the heart of it all, we find a great mystery, and this is the point: the stream of wisdom that is transmitted through a living (not necessarily incarnate) lineage is ultimate *bartaman*.

Exploring essential differences of important aspects of practice, philosophy, teaching, or spiritual clan (*sampradaya*) may give rise to deeper insights and appreciation of the dharma. This deep enjoyment and love of the teaching is found in the Baul practice of *Baul gan*, a kind of "dharma combat," to use a Buddhist term, which is undertaken in the spirit of camaraderie and shared engagement with the path. In *Baul gan*, a question is asked which is then answered with a song. If the answer is unsatisfactory or if someone has a different view, then another song will be sung, and another—until the consideration has been given full and satisfactory attention.

One thing the Bauls seem to agree on is the necessity for absolute reliance on the guru and *deha-tattva*, or the truth in the body—which leads back to *sahaja* and the radical instinctual knowing of the *bartaman* experience. Most of all, Bauls around the world agree about the key element of *bhava*. The cultivation of *bhava* and *rasa* is all-important; it is in the divine mood of their soaring songs and stirring rhythms that we receive the transmission of the Baul message.

MEETING THE BAULS

In 1986 Lee sent two of his students to Bengal to seek out the Bauls, and it was with Sanatan Das and his clan that a lasting connection was forged. Khepa Lee and Sanatan Das Thakur Baul met in 1991, when Sanatan Baba came with his sons, Biswanath and Basudev, to visit Lee at his ashram in Arizona and perform on tour in the American Southwest, hosted by Lee and his students. While Khepa Lee developed connections with various Bauls, it is with the *sampradaya* of Sanatan Das Thakur Baul that Lee maintained very deep connections that have endured beyond Lee's physical lifetime.

Sri Guru Sanatan Das Thakur Baul was born in Khulna, Bangladesh. His family had embraced the Baul tradition for at least four previous generations, so the young Sanatan was immersed in the culture of Baul dharma, theatre, song and dance from an early age. His initiatory guru in the tradition was Nitai Khepa, who introduced him to Baul *sadhana*. Later, the great Monohor Khepa gave him instruction in the intricacies of the music. Today, he lives on a small ashram in Khayerbhani, a village in the Bankura district of Bengal, with his wife, Mirabai, his sons, grandchildren, and a large extended family.

Many people come to Sanatan Baba for spiritual guidance in the Baul tradition. Over the years he has traveled occasionally, communicating love and longing for the Beloved (the "man of the heart," in the Baul tradition) through his music. Sanatan Baba is especially known and appreciated for his unique dancing which, like his singing, has more conscious artistry about it than that of most Bauls. He is one of the few Bauls who is occasionally asked to perform on All India Radio Calcutta.

At the time of this writing, Sanatan Baba lives and practices yoga—at the venerable age of over ninety years—every day on his ashram. He continues to inspire and guide his students, family, friends, and community in Bengal and in the West.

During their visit in 1991, the Bauls of Jagabhandu Ashram lived for six weeks on Lee's ashram in Arizona in between public concerts; it was a rich time of sharing between East and West, frequently interspersed with *Baul gan*—spontaneous events of *bhava* and *rasa*, of song and dance performed by the Bauls on bare ground on the ashram under trees and sky or in private homes.

In Sanatan Baba we discovered a formidable spiritual elder and fierce yogi; stern but compassionate, he is wholly committed to Baul *sadhana*. A friendship blossomed naturally between Sanatan Das and Lee, growing effortlessly out of a ground of shared purpose, integrity, and inherence in the principles of the path. At the time, Sanatan recognized Lee as a Baul guru, affectionately calling him the "Baul emperor of the West," and enthusiastically watching performances of Lee's band at the time—liars, gods, & beggars—in venues in Phoenix and Los Angeles. Almost twenty years later, in December 2007, Sanatan Das Baul and his entire family drove from their remote ashram in rural West Bengal to be reunited with Lee and company in Kolkata.

Khepa Lee and Sanatan Baba, Arizona 1991.

BAUL GAN

As we walked across the tarmac at the Kolkata airport in late December 2007, our senses were inundated by the thick, haunting atmosphere—a collision between the cool misty morning air and a heavy pall of gray smog. Driving into the city, we passed dust-laden tropical canopy and glistening pools, where people squatted with bronze pots to draw water or wash clothes. Having just visited friends in the urban sprawls of Mumbai, Varodara and Ahmadabad, I was keenly aware of rapid changes that are occurring in India's timeless sacred culture and natural environments. And yet, even with the pervasive influence of techno-culture and Western value systems, India is a place of ancient rhythms and flows, and this was apparent right away in Kolkata.

Kolkata is Kali's playground—a city in which the *ishta devata* is alive and thriving. Shrines to Kali Ma adorn every other street corner, where she resides in ecstatic four-armed form with lolling tongue and primordial eyes, beautifully adorned and freshly garlanded with the evocative golden yellow marigolds and red hibiscus flowers. Ghee lamps burn brightly at her feet in the smoky, soot-blackened air while people hurry past, wrapped in shawls against the chilly night air.

Kali's influence brings the transient nature of all things into sharp focus on the streets where life unfolds, where her images remind us that this fragile existence—miraculous in its exquisite beauty but also raw and cruel—is ephemeral. In Kolkata, it is important to pay respects to the Mother Goddess as soon as you arrive, and indeed, Kalighat—Kali's ancient temple—was calling. After making *yatra* (pilgrimage) to Dakshineswar and Kalighat, we turned to the primary mission of our sojourn: encounters between the Bauls of the West and the Bauls of Bengal.

Khepa Lee was traveling with an entourage of students, including his blues band, Shri, who would perform a two-week tour in Kolkata hosted by Purna Das Baul. After over twenty years of singing his original music for Americans and Europeans, Lee was finally bringing traditional American blues and rock & roll—Lee's unique permutation of Baul music in the West—home to

Lee and Shri on stage with Purna Das and Bauls in Kolkata, 2008.

Parvathy Baul looks on as Sanatan Baba and Lee greet.

Mother India. They would play ten concerts in the Kolkata area to Bengali audiences.

As our sojourn in Bengal unfolded, we found ourselves connecting with Bauls from diverse places—from the vast sprawl of Kolkata to rural West Bengal, Joydeb (the village of Jayadeva, where a Baul mela is held every year), Shanti Niketan, and Tarapith in Birbhum. Dressed in pale orange or pink and wearing a handmade patchwork jacket, or in white or ordinary dhotis and kurtas, with *ektara* or *anandalahari* in hand, wherever Baul musicians gathered to play their songs and dance there was a sense of freedom and elation.

Close to our hearts was the anticipated reunion of Khepa Lee and Sanatan Baba after their many years apart. Sanatan Das Baul arrived with most of his clan—his sons, Biswanath and Basudev and their wives, and two grandchildren. Sanatan Baba's wife, Mirabai, had stayed on the ashram, keeping the hearthfires burning while the rest of the clan traveled. Sanatan Baba also brought his "spiritual daughter" and disciple, Parvathy Baul, to this heartfelt reunion—a meeting that would initiate an ongoing friendship between the next generations of Bauls in the East and West. For the next two days, we

Kolkata reunion: Sanatan Baba and Khepa Lee, 2008.

Baul Gan, Kolkata, 2008.

were treated to spontaneous *Baul gan* in the home of friends.

In between songs, food, and basking in the enjoyment of good company, Sanatan Das graciously agreed to an informal interview.

"What is a Baul?" I asked.

"Baul is to know yourself. To know, to search, 'Who am I?' In Sanskrit, *atma -tattva*. This doctrine: to know this body as a temple. To know all the [subtle] bodies," Sanatan Das replied in Bengali. With Parvathy Baul translating into English, he continued, "This body is given by God. Like people have fields and they grow crops, and with those things that can be grown from those fields, they feed themselves and others. This body is also like that field."

Just then Biswanath suggested that it was time to sing and dance—a hint that this was the best way to answer the question. Within moments, we had the opportunity to participate in the best kind of *Baul gan*—performed in an intimate environment—-beginning with an invocational mantra and the traditional Baul salutation, "Jai guru!" (Victory to the Guru!)

Incense was lit and a large, two-headed drum appeared in Basudev's hands as if by magic. Out of a cloth bag Parvathy brought an *ektara*—a simple instrument made with a calabash for a base and bamboo strips to hold up its one string—while Biswanath got out the *kartals* (hand cymbals), handed them to his oldest son, then got out his own *anandalahari*—a kind of handmade plucking drum that is unique to Baul music. Its name, *anandalahari*, means "waves of bliss" in Sanskrit—an apt description of its effect upon the listener.

"Khyapa Re …." Biswanath's voice rang out in song as he raised his arm toward the sky calling for *khepa*, the one who is divinely mad. Then he began to dance, turning his body in a circle with delicate, small steps that fell in an exquisite pattern on the heavy cotton rug. With the simplest instruments and dance, rich polyrhythms and evocative melodies, we were enveloped in sound; ease and harmony flooded our road-weary bodies as we were carried along on the wave of song, awash in *ananda bhava*. The song unfolded as a sensual weave of rhythm and melody rooted in the body, the earth, sun, moon and that stars that drew the listeners into its *bhava*. Biswanath began to bounce gently up and down, connecting heaven and earth.

The mood Biswanath had invoked lingered as he sat down and Parvathy Baul translated, "Oh my heart, it goes to the city of *ananda*. If you want to see that *rupa*, that form, that beauty, there is no day or night. There is a full moon there, and it brightens the room. *Bindu*! It is surrounded by the *bindu*. It's beyond comparison. It is intense, and also very magical, like the moon. The fine path of *sushumna* lights; you pierce the lotus, the middle path, and reach the higher place. The essential man hides there, in *triveni*, the meeting place. He is the essence of everything, he is the truth, and he is the one who never perishes. You enjoy it, you play there, and you find the man of the heart there. That is *ananda*."

Playing nothing but a simple, small drum called a *dubki*, Sanatan Das got up to sing and dance. His drum seemed to be at the center of the Universe. He looked directly into our eyes as he sang, and the language difference was not a barrier to the communion that flowed between us. It was a rare moment when we drank in the tender, loving mood that arose among the gathering, as this spiritual elder and revered Baul master's *rasa* filled the atmosphere and captured our hearts once again.

When the dance and song were done, Sanatan Das sat down beside Lee, *pranamed*, and took his hand. Later, he said, "We dance and sing to become egoless. We dance and jump to lose our egos. Hari flows downwards; Radha flows upwards. That's why we leap with joy, because it's the upward flow of Radha." ✻

CHAPTER 6

Lineage (Parampara)

ONE OF THE MOST ESSENTIAL TENETS OF THE BAUL PATH is the principle of *guruvada*—the yoga of radical reliance on the guru or spiritual preceptor as the conduit of Grace. The *parampara* or spiritual lineage of the *sampradaya* is the central jewel in the mandala, for the lineage carries the living wisdom of the traditional path. Among the Bauls of the West, the lineage flows from Swami Ramdas to Yogi Ramsuratkumar to Khepa Lee to his initiated disciples.

It is not uncommon for Bauls to have a guru who is not strictly Baul but who is an authentic source of transmission from any tradition. Even so, parallels and similarities are easy to find between the Bauls and the lineage stream of Ramdas and Yogi Ramsuratkumar: their years on the road as wandering beggars, their love of God, trust and surrender to guru and God, renunciation, and their joyful, ecstatic chanting of the Name of God. The creative marriage between these facets of the jewel was one of the most brilliant hallmarks of Khepa Lee's life and work.

SWAMI PAPA RAMDAS

Swami Papa Ramdas (1884–1963) was a south Indian saint who gave up his worldly life and possessions at a young age to become a wandering sadhu. Born as Vittal Rao in Kanhangad, northern Kerala, India, he worked as a spinning master in a cotton mill and was married in 1908. Difficulties with conventional life soon ensued, and he began to chant "Ram," a name of God, to find some relief. Before long, he was initiated by his father in the sacred Ram mantra, *Sri Ram Jai Ram Jai Jai Ram.* An inner revelation inspired him to add "Om" to each repetition, so that the mantra in which he later initiated his disciples became *Om Sri Ram Jai Ram Jai Jai Ram.*

Striving to repeat this mantra "all the twenty-four hours," Rao was quickly detached from his former conventional life of seeking temporary pleasures and satisfactions. He soon left to wander as a mendicant beggar, took the name Ramdas, and lived on the alms and charity of others. Ramdas cultivated the view that everything that came his way was the Divine, which he referred to as Ram. When there was no food for days, it was "Ram in the form of no food." Every relationship, good or bad, was Ram in the form of whatever or whoever appeared before him—an embodiment of radical faith. Ramdas' demonstration of the essential state of surrender to God's Will was an expression of what Khepa Lee would later call Spiritual Slavery.

In 1922, Ramdas the wandering sadhu encountered the great sage of Mt. Arunachala in Tiruvannamalai, Ramana Maharshi, and, having his darshan, received his grace. Years later, he wrote about this meeting as a definitive turning point in his *sadhana*, speaking of himself as "Ramdas" rather than the first person "I." Years later, Ramsurat Kunwer (the young man from northern India who became Yogi Ramsuratkumar) would have a very similar encounter with Sri Ramana.

As a result of this meeting with Sri Ramana, Ramdas went into his first retreat, living for twenty-one days in solitude in a cave on Mt. Arunachala, at the base of which was Ramanashram, the ashram of Ramana Maharshi. It was during this time that a profound illumination suffused his being. When Ramdas left this cave, he was reverberating with the realization that, "All was Rama, nothing but Rama." As Ramdas continued his wanderings, another profound spiritual awakening occurred near Mangalore, which obliterated his personal identity. Only an abiding sense of oneness remained.

After he had been wandering the roads of India for many years, devotees began to surround Ramdas, including one particularly bright light, Krishnabai, who became his feminine counterpart. Together they established Anandashram in Kanhangad in 1931. The

---

God is in the World

Spirituality that cannot be applied in actual life is no spirituality. God is in the world and is acting through every one of us. God-realization does not mean disappearing into some unknown realm beyond the world. True spirituality consists in our living in this world, moving in it and serving all beings, all the time being conscious of the Divine within us and everywhere around us.

— Swami Ramdas

Meeting with Sri Ramana

When Sri Ramana intently gazed on Ramdas and the eyes of both met, Ramdas felt He was pouring into him His spiritual power and grace in abundance, so much so that Ramdas was thrilled, as His divine light shone on his mind, heart and soul. Sri Ramana's eyes always radiated a splendor, which was simply unique and irresistible—a splendor mingled with infinite tenderness, compassion and mercy. The few minutes that Ramdas spent in His holy company meant a momentous impetus in his spiritual career.[1]

— Swami Ramdas

---

[1] *The Essential Ramdas*, p. xlvii.

What is sweeter in the world than to hold communion with your Eternal Beloved? He is your never-failing companion and friend. He resides in the inner chamber of your heart and is also present everywhere about you. He is the soul of your soul, the life of your life. In the absolute sense, you and He are one.

If this love of intimate comradeship with your Beloved does not inspire your life, even if you have all other things, your life is lived in vain. See your Beloved in the face of all beings and creatures. Verily, He has become the whole universe. Wherever you turn, there He is. The bliss of His presence is inexpressible. Why run away from Him and seek to attain peace in aloofness? Allow your life to mingle with His life, which is the universal life. He is a calm, serene, changeless Spirit and, at the same time, He is a world player. He dances in the hearts of all beings and creatures. He is at once wisdom, power, and love....

Seek the Beloved. Feel His presence. He is thy own Self. Have Him at any cost. Find Him and enjoy eternal felicity.[2]

— Swami Ramdas

Swami Ramdas.

known as Papa Ramdas, his renowned devotees include Mataji Krishnabai and Yogi Ramsuratkumar, who are adored by devotees in their own right.

After over thirty years of teaching, guiding his devotees, and providing a sacred sanctuary to sadhus, wanderers, and pilgrims of many faiths from around the world, Swami Papa Ramdas took *mahasamadhi* in 1963. After his death, Mataji Krishnabai became the spiritual preceptor of Anandashram. The current preceptor is Pujya Swami Muktananda—who followed Swami Satchidananda, the great devotee of Ramdas and Krishnabai.

ashram was dedicated to improving the living conditions of the local people, and continues to this day to share Swami Ramdas' vision of universal love and service. Affectionately

---

[2]   Ramdas, *The Divine Name*, p. 22–23.

Today, the teachings of Swami Ramdas are explained and encapsulated in three main parts:

1) Nama: Taking refuge in the Divine Name.
2) Dhyana: The inward journey
3) Seva: Service to God through humanity.

In chanting the mantra of the divine *nama* of Ram, *Om Sri Ram Jai Ram Jai Jai Ram*, one is aligned with the Absolute Godhead or *nirguna,* and with the Beautiful One—the personal, *saguna* aspect of Ram. Ramdas taught that chanting the name of God eventually leads to inner stillness, and in this stillness we find direct relationship with the Divine.

Chanting *nama* leads one to realize that everything in creation is interrelated and interdependent. Ramdas taught that the liberation and peace of the individual depends upon his or her contribution to collective human happiness and harmony, and that chanting the divine name puts us in direct touch with this universal law. The practice of *nama japa* or *sankirtana*, especially when it dovetails with the inner journey of meditative insight and self-honesty, makes us intellectually aware of the truth that at the center of our being is unbounded love, and our deepest wish is to serve creation.

As we travel down the spiritual road, it becomes obvious that in order to sustain these feelings of unity, peace, and love we must make an inward journey of radical transformation. To become stabilized on the spiritual path, we must go within. And so we take on practices of meditation (*dhyana*) and contemplation.

Swami Ramdas was utterly convinced, through his own personal experience, of the power of the Divine Name. Well-educated and a prolific writer, Ramdas wrote many excellent books in English that provide a compelling account of his spiritual journey

---

[3] *The Essential Ramdas*, pp. 77–78.

and his subsequent teachings and function as guru. Today, Anandashram is a profound spiritual environment that has thrived for over eighty years, where the repetition of the Name of God continues unabated.

YOGI RAMSURATKUMAR— THE GODCHILD OF TIRUVANNAMALAI

Ramsurat Kunwar was born in Nardara, a tiny village on the Ganges near Varanasi, on December 1, 1918. A brilliant student, he graduated from university and became a teacher and then headmaster of a tiny village school in Bihar, where he lived with his wife and four children. At the age of thirty, he was driven by a fiery longing for the Divine that changed his life forever.

Known as a loving family man, he responded to that powerful inner call, traveling south on several pilgrimages; in these journeys he discovered his three "spiritual fathers, Sri Aurobindo, Ramana Maharshi and Swami Papa Ramdas. Returning to Bihar, Ramsurat resumed his family life and post at the school. Hearing of the deaths of Sri Aurobindo and Ramana Maharshi and grieving the loss of his spiritual mentors, Ramsurat returned to Swami Ramdas, with whom he discovered a renewed ardor for the spiritual path.

After several trips south to Anandashram to visit Ramdas and Mataji Krishnabai, Ramsurat was initiated by Ramdas in 1952 into the mantra, *Om Sri Ram Jai Ram Jai Jai Ram.* After only one week of repeating the mantra, he was thrown into a state of God-intoxication. He often said, "In 1952 Ramdas killed this beggar; this beggar is no more," referring to the annihilation of personal identity that surrendered him into the Divine.

By 1953 Ramsurat was living in a state of divine madness that caused him to break into spontaneous fits of ecstasy in which he would sing the name of God and dance. No longer able to function as a headmaster and householder, he returned to Anandashram with his wife and two youngest children. There his states of divine madness only increased; he became unruly and often threw himself at the feet of Ramdas and Krishnabai, much to the dismay of the other devotees.

At that time, Ramsurat begged Ramdas to allow him and his family to remain at the ashram with his beloved Papa and Mataji. Instead, Ramdas sent him away, saying, "You cannot live in the ashram … Remember, under a big tree, another big tree cannot grow. Go and beg." This seemingly fierce instruction echoed what Ramdas himself had done, and to a very good end.

A divine madness had taken over Ramsurat. At the cost of great personal anguish, he sent his family back north to Bihar, where they would live with his wife's parents. Compelled to enter the life of a mendicant beggar, Ramsurat wandered for seven years and finally arrived in Tiruvannamalai in 1959. There he lived until his death in February 2001 under the powerful spiritual influence of Mount Arunachala—the legendary mountain famed to be an embodiment of

Shiva and the catalyst of the awakening of Ramana Maharshi amd Swami Ramdas. It was in Tiruvannamalai in 1960 that the beggar's sanctity was noticed and he was given the name, "Yogi Ramsuratkumar" by an ardent devotee of Ramana Maharshi.

For many years Yogi Ramsuratkumar lived on the streets of Tiruvannamalai and in the Shiva temple as a beggar and hidden saint, subsisting entirely on the good will and gifts of food and clothing given by the village women and later by a growing number of admirers and devotees. The sublime countenance of the yogi, his spontaneous outbursts of ecstatic song and dance, his chanting of the name of God and blessing all who were drawn to him began to captured the attention of many seekers.

The numbers of devotees continued to swell until it was no longer possible for Yogi Ramsuratkumar to move freely about Tiruvannamalai without being inundated by hundreds of well-meaning devotees. In the mid-seventies the devotees of Yogi Ramsuratkumar acquired a small house for him on Sannadhi Street near the temple in Tiruvannamalai. It was during these years that Lee Lozowick first encountered Yogi Ramsuratkumar and was so deeply affected by the influence of the saint that he became an ardent disciple.

And so, after living in the streets for many years, in rain and sun and storm, Yogi Ramsuratkumar was finally willing to accept a permanent shelter from his devotees. His house was messy and strewn with many seemingly unnecessary things, including piles of newspapers, dried flower garlands and odds and ends given to him as prasad. Dressed in rags with palmyra fan in hand, he often sat for hours with those who came—regardless of caste or station in life—conversing with them and listening to their stories, smoking cigarette after cigarette, and raising his hands in blessing with his characteristic phrases, "My Father in Heaven blesses you," and "Ram, Ram!"

On many occasions his devotees were thrilled to see Yogi Ramsuratkumar enter into ecstatic *bhavas,* in which he danced and spontaneously chanted, *Sri Rama Jaya Rama Jaya Jaya Rama* or *Sita Ram, Sita Ram, Sita Ram.* These irresistible, compelling dances—reminiscent of Lord Nataraja—have been the source of many devotees' most cherished memories of Yogi Ramsuratkumar from his early days in Tiruvannamalai.

Over the years, his work grew and evolved—from the intimate atmosphere of small gatherings to vast numbers of pilgrims and people who came seeking a glimpse and a touch of the blessing power that emanated from a great saint. Over time, thousands of people received the darshan of the Godchild of Tiruvannamalai (as he was affectionately known), in the tiny house on Sannadhi Street. Most of them came seeking help for basic problems in their lives: "Heal my sick father," or "Bless my childless wife with children."

After seeing the lines of devotees standing in the sweltering sun outside his house—sometimes for hours—in hopes of receiving his darshan, in 1993 Yogi Ramsuratkumar finally gave his devotees permission to buy land and build an ashram in Tiruvannamalai where his devotees could worship. "For the devotees," he said, not promising that he himself would be willing to actually live there.

While the plans for the ashram were underway, another significant event occurred: An ardent devotee named Devaki, a former professor of physics at the university in Salem, became the new attendant of Yogi Ramsuratkumar. He called her his "eternal slave" and referred to her as a "Ma" or divine mother; clearly he saw her ultimate role as being similar to that of Mataji Krishnabai's with his own guru, Papa Ramdas.

In November 1993 Yogi Ramsuratkumar took up residence in a house that had been acquired by Devaki and three of her close friends, Vijayalakshmi, Vijayakka and Rajalakshmi—ardent devotees also from Salem, who the beggar called "the Sudama sisters." These four women became a spiritual family for the beggar, attending to his needs twenty-four hours a day. At the Sudama House, as their dwelling was called, this small group created a sanctuary in which the beggar could continue his work while the construction of the Yogi Ramsuratkumar Ashram was underway, beginning in the spring of 1994.

Dressed in layers of ragged, stained *dhotis* and copious shawls in the scorching Indian heat, and with a palmyra fan and coconut begging bowl, Yogi Ramsuratkumar

> ### My Father Alone
>
> *My Father alone exists! There is nothing else, nobody else—past, present future—here, there, everywhere! Anywhere. There is nothing else, nobody else. My Father alone! My Father alone! That is the only existence. Nothing is separate, nothing isolated. All in Father, Father in all—near, nearest, far, far, farthest, Father alone! There is only one existence of my Father, indivisible, total, whole, absolute.*
>
> — Yogi Ramsuratkumar

held court as a beggar king, giving darshan twice a day in the vast temple of the ashram from 1994 through 2001 while continuing to live at Sudama House. Throughout these years, the utter simplicity of perfect surrender and the innocence and spontaneous ecstatic joy of his communication never changed. Within the divine madness of the beggar saint one experienced a being of profound spiritual majesty, whose countenance was imbued with a captivating, transcendental beauty that transmitted the rare blessing of a divine indwelling.

Like many who are Baul, Yogi Ramsuratkumar did not teach in linear terms, but through the transmission of presence in everyday circumstances. Although he often laughed, joked and enjoyed the company of his devotees and visitors, his eyes were ever turned inward toward the Divine. In the moments that he spoke of the dharma, his all-consuming vision of the unity of life spontaneously poured from his lips as ecstatic blessings.

Sweet Slavery

Yogi Ramsuratkumar lived in a state of what he called "sweet slavery" to "Father in Heaven"—a realization that resounds in Lee's articulation of Spiritual Slavery as one of the primary threads of continuity that runs through the lineage. Similar to countless Baul masters of antiquity, Yogi Ramsuratkumar did not leave any written teachings, but he expressed a great love for poetry and wrote a few precious poems in the early seventies, perhaps inspired by Papa Ramdas, who wrote many poems. Later, Yogi Ramsuratkumar reveled in the prolific flow of poetry that came from his heart-son Lee. For the greater part, he simply asked his devotees to praise God, and although he did not write books or give dharma talks in a formal sense, he frequently burst into praise of God in spontaneous speech.

Ma Devaki recounted the story of an exchange that occurred in the early 1990s, when several people were sitting with the master under a tree at the home of a devotee. Yogi Ramsuratkumar looked at the doctor who was attending to him and, in ecstatic tones of childlike innocence, said:

God alone exists. There is nothing else and no one else. He is all-pervading. He alone exists, nothing else, neither in the past nor in the

present nor in the future. He is everywhere— here, there...everywhere! He is indivisible, indescribable, beyond ordinary intelligence. He is total, beyond words, complete....No one is separate.

While he spoke, the eyes of the beggar saint looked around at each person. Then he said:

It is for people, for ordinary mortals who do not understand this, that name and form are necessary. All are in Father. Father is in all of us. This beggar does not understand advaitic philosophy, but he remembers the lotus feet of his master, Swami Ramdas. Ramdas gave this beggar Ramnam. For this beggar, the lotus feet of his master and Ramnam will do!

These words of inspiration come from a human being whose life was an example of faith. The profound awakening and divine madness that seized his being and transformed his life came through the auspices of Grace—through devotion to the guru and chanting the name of God. Yogi Ramsuratkumar's frequent nondual declarations of the unity of all life were expressions of the *sahaja* ideal: he embodied a lucid, natural, unpremeditated relationship to the world around him, which he ever viewed from the eyes of God-realization.

During the years when the ashram was under construction Yogi Ramsuratkumar was a constant presence on the site, blessing the progress of the work and giving formal *darshan* twice a day in a small building near the gate. It was in 1994 that Yogi Ramsuratkumar also asked his Western devotee, Lee Lozowick, to build an ashram adjacent to his—a project that finally came to fruition years later.

Yogi Ramsuratkumar was unique in his ability to relate with Westerners and Indians alike. He had an uncanny instinct that gave him a deep understanding of each individual. He worked with many Westerners, particularly Lee's students, in ways that imparted a lifetime of powerful, enigmatic, teaching communications that continue to reverberate as time goes on.

A Beggar King

Yogi Ramsuratkumar was a regal beggar in the greatest sense of the word; from beneath his simple, humble dhotis and shawls shone a kingly presence. His "court" was one of rich, full silences and the beauty of song, the chanting of the Divine Name while the qualities of innocence, purity, and wholesomeness pervaded the ambiance around him.

The sweet sound of Yogi Ramsuratkumar's extraordinary laughter frequently echoed through the temple as he delighted in the antics of a devotee or a guest, or at a story he had just heard. His sense of humor and irony was pure and childlike, both virtuous and marvelous, while his spontaneous depth of wisdom and skillful means in relating with many different types of people, particularly Westerners, was unparalleled.

And yet, from the time he renounced the comforts of worldly life, leaving his family and teaching responsibilities back in Bihar, Yogi Ramsuratkumar was a beggar. As he once said of himself, "This beggar is born a beggar, will remain as beggar, will die as beggar." Despite the vast temple and beautiful ashram that was built for him, he remained as he always was: a man of noble simplicity, totally unconcerned for himself, living as a beggar even among the riches his devotees sought to heap upon him. The delight of his many lovers, Yogi Ramsuratkumar's laughter and tears and the lilt of his melodious voice carried the power to uplift, purify and transform those who turned their hearts toward him.

His was a demonstration of freedom from all personal desires, motives or plans; his one wish was for the welfare of all beings. He has been quoted many times for having made the following universal declaration of the bodhisattva:

I do not seek for happiness. I only want to do my Father's Work. If even one being has benefited from my life, that is enough. It has been worthwhile. And if this body dies, the soul that may remain, may it be born again to do my Father's Work.

The "Work" that Yogi Ramsuratkumar referred to had profound and universal dimensions. It could be experienced as a tangible force, a powerful mood around him that was sometimes perceived as joy, sometimes as sorrow and on rare occasions as fleeting anger—but always there was the penetrating communication of compassion and love. Oftentimes it seemed that Yogi Ramsuratkumar was engaged in a powerful inner work that commanded all of his formidable energies to bless all beings, to focus on a specific problem in the world, or on something that troubled one of his devotees. Of his work he once said, "Ever since this beggar died in 1952 he hasn't been able to do anything. Now Father in Heaven does everything. I do only His work. Only what He tells me. It's slavery—sweet slavery."

When Yogi Ramsuratkumar was working in a particular way that his friends and devotees came to know well, he smoked. During the ashram years Yogi Ramsuratkumar sat in darshan for four hours a day, listening while his devotees chanted, smoking cigarette after cigarette, slowly, with great care and meaning in every nuance of movement.

Smoking came to Yogi Ramsuratkumar after he was taken by divine madness, and at times he commented that he never liked smoking "before this madness came to this beggar." As an aid to his work, smoking became a ritual of singular elegance for Yogi Ramsuratkumar, as his movements were perceived by many as a pure expression of the Divine in form. Each cigarette became a prayer in his hands, and his silence and deep inner stillness was rich with the thundering, soundless sound of praise. Within the fire and air and smoke of each inhalation, in the transformation of matter into spirit,

Yogi Ramsuratkumar consumed and transformed *samskaras*. With each exhalation a new Universe of possibility unfolded once again, and the whole of it—inhalation and exhalation—became a guileless and impeccable breath of the heart.

Chant This Beggar's Name

Like his master, Swami Ramdas, Yogi Ramsuratkumar gave one basic instruction for *sadhana* to his devotees: Chanting the divine name in the mantra, *Yogi Ramsuratkumar, Yogi Ramsuratkumar, Yogi Ramsuratkumar, Jaya Guru Raya.*

It is said in the Indian tradition that in the *Kali Yuga* (the dark eon or age in which we live), the only effective recourse of *sadhana*, the only hope of liberation, is to chant the name of God. This yoga is an all-consuming practice of repeating the mantra using a *mala* (beads), written repetition, speaking, singing or thinking. Yogi Ramsuratkumar himself said on many occasions that to chant his name once would bring unfailing divine "help." When a mantra is chanted, the practitioner becomes resonant with the vibration or essence of that which

---

Faith

To the Baul, who is an individualist by nature, faith is spontaneous because it springs from trust. It is related to the Adhar-Manush, the "Unattainable Man" who dwells in the human form.

— Deben Bhattacharya

---

the mantra represents. The gift of his name, Yogi Ramsuratkumar, as the invocation of Grace, reflects the inner condition of the beggar king of Tiruvannamalai: His complete Surrender to the Divine.

Yogi Ramsuratkumar shed his physical body on February 21, 2001, and yet his presence is vivid and bright for those who knew and loved him and for the many who meet him for the first time through the legacies he has left behind. The physical form of the Godchild of Tiruvannamalai has passed away, impermanent like all things, but his blessing is alive in the world today. He is alive in the sacred ground of his ashrams, in the chanting of his name, in his sacred image or *murti*, in the poetry written to him, and most especially, in the many people whose hearts have been touched, irrevocably changed and sweetened by the *rasa* of Yogi Ramsuratkumar, which flows from the benevolence of his slavery to the Supreme Reality.

Yogi Ramsuratkumar as Sahajiya

Central to the Bauls is the potential of the *sahaj manus*, or the natural man—a human being who has realized the state of awareness that flows spontaneously, smoothly, easefully.

The Sahaj Manush

Even if it's very difficult, you chant the nama many times for many, many years and then it becomes organic and continuous, so that you don't have make any effort to do that. When you don't have effort and it's happening just naturally, spontaneously—that's sahaja.

We cannot say that we have become sahaja or Sahajiyas; it's only a person like Yogi Ramsuratkumar who can say that he is a Sahajiya practitioner, he is a Sahaja, because he has made it continuous. He is never stopping, even when he is giving darshan or he is smoking, he is working. But this work has no effort because from the outside, if you see him, he is just sitting very relaxed. He is not saying, "I do chanting sometimes and then suddenly it stops."

When the chanting doesn't stop, that is sahaja—to live with that effortlessness every day, every moment, so that they don't even need to light a lamp or put a flower to the picture. At the same time, don't try to adopt it unless you are there, because it's very tricky—again the mind will come!

Another way of telling what is sahaja is that it is like the rays of sun when it touches the lotus in the morning. The lotus will open, and this opening has no effort. It opens very, very spontaneously, naturally. Same way, when the light from the guru's sun—the rays of compassion of the sun guru—when it touches us, it really enters our heart and the heart is open without any effort. That is sahaja.[4]

— Parvathy Baul

---

4   Interview by the author with Parvathy Baul, August 15, 2013, Ferme de Jutreau, France.

Yogi Ramsuratkumar at the Arunachaleswara Temple in Tiruvannamalai, early 1970s.

The one who dwells in *sahaja* abides in changelessness in the earthly realm of change; therefore they are "dead" to the seductions, distractions, and fascinations of this world. Although they are engaged with the world in a benevolent way, their mystic gaze is turned inward toward the Supreme Reality; they are self-contained, self-luminous, self-abiding.

One who has realized the *sahaja* naturally cares for the welfare of others and is of a deeply humble and devotional nature, a state of being that radiates from deep within. They are servants of God and seek always to assist in the evolution and development of other souls. They are concerned if harm is done to another, and practice kindness, compassion, and generosity, perhaps even to a (seemingly) extreme degree.

A *sahajiya* has reclaimed the state of original innocence in which he or she resides beyond the constant influences of the three *gunas* or qualities of primal nature that work at the foundation of all Creation. Such an individual is the master of himself or herself, and from that consistent, steady place of equanimity, is turned toward serving others. Such a one naturally exudes the noble qualities of selfhood and is not swept away by the common flux and conflict of emotions and entanglements that characterize the *maya* of ordinary life.

Love flourishes in such a one; love arises from the wellspring of being in a never-ending fountain that showers its nectar on all who come near. Chandidas said, "Love makes the man"—a superb love that is not of this world. Such human beings are rare indeed. It is said of the *sahaja* man that because of the perpetual union of masculine and feminine, or Krishna and Radha within him, he has realized the Supreme Reality and is also known as the "man eternal" who has gone beyond life and death. These descriptions accurately characterize the true guru, who is the epitome of the natural human being.

KHEPA LEE LOZOWICK

American spiritual teacher Lee Lozowick was known by many people the world over as the heart-son of Yogi Ramsuratkumar and the only recognized Baul master in the West. Lee entered into the role of guru in 1975 with the advent of a profound awakening that left him in a state of consciousness he characterized as "Spiritual Slavery"—a radical and complete surrender to the Will of God.

Lee's awakening was not mediated by an affiliation with a specific teacher, path, or religion. It occurred in the spirit of the Bauls—iconoclastic, fresh, untamed, and original. For years Lee had passionately immersed himself in the Indian traditions, absorbing and integrating what was resonant with his own experience, and in this process he was deeply called toward the Hindu *bhakti* path. One year after this awakening, he was drawn to India, which led to the revelation of his relationship with Yogi Ramsuratkumar, who he met for the first time in January 1977. This encounter sowed the seeds of an earth-shaking realization

Khepa Lee at his ashram in Tiruvannamalai, 2004.

that the beggar saint was in fact the source of Grace and Benediction in Lee's life and the spiritual power behind his awakening and his teaching work.

In an outpouring of devotion, longing, and praise catalyzed by the powerful symbolic interactions of their second meeting in India in 1979, Lee began to send poems across the sea to Yogi Ramsuratkumar. The relationship between spiritual father and son developed over the next decade in a wondrous *lila* described in depth in the biography, *Yogi Ramsuratkumar—Under the Punnai Tree*, and Volume I of Lee's biography, *Spiritual Slavery*, as well as in the biographical tomes, *Only God* and *Father and Son*.[5] In 1993 Lee's poems to his master were collected and published—at the request of Yogi Ramsuratkumar—in Chennai by the master's Indian devotees, under the title *Poems of a Broken Heart*.

In early December 1993, Lee and nine of his students visited Yogi Ramsuratkumar in Tiruvannamalai. At that time, the poetry became a matter of public knowledge when the paperback volume of *Poems of a Broken Heart* was presented to Lee, and he placed it in the hands of his students, to their awe and great joy. It was during this visit that Yogi Ramsuratkumar declared his American devotee's poems to be the definitive statement on the beggar's life and work.

Speaking ecstatically, he said, "Lee Lozowick has done a great work for this dirty beggar with these poems. The name of this dirty beggar will be scattered all over the world with these poems, written in English by Lee. Lee Lozowick has given a gift to this beggar. Now this beggar won't have to beg anyone to write about this beggar anymore. No more. It is done now. Lee Lozowick and his reign of love will be all over the world!"

The extraordinary affection and intimacy that was shared between Lee and Yogi Ramsuratkumar continued until the end of their lives and beyond death. It was and is a relationship with very deep roots, as Yogi Ramsuratkumar said many years later, "Lee and I have been together in many lives."

Over the decades that followed their first meeting in 1977, Lee elucidated and embodied a timeless and contemporary teaching of diamond-like brilliance that blended his devotion to Yogi Ramsuratkumar and his certainty about the necessity of the guru with his realization of nonduality and awakened perception of reality as "Enlightened Duality." Underlying all was his invitation to discover the innate relationship with the personal Beloved and his insistence upon faith and the reality of Grace.

Lee's communication as guru and Baul *khepa* was multifaceted, original, and unique: even while he was foremost a true devotee of his master, Yogi Ramsuratkumar, and a great yogi in his own right, he was also a spiritual friend to many. He became particularly known in Europe as a provocateur, poet, lyricist and rock & roll singer, a merchant of sacred artifacts, and a captivating storyteller. Through a flow of stories and spontaneous teachings, his talks offered the listener a practical, humorous, sometimes outrageous and often sublime transmission of universal truths—all aimed toward the actual living of the spiritual path in the gritty, challenging,

---

[5] Regina Sara Ryan, *Only God*, Hohm Press, 2004, VJ Fedorschak, *Father and Son*, Hohm Press, 2009.

and sometimes heartbreaking circumstances of daily life.

Like many *khepas* before him, Lee was at times enigmatic, cryptic, difficult, and irascible. Because Lee assumed in 1975 that he had awakened purely by Grace, without a teacher or guru for many years, there was a heretical element to his work that never completely disappeared, but was always present in his sharp, uncompromising criticisms of conventional religious dogma as well as the contemporary spiritual scene. Lee was extremely vociferous in his view of false teachers and the superficial, vain, materialistic aspects of modern seekers and spirituality.

From the beginning, Lee was provocative and irreverent, calling seekers to pierce the illusions that hide not only in conventional society but in the labyrinth of the spiritual path. In subsequent years, Lee as maverick was tempered by the gentle and strong hand of his master; even so, Lee often referred to himself candidly as "Your wild Heretic," in his poems to Yogi Ramsuratkumar. Lee's wild heresies showed up in his inimitable style of teaching, which comes across powerfully in his nine published journals, in his music and lyrics, and in his resonance with the Bauls.

"Getting" Lee Lozowick has always been (and continues to be) a process that occurs in the mysterious byways of the human heart. Understanding or connecting with Lee—as guru, teacher, guide, contemporary prophet, friend, or family—requires an openness to resolve the seeming paradoxes of what Lee called "my style." A naturally shy and retiring man, Lee cultivated a way of teaching that created a labyrinth that must be traversed with the wisdom and instinctive knowing of the heart. Similarly, some have found Lee's teaching complicated and difficult to sort out, not only because of his style, but also because his teaching resounds with depths and mysteries that must be pondered and lived if one wants to come to know them.

Lee often said that he spent many years cultivating his unique way of teaching, which he used to great advantange as a vehicle of spiritual transformation. His ability to translate the ancient wisdom of the spiritual path—and of the Bauls in particular—into a contemporary perspective offers a powerful view of compassion and practical wisdom applied to the greater potentials within ordinary daily life: in relationships, marriage, sexuality, conscious parenting, careers, money, friendship, food, music and all forms of artistic endeavor. Lee funneled his instinctive understanding of the transformational power of music into rock & roll, and he brilliantly used this to keep many of his students, born and fully entrenched in the Western milieu and culture, fully engaged with him in musical projects. Secondarily, he used this art form to deliver his message as poet of the truth.

The multidimensional and multifaceted character of his teaching is both exalted to the peaks and resolved in the sweet valleys that are experienced in the presence of his being—during the years of his life and now after his physical death. All complexities or conundrums naturally fall into place in the divine mood that permeates the guru's transmission, both in life and in death. It is the living presence of the eternal guru and the pure transmission of Grace that has been discovered beyond his physical departure to be the continuous mystical gaze of the guru.

Being in resonance with Khepa Lee, then, leads eventually to the most essential theme of Lee's legacy—his view of guru yoga, or *guruvada*, as the doorway to adoration of the Beloved, which is inseparable from his communication of the realization of non-duality arising as an Enlightened Duality. It is this perception of the Supreme Reality, immanent and indwelling in existence itself, which Khepa Lee lived and transmitted, whether it was through his presence, his prolific writings, his music, or the example of his life and love for Yogi Ramsuratkumar.

In November 2010 Lee left his body and entered into *mahasamadhi*, leaving his devotees, friends, and acquaintances an immense legacy: three thriving ashrams in Arizona, France, and India; a rich teaching spanning more than thirty-five years, including thousands of recorded talks, over forty published books and thirty-five CDs of original music recorded by his rock & roll and blues bands; and a mandala or *sampradaya* of initiated disciples who continue to live and teach the Baul way in the West. ❀

Yogi Ramsuratkumar and Lee, 1997.

The Mystic Gaze

It has been reported by those who should know that the gaze is one of the direct access points, or channels, to the Transmission of Blessing force. In the Guru traditions, of course, the way, one of the many, that the Guru transmits is through his or her gaze upon the devotee. In the more generalized Bhakti traditions, another way in which this word "gaze" has been used is the devotees gazing on the Teacher, or traditionally as well, the Divine Object, be that SitaRam, Krishna, Shiva, Ganesha, Hanuman, Kali and Her many forms of Shakti Devi, and so on. Through this gaze the devotee draws from the object of that gaze, and this drawing has often cited not only Blessings as the result but also energy, knowledge, Siddhi, and other sorts of manifestations.

In the Bhakti traditions as well, or in the Tantric arms of those traditions, the Gaze has been considered as one of the highest forms of relationship, communication and communion as well, not to mention perhaps the highest of highest forms, Adoration (of lover to Beloved and Beloved to lover, ideally between the two. I say ideally because in the struggling domain of human realities, it is often the Beloved's Gaze upon the lover that goes completely unnoticed by the confused, conflicted, neurotic ego of the "lover"). So an obvious question that might arise is: of what nature and from what Source is this Gaze and does it arise?

The gaze of the heart is a whole-being attention, alert and open, sensitive and exclusive in its total non-exclusivity. This gaze may produce various affectations, such as swooning, sighing or moaning, various other forms of or demonstrations of ecstasy or bliss, the hair standing on end, thrills of the body, visions of dancing and playing Gods and Goddesses, demi-gods, celestial musicians and so on. The gaze of the heart is a mood, indistinguishable from Unity, the Oneness of lover/Beloved even as lover/Beloved remain as a non-problematical and non-paradoxical dichotomy. There is at one and the same time, seamless and undifferentiated, the gaze and the object of that gaze, not two in one but two-as-one.

This mystical gaze is the core foundation of all worship and all prayer, in their also objective forms, and so is a consideration that should not be overlooked even if one's disposition, or inclination or bias, does not lean toward the devotional types of practice. Even if we lean toward worship of the nondual, abstract Absolute, the is-ness of it all, nonetheless, this mystical gaze is at the seat of our inherence in Truth, Reality-as-it-is, or we could even say the state of Awakening, Realization or Moksha (Freedom). In fact we could even say, without getting ourselves out on a limb, that the mystical gaze is Worship, is Prayer, as all of our ritual frameworks, technical as well as verbal, are just that, frameworks in which we are creating, or allowing, the possibility for the arising of Objective Prayer or Worship, which is the mystical gaze.

So of course the eyes take part in this Miracle of Incarnation, our attraction to not only beauty in its many forms but to the objects of our human love as well as our Divine urge, our Ishta Devata as is said in Sanskrit, being a sure gateway, an instinctual encouragement to gaze, not just to look and reflect, but to gaze in a way that all reflection is obliterated, incinerated in the fire of Love-without-an-object (even as mentioned before this may include the lover/Beloved dynamic).[6]

— Khepa Lee

---

[6]   Lee Lozowick, "A Tale Told by an Idiot, Full of Sound and Fury, Signifying...", pp. 22–25.

Swami Ramdas (above) and with Mother Krishnabai (below).

Yogi Ramsuratkumar.

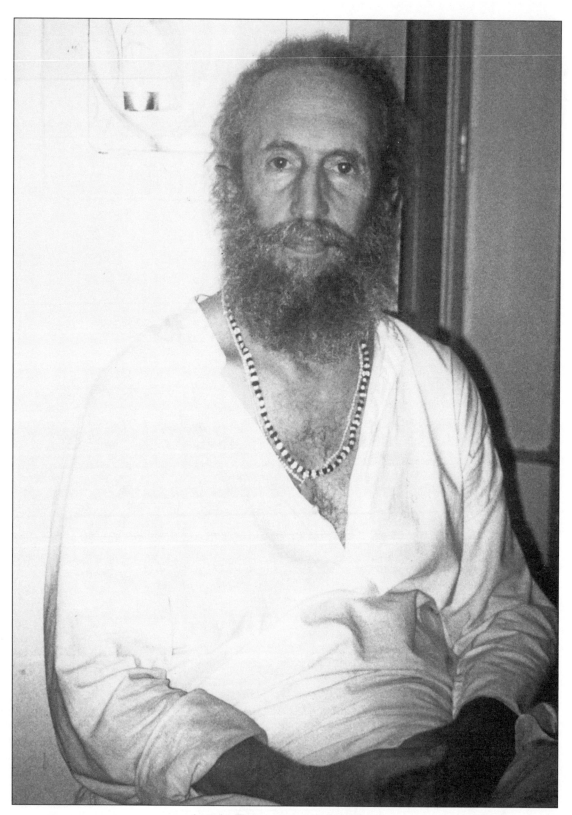

Lee in Tiruvannamalai, 2004.

Yogi Ramsuratkumar and Ma Devaki with Mt. Arunachala in the background.

Front row (left): Outside the temple at the Yogi Ramsuratkumar Ashram in 2014—Ma Devaki, Sharana Lhaksam, Mari Angelon Young, Purna Steinitz, Justice Arunachalam (spiritual head of the ashram), Mirabai Lodro, Rose Volckhausen, Vijayalakshmi Ma, and Rajeswari.

CHAPTER 7

The Name of God (Nama)

Chant this beggar's name only once with faith and he will be there.

Yogi Ramsuratkumar

IN KOLKATA WITH SANATAN DAS AND HIS CLAN in 2008, Lee and his traveling party gathered for *Baul gan* in the home of a friend. They had made a great effort, traveling many miles to be reunited with Lee, and as we all settled in together I became acutely aware that despite performing tours in Europe, the U.K. and U.S., Sanatan Das and his clan are country Bauls. Their ashram in rural West Bengal is a cluster of handmade mud-brick huts with thatched palm roofs and dirt floors set amidst rice fields, skirted by thick networks of banyan trees and jungle growth. Sanatan's sons, their wives and children, are earthy, simple people of natural beauty. He and his spiritual daughter, Parvathy Baul, glowed with essential realness and embodied the sahaj vision.

Their clothes were well-worn, faded, and obviously had been washed many times, but they carried the unmistakable power that clothes take on when worn repeatedly in sacred spaces of one kind or another. There was nothing artificial about them, and because of that they touched the truly essential within us. Their music infused us with energy and inspiration, and after three weeks of grueling travel in India, we were rejuvenated in their company.

The next day we had a whole afternoon and evening with this Baul clan. As Parvathy Baul told stories of her apprenticeship with Sanatan Das, who was in his late eighties at the time, his watchful gaze did not miss anything that was going on in the room around him. He had the childlike grace of the very old and very wise, which reminded me of being in the divine presence of Yogi Ramsuratkumar during his lifetime and catalyzed a flood of sweet memories and a mood of longing. At one point I asked Sanatan, "What is the most important practice of the Bauls?" Sanatan Das replied:

Finally, there is only Nama. Name. In the beginning, you are like all the other people, feeding yourself and your desires. Over time, your needs become smaller and smaller. You can sit in one place and everything comes to you. In the final stage, you realize oneness with the master. You find your master in yourself.

Finally, it is a very lonely path; the guru may instruct you in a specific practice to do in solitude. After many years of rigorous practice, the student may realize the truth in the master's words. The student will realize that the master is not a common worldly man—he is the Beloved. You think of your guru as your God; to offer service to the guru is equal to offering service to God. You cannot see God, so God said, 'I will visit you in the form of your master.' Believe in what the guru says. Remain constant. Do not defy the guru. Nama. There is something beyond, when you reach this place of supreme joy, you find the master and you become one with the master. So, finally, the Name. Nama. Only a few people find it.

His sons, Biswanath and Basudev, were poised for the songs to begin; they quickly distributed small percussion instruments around to everyone and invited us to play along. With the *ektara* held to his ear and the *dubki* at his side, Biswanath began to whirl. "Jai Guru!" he exclaimed joyfully. Within seconds we were transported by the storm of sound that came from the amazing

Lee and Sanatan Das.

In the Padma Purana, it says:
"Krishna's Name is complete in itself,
and it is the essential form
    of all spiritual relationship.
It is not a material name
    under any circumstances,
and it is no less powerful
    than Krishna Himself."
Ah, yes, my Lord, our Yogi Ramsuratkumar,
    I believe this defines You
quite exactly, does it not?
    In fact, my secret Krishna,
was this Purana written to You?
    You, in Your great Mercy
and infinite generosity, in
    Your Radiant Grace and
Motherly care for Your infants,
    have given us Your Name,
and how true, how true, for
    it is not other than You.
How fortunate, how fortunate we are,

little chelas, to have this
great Blessing, Your Name, the Name,
    to guide us, protect us,
to elevate us in our aim.
    All we need to do is repeat It,
Yours, This, the Name of God,
    Father's Holy Son, You, You,
Yogi Ramsuratkumar, our Guru,
    our Only, our One, our Light.
Father, our Father and my Father,
    this is Your Heart-Son lee,
still a "me," still with a "my,"
    and ever Yours, without doubt
or question, ever repeating
    Your Name, always keeping You
in mind, even into these very cells
    themselves, vibrating with You,
Lord and Master, Your little beggar
    washes Your Feet with his tears of love.[1]

— Lee Lozowick

anandalahari and drums—simple, hand-made instruments of the earth.

After a rousing Krishna chant with everyone in the room up and dancing, we sang "Anonde Bawlo, Jai Guru Jai"—a song in praise of the guru and the Baul *sampradaya*. The room and its occupants were suffused with brightness and joy; the rhythms and their potent soaring voices, the elegance of their dance, were the *nama* and *rupa*—the name and form—of which the Bauls had spoken, and they had transported us into it. Most important of all,

Sanatan Das had brought us full circle, back to the essential instruction of our lineage guru, Yogi Ramsuratkumar: "Chant this beggar's name."

Sanatan Das used the word *nama* in its transcendent meaning: the name of God as a mystical formula that encapsulates the Supreme Reality. In this sense, *nama* lies behind all appearances: it is the "Word made incarnate" of the Christian tradition, the Logos principle, and the primal sound, Om, from which it is said all of creation emanates.

---

[1]   Lee Lozowick, *Intimate Secrets of a True Heart Son*, 19 November 2008 I, pp. 130–131.

SHABDA

In August of 2013 Lee's ashram in France hosted Parvathy Baul during one of the monthly seminars held there. Amidst the rolling green hills and patchwork fields of yellow sunflowers, in the pastoral beauty of Douce France, we spent a week talking about the Baul Way, East and West, and sharing hours of conversation on the road to one of her concerts on the Atlantic coast of France. Along the way, she said, "For the Bauls, it's all about the sound. *Shabda*. Mantra practice. The *nama*—the divine name. This is the one practice that all Bauls have."

For Bauls of both East and West, *sankirtana* is a natural part of our lives. Whether one is chanting the name of Krishna, Govinda, Ram, or Shiva doesn't matter, as Yogi Ramsuratkumar said many times—just pick one and cleave to it! It is the vibration of the name of God that purifies, comforts, transmits Grace, opens to infinite possibility and transforms the soul.

Yogi Ramsuratkumar Speaks on the Divine Name

My Friends!

This beggar learned at the feet of Swami Ramdas the Divine Name of Rama, and begs you—begs all of you—not to forget the Divine Name Rama. Whatever you do, wherever you are, be like Anjaneya Maruthi, thinking of Rama and doing your actions in this world.[2] At every stage we face problems—today one problem, tomorrow another problem, the day after tomorrow another problem—and on account of facing these problems, often we get dejected, disappointed, psychologically sick, if we don't remember the Divine Name. So this beggar will beg all of you not to forget the Divine Name, Rama.

There are people who like to remember the name of Siva; it is equally good. There are people who like to remember the name of Ganapathi— equally good. Whatever name you choose, whatever form you choose, but give to this beggar what he wants. Never forget the Divine.

Live in the world and the problems will be there. If we are remembering the divine name, we are psychologically sound. Maybe, we may feel some of the problems; even then the intensity with which we feel, if we don't have faith in God, is much more than a man of faith—a man who remembers the name of Rama.

So this beggar is always begging, begging for food, begging for clothes, begging that you should compose songs on this beggar, build a house for me, buy a house for me, a cottage for me, this thing, that thing—so many things. But this beggar will beg of you this also, and you are

always giving what this beggar has begged. So this beggar begs, please don't forget the name of God. This Divine Name has always been of great help to all the world.

You read Kabir, Tulsidas, Appar Swami, Manickvasaga Swami: how they all emphasized Namasivaya.[3] Don't forget it! This is your heart. This is your soul, whether it be Om Namashivaya or Om Namo Narayanaya, whether it is Rama, Siva, or Krishna—whatever name you choose, whatever form you choose doesn't matter. Remember the Lord with any name, with any form of your choice. Just as when there is heavy rainfall, we take an umbrella and go on doing our work in the factory, in the field, go to the market, we catch hold of the umbrella and go through the rain that is falling there. Still we do our work.

Similarly, we have got so many problems all around. The Divine Name is just like an umbrella in the heavy rainfall. Catch hold of the Divine Name and go on doing your work in the world. This beggar begs of you, and this beggar has received all he has begged of you. So I think none of you will shirk away when this beggar begs of you, "Don't forget the Divine Name." This beggar prays to his Father to bless you all who have come here. My Lord Rama blesses you, my Father blesses you! Arunachaleswara blesses you! It doesn't matter to me what name it is. All the blessings of my Father for all of you! Well, that is the end. That is all.

—H.H. Yogi Ramsuratkumar, the God Child,
Tiruvannamalai, 1988
Divine Message to Humanity

---

[2]   Anjanyea Maruthi is a name for Hanuman.
[3]   The Divine Name of Shiva.

"Remember this beggar's Name, Yogi Ramsuratkumar. The Name Yogi Ramsuratkumar is not this beggar's Name, it is my Father's Name."

The Sanskrit word *shabda* refers to sound—the primordial root power of God's universes, which is the vibratory power behind all mantric practices. Shabda is the eternal vibration of the Divine which manifests in eternal unmanifest (silent) sound and the external spoken sound. Lee often instructed that mantra may be spoken aloud, written down, or spoken internally; it is this last form of mantra practice— internalized and yet vibrating within the organic complex of body and soul—that is the most powerful. This is really good news for busy people; we can be doing mantra practice internally no matter how much we have to do in the external world of karma yoga—work, creative projects, families, children, careers, and service.

THE SEED PRACTICE

Yogi Ramsuratkumar gave his devotees two basic instructions: only praise, and repeat the name of God. He often said that any of the names of God or true mantras—such as *Om Sri Ram Jai Ram Jai Jai Ram, Hari Om* or *Om Nama Shivaya*—were equally effective, depending upon the faith or *ishta devata* of the devotee. He also gave his own name as mantra. It sounds simple, and yet Yogi Ramsuratkumar lived in a sacred milieu

On Sankirtana

Chaitanya brought the sankirtan movement to everyone; from him all this chanting started. He is the first person who started the chanting that we do all the time—the name, repetition of name.... He started this big movement because he brought a totally new style of singing to Bengal. It is called kirtan. It was a total revolution in the society because he brought together all the lower class and upper class people, the Islamics, everybody.

The mirror of "you" has gathered a lot of dust through the years and years and years. Clean your mirror by chanting the name of the Beloved, Sri Krishna, in here [in the heart]. If you chant the name, you will clean this dust from the mirror, and joy and buddhi will increase. Buddhi is from the word bhodhum, which is awareness. You will become more aware. Once you are able to clean this dust from the mirror, it will extinguish conditional life... Let Sri Krishna sankirtanam win over all that dust! Every day in the morning, in the evening, do the nama, chant the name....

It is just like in Baul practice, when we sing and dance. We don't do the Sri Krishna sankirtanam in the sense of how it is done—only the name—but we sing the poem of the master. Then there is this presence of singing and dancing, which helps to transform the space and time and what is in the mind.

Chaitanya brought this way of doing meditation, because sometimes for some, when we sit quietly, we just cannot let our mind be quiet. It doesn't happen. So we make a lot of noise outside—singing—and we start dancing like a mad man or woman! Sometimes we look like a child, just turning around. We become so active with our body, it's just the opposite of sitting quietly, but you can still find the stillness inside.

So, be respectful to all and sing kirtana, sing the praise. Why is it important to sing the praise? And why is it important to chant the name every day? Because sometime we feel that we are doing the same thing again and again. But once we get into that intoxication of name, every time we chant, it is new, ever new!

It's like turning your mind and turning your speech in one direction; everything is oriented to one direction, towards this praise. And so, in that way, through the speech and through the mind, we are able to become one. There is just no duality anymore.[4]

— Parvathy Baul

---

[4]   Interview by the author with Parvathy Baul, August 2013, Ferme de Jutreau, France.

in which his devotees were steeped in the vast resource of India's Vedic and Sanskrit wisdom traditions. Countless sacred texts—including the *Srimad Bhagavatam* and the *Mahabharata*—extol the virtue and efficacy of chanting the name of God. In the India of Yogi Ramsuratkumar's time on Earth, the perennial *dharma* was known to all, rendering the seemingly simple instruction to repeat the *nama* of God into a profound yet practical, useful—and, at the same time—subtle, multi-dimensional practice.

In the West, we must carefully build a matrix of understanding by educating ourselves about the wisdom of the path and dharma, which gives the practice of study a vital importance. As an example, Lee's poetry to Yogi Ramsuratkumar is a testimony of Lee's own inner practice as well as a roadmap of how to proceed on the path. While the majority of Lee's instruction on the use of *nama* is found in over two thousand poems that he wrote to his master, on Lee's ashrams the *nama* of Yogi Ramsuratkumar is sung in *kirtan* to countless melodies—a practice inherited many years ago from the Indian devotees of Yogi Ramsuratkumar.

There are times in life when God's grace seems very far away, and the disruptions of impermanence and suffering cause the nature of life on Earth to come into focus. In this world where war and greed and power conflicts are our daily fare, where whole species are dying along with rivers, lakes, and oceans and indigenous people, where a child's innocence meets daily cruelties and relationships

are degraded or agonizingly painful, we come to know the truth of the Buddha's teaching: "All life is suffering." Harsh realities seem to crash in upon us, and in the uncertainty and groundlessness of these times, the need for the rare, precious pearl of sanctuary becomes most apparent. Turning to the name of God, we find refuge and mercy; simply to repeat the name of God is to invoke blessings and ultimate Grace.

Lee's words, "You cannot dispel the darkness, but you can light a candle," ring with a simplicity that hints at the depth of their meaning. The primary practice of the Bauls, chanting the name of God, is lighting a single candle. On the temple walls in the Yogi Ramsuratkumar Ashram the master's words resound: "No nama goes wasted. Every nama chanted helps this beggar's work." We can make a difference in this world through the simplicity of cultivating the life of the soul by repeating the name of God.

The pristine essence of sahaja is underlying all phenomena. Even when life seems so fragmented and dark, so full of breakdown and conflict; in times of happiness or sorrow, we can choose to cleave to the timeless truth of the Path: the power of *nama*, of the Divine Name.

REMAIN CONSTANT

Sanatan Baba said, "Believe in what the guru says. Remain constant." One simple and easy act of obedience to the teachings and the way, no matter how busy we are, is to repeat the Divine Name. It is the remedy against the endless forms of distraction, seduction, and fascination that lead us down the back roads of this crazy world, where we can get lost and wander in a forgetful state, sometimes for years at a time.

In the last year of his life, Khepa Lee said, "The name of Yogi Ramsuratkumar is the seed practice of all of our practices." Throughout Lee's poetry, he begs and asks us to "take the Name of Yogi Ramsuratkumar" into our daily lives and daily practice. He describes—in hundreds of ways—his own practice of repeating the name of his master. In his great generosity, we are given both the simple *nama* of Yogi Ramsuratkumar and the formal mantra:

Yogi Ramsuratkumar
Yogi Ramsuratkumar
Yogi Ramsuratkumar
Jaya Guru Raya

Here the extended communities of the Western Bauls find an easy resonance with the Bauls of Bengal; in this practice, the lineage and *nama* of Yogi Ramsuratkumar blends seamlessly the Baul *sadhana*, dovetailing our paths in harmony with ancient tradition and practice. ✤

Khepa Lee with Yogi Ramsuratkumar.

CHAPTER 8

The Western Bauls

*Inner practice, like doing mantra, is designed to be completely seamless.
It is the natural interior process as you live your life. The inner practice
always bears fruit, which is when the practice ceases to be separate from
you. Whoever you are and wherever you are, you are just carried by the
wave, radiating in whatever comes along.* Khepa Lee

NEW INSIGHTS INTO ANCIENT, ENDURING, TIMELESS TRUTHS are the province of the unexpected prophet—a seer, a fiery lover of God in whom primordial *sahaja* awakens, leaving the visionary with the work of integrating the divinity that has erupted within his or her humanity. While there has been a vast migration of wisdom teachings and teachers from East to West in the last fifty years, the spontaneous arising of *sahaja*—like that which occurred in the West in the sudden awakening of Lee Lozowick in 1975—is a rare event.

Lee's street-wise message of the natural wisdom of the body, its "already present enlightenment," and the human potential for loving God carried the noncomformist, iconoclastic, enigmatic, and at times provocative touch of the Bauls and Sahajiyas. Like the Bauls, Lee also enjoyed and easily interacted with many traditions; his eclectic love of study and his dedication to the path of transformation added many universal and all-inclusive elements to his teaching, which paradoxically is extremely traditional and in some ways quite conservative. Regardless of its so-called "wild heresy," Lee's work was always blessed by Yogi Ramsuratkumar.

In 1980 Lee moved from the East Coast to Arizona, where he established his first ashram with a small group of students. For the next eight years, he lived in relative seclusion; it was a time during which his teaching was in a process of both revelation and germination. After Lee enigmatically claimed in 1985, "Tell them we are Bauls," he entered into a phase of creativity that would grow and evolve into many arenas during his lifetime. After a few early, short-term musical experiments (Lee had been writing lyrics since 1976), he formally initiated his first rock & roll band in 1987. This was the beginning of a long love affair with communicating and transmitting the teaching through his poem-lyrics and the power of musical performance. It was also the beginning of Lee's collaboration with students who composed music to his lyrics to create the songs that would be sung before audiences.

Lee had been writing devotional poetry to Yogi Ramsuratkumar since 1979, and in the mid to late 1980s the seeds that had been planted and nurtured for many years began to show signs of growth. In 1988, Yogi Ramsuratkumar initiated a more active, dynamic relationship with Lee, which catalyzed a deep intimacy between the master and his devotee. Lee's attention was entirely focused on Yogi Ramsuratkumar, who became the inspiration and blessing force behind all activities of the growing community of Bauls in the West. Yogi Ramsuratkumar was the spiritual influence behind everything Lee engaged—his public role as an international teacher, the founding of ashrams in France and India, the music and bands, the tours, travels, and teachings.

Creativity is a hallmark of Lee's life and his teaching. His lifetime passion for the arts in all forms inspired his involvement with the creativity of his students and permeated his own writing and poetry. Many individuals of refined artistic talent in all domains—painting, music, poetry, literature, sculpture and more—were guided and supported in their artistic unfolding by Lee as their guru and by Yogi Ramsuratkumar as his *ishta devata*. And so, when Lee's students' books were published, they were dedicated to Yogi Ramsuratkumar; if art was the pursuit in any form, from paintings and sculptures to books

and poetry, it was another form of praise for Yogi Ramsuratkumar. In Lee's world, it was and remains Yogi Ramsuratkumar as *maha-guru* who is given the seat of honor.

In this way Lee responded to his master's instruction, "Only praise," with no hesitation. When poetry was written and published, it was for Yogi Ramsuratkumar; when lyrics were made into songs that were recorded and performed, it was all for Yogi Ramsuratkumar. When the bands went on tour each year in Europe, or in Lee's long-time collaboration with Arnaud Desjardins (the renowned French filmmaker and spiritual teacher), this too was another way of making the spiritual presence and blessings of Yogi Ramsuratkumar available in the world.

Across the span of his teaching work, Khepa Lee churned out lyrics, over five hundred of which have been put to original music (composed by a number of his students) and recorded on CDs.[1] As the teaching-in-action, Lee's bard poems are ultimately human and natural and flow in *sahaja* waves that express the way life is: some of them are absolute perfection—an objective expression of the moment—while others might be considered good, mediocre or "bad" by the conventional critical standards of a schooled and sophisticated intellect. He often criticized himself for not editing or fine-tuning his poems and lyrics—however, this kind of spontaneity is the way of *sahaja*, which also yields the gem of an unstudied, perfect poem.

---

[1]   See the discography at the end of the book.

Yogi Ramsuratkumar said so, so often: "Only Praise, only Praise." And although I am smart enough to argue that [all of my work is] Praise, in a certain context, obviously, I do have some small concern for I am both dedicated and devoted to obeying my Guru's Word and in bringing honor to His profound trust in me, and His Trust was and is truly profound, of this there is no doubt....

The main concern is that I please Yogi Ramsuratkumar through this mission, a mission that He gave me, a mission that He Praised me for countless times and a mission that I value with the utmost seriousness and mean to bring integrity to. I have no need to "strike out on my own" as so many students of powerful Teachers seem to do. I guess the whiff of authority they mistake for worldly power goes to their egos. I am quite happy being nobody and nothing in His shadow. Let His Light shine and I am thrilled.[2]

— Khepa Lee

Never one to flinch from praise or blame, Lee once humorously recounted how someone had said to him, many years ago, "You're a bad poet." In the so-called "bad poetry" to Yogi Ramsuratkumar, Lee demonstrates a powerful example: without apology or explanation, he refers to himself as Yogi Ramsuratkumar's "bad Poet." This misnomer became a powerful metaphor that has had the effect of objectifying and even mythologizing aspects of Lee's *lila* with Yogi Ramsuratkumar. Whether poems or lyrics are "bad or good" does not matter from the *sahaj* view, because it is their unstudied simplicity that communicates an authenticity, a fresh quality, which is disarming in a way that goes directly to the heart.

Such simplicity can easily be the very thing that opens us up—we are perked up, momentarily awakened, and given cause to reflect—if for no other discernible reason than by the fact of a poem's irritating orneriness or a nuance of its everyday language. Regardless of form, even the poems that come across as hastily cobbled, stunted, or absurd have a lot to say to us.

More significantly, Lee is a *sahajiya* poet: he writes because he is moved to write. Writing is what occurs. Writing is Just This. The result is that *bhava* is created through the medium of the word. The touchstone of *bhava* and the traditional way of Baul *guruvada* are found in abundance throughout Lee's work—in his lyrics and poetry as well as in his performances onstage with his students.

In the early 1990s, during a time when Lee's relationship with Yogi Ramsuratkumar was deepening into the graceful intimacy that characterized their last twenty years

---

2   Lee Lozowick, *Chasing Your Tail*, pp. 116–117.

together, Lee was also getting to know—with the blessing of his spiritual Father—his Bengali Baul cousins. During the visit with Lee on his ashram in Arizona in 1991, Sanatan Das Thakur Baul wrote the following song for his friend:

> I salute you,
> oh guru of LGB.
> You and I will meet again and again.
>
> You, Baul of America,
> travel from country to country,
> but I came and met you at your ashram.
>
> You always fight the war of justice,
> Now conquer the hearts of all.
> Initiate everyone with the mantra of
>   renunciation;
> Teach the worship of the natural way.
> Beg at the door of love.

As Western Baul poet "begging at the door of love," Lee was a prolific writer. His pen was always steady: there were no prima donna antics or emotional fluxes that kept Lee from his ever-present muse, Yogi Ramsuratkumar. The poetic flow of Khepa Lee was much like a river that diverges into two streams on their way to the same ocean:

I. Poems and prayers to
    Yogi Ramsuratkumar
II. Lyrics—the teaching encoded in
    the contemporary Western forms of
    music, rock & roll and the blues.

Ultimately, it was and is all about "Lee's mission," as Yogi Ramsuratkumar called it—bringing the blessings and the divine name of Yogi Ramsuratkumar to the Western world. In the process of achieving that mission, Lee was a messenger who encoded his message in lyrics and songs. The mission and the message were one and same.

BAD POET WITH A MISSION

In thirty-five years of teaching work, Lee's expression went through many changes and stages, in which he began to place a stronger emphasis on the power of those great intangibles that are so tacit to the actual living or *bhava* of true spiritual life—adoration, prayer, faith and praise. He gave a great deal of consideration to these in both verbal and written dimensions of his teaching, and most powerfully, he demonstrated it in his poetry—which he also called "prayers"—to Yogi Ramsuratkumar.

Lee's "mission" is most fully encoded in the poems; taken as a whole, they contain a perfect map of *sadhana* and all the instruction needed to walk the path. The poems to Yogi Ramsuratkumar are a living *vidya* (knowledge) that contains and expresses, by the objective power of the divine word, the timeless truths of the spiritual path. They exist as a template of *guruvada*, or guru yoga, and a guide to supreme love between human being and Divine.

At a deeper level of potential, Lee's poetry to Yogi Ramsuratkumar contains a direct transmission of the spiritual power of the lineage, which may be easily accessed by the serious student. Lee's poems communicate the fulfillment of the true devotee while they simultaneously transmit the heart of the master.

The story of Yogi Ramsuratkumar's acknowledgement of Lee's poetry is one that must be told here. Lee wrote his first poem to Yogi Ramsuratkumar in February 1979 while he was visiting his master in Tiruvannamalai. Over the next years, Lee sent poems through the mail to his master regularly. As early as 1987, Yogi Ramsuratkumar began to give Lee's poems to his devotee, Sadhu (Professor) Rangarajan, to be printed in *Tattva Darsana*, a small dharma magazine published in Chennai. When Lee arrived in India in 1988 with nine of his devotees, he was surprised to find that one of his poems had appeared in the publication, along with a short article about himself as the author of the poetry. Still, Lee did not reveal anything to his own devotees about the poetry he was writing to his master.

> You, Yogi Ramsuratkumar, have always been the same
>   to Your bad Poet and wild Heretic.
> Before I met You in the body, You were,
>   guiding, teaching and fully Blessing.
> Before this birth, You were,
>   always with me, Present, always True.
> And then after we met, flesh to flesh, face to face,
>   You were still That same One, the One
> Who was always, always there, here, and only God.
>   Of course, I love the personal contact,
> Your words of wisdom and humor, Your caresses,
>   Your mild scoldings, Your laughter and Your tears.
> And yes, I love to gaze at You, at Your beauty,
>   in which I can get lost for hours or ages.
> But You were also That before I met You
>   and You will be That after Your Body dissolves
> in the Infinite Field of Father's Being.
>   Yes, this lee lozowick, insignificant except for
> his Faith in You and his Obedience to You,
>   calls himself your son and calls You his Father.
> Paradoxically this is also true, even though You
>   have always been and are and will always be the Same,
> One, Total, Indivisible, Unitive, Yogi Ramsuratkumar.
>   For this, because of this, Praise flows, unstoppable,
> and song arises in the various melodies and tones,
>   chanting Your Name with sweetness and abandon.
> Lost in You, even found in You as well, Your little beggar
>   falls at Your Feet crying, "Light, Salvation, Wonder, Awe,
> Yogi Ramsuratkumar, have Mercy on Your worshippers
>   who live only to please and Praise You."[3]
>
> — Lee Lozowick

---

[3]   *Gasping for Air in a Vacuum*, 4 October 2000, p. 520.

Very soon after this, Yogi Ramsuratkumar gave all of Lee's poems to Sadhu Rangarajan, asking him to publish them all. They appeared in a slim paperback volume with written introductions by the poet and by Rangarajan, in which the publisher called the poetry a form of *ninda stuti*—the classic Indian form of devotional poetry called "ironic praise." In November 1993, when Lee made the trip to India with nine students, he was received by Sadhu Rangarajan, who soon presented boxes of the small books, which were then distributed among his traveling party. Taking the small volume in our eager hands, we were surprised and thrilled to immediately immerse ourselves in *Poems of a Broken Heart.*

Glancing at Lee and each other with wonder and delight, we soon discovered that our teacher's heart was speaking directly to our own through the medium of his poems. In the days that followed, Yogi Ramsuratkumar had the poems read over and over again on the porch of Sudama House, where he sat for hours at a time with his attendants, Ma Devaki and the Sudama sisters, and Lee and his students.

The poetry was not only an unveiling of Lee's inner life with his master but also

Oh Father,
    Yogi Ramsuratkumar,
I have brought Your Name
    around the world.
This is as You have wished,
    is it not?
But You have said,
    and tell me if I am mistaken,
that This is the Name of God,
    of Your Father in Heaven.
Alright! Well and good,
    but lee is his Father's son
and doesn't know
    his Grandfather very well.
I want the Bliss of You
    to flood the hearts of the sad and lonely.
Maybe I am just selfish,
    for after all,
since my heart has been shattered
    on the mountain of Your Love
perhaps I want other hearts
    shattered as well,
so I have some company
    on the long nights when I am missing You.[4]

— Lee Lozowick

signaled the revelation of Lee's teaching as scripture, an embodiment of lineage and transmission. At the time, Yogi Ramsuratkumar said, "No one needs to write anything else about this beggar, now that Lee has written these poems." It was then

---

[4]   Lee Lozowick, *Death of a Dishonest Man*, March 31, 1994, p. 515.

that Yogi Ramsuratkumar instructed, "Everyone should read these poems every day." This was the origin of the practice of reading one poem—or a few or several—as an important element of daily *sadhana* for many of Lee's students.

Two years later another volume was published in India, again at the request of Yogi Ramsuratkumar, titled *Poems of Broken Heart, Part II*. In 1997 Lee gave his students permission to publish his poems to Yogi Ramsuratkumar in the U.S. in a large hardback volume titled *Death of a Dishonest Man*. Six years later a second volume was published in the West under the title *Gasping for Air in a Vacuum*. After Lee's death, his poems to Yogi Ramsuratkumar—written from 2003 through September 2010—were collected and published in the third and final volume, *Intimate Secrets of a True Heart Son*.

BAD POET WITH A MESSAGE

Khepa Lee spilled out poems and lyrics as naturally as the rain falling, the sun rising, the stars shining. As a *sahajiya* poet, Lee had no premeditated time, ritual or special place where he contacted his muse, as many writers have claimed to be necessary. He wrote at any time, in any place. Not one to rewrite, edit, polish or otherwise improve upon whatever came out, his words are true to the moment of their arising—original, fresh, plain and simple, rough or smooth, lyrical or prosaic.

Lee had a talent for hiding the teaching in lyrics that were turned into rock & roll or blues songs—the Western forms of music that sprang spontaneously from the cultural melting pot of America, where African slaves and European immigrants mingled and music was born from their suffering on the porches and juke joints and back streets of the south.

Like the traditional American Blues, over the years, Lee's music has touched ordinary people from all walks of life, from urban to rural enclaves. Even so, Lee's lyrics remain a largely unknown but significant and rich source of dharma teachings. Their very nature as songs renders them into informal teachings, and yet they follow the rich tradition of the *caryapadas, dohas* and *padavalis* of the Buddhist and Vaishava Sahajiyas as classic vehicles for the teaching. Because they reach us in the medium of music, in seemingly casual, ordinary circumstances when the mind and body are relaxed and receptive in a different way than in a formal teaching space, they sink in. While the songs speak to the mind through language mingled with music, they saturate the cells of the body.

Lee had a unique talent for getting the point across in his songs. The lyrics are yet another form of praise, even when they are a searing penetration into the opaque world of illusion. In fact many of them are prayers that resound into the world through the notes and melodies of the songs in which they are contained and brought to life. They bring us to the brink of true feeling and release us into *bhava*.

CRUSHED BY LOVE

In 2006 Lee was answering a question posed by one of his students who wanted to know more about the enigmatic title of his new CD, *Crushed by Love*.

"What does it mean to be crushed by love?" she asked. Lee answered, "It's about Reality. Reality is Love, and we are crushed by Love to the degree that we are not defended against Reality."

Lee's statement, "Reality is Love," provides another inroad into the *sahaj* vision, which yields those poems and songs that spring from the undefended, open heart. The phrase "crushed by love" describes the natural vulnerability of the awakened state, which leaves the innate nature of the visionary or seer open to the searing, transformative force of love—a fiery crucible in which the heart and body are made tender and caused to tremble at times with awe at the flow of objective feelings. Being crushed by love occurs as a way of life—of *sahaja* expressing through one individual—when we know, without a doubt, through direct experience, that we are one with every other aspect of Life.

In contemporary times, we could say that we all have the blues. This was one of Lee's favorite metaphors because it aptly conveys the teaching of Buddha, "All life is suffering." One could say that Lee wrote lyrics and sang in the musical form of the Blues as an expression of this truth. Out of the heat and fermentation of that sweet and bitter alchemy—which on the path results in

an objective heartbreak—words arose, spilled out, and were written down on paper. The great bluesman Leadbelly said, "It takes a man that have the blues to sing the blues." To be crushed by love in this way is to feel the suffering of the world and to respond with love, because love is the supreme force that causes the stars to burn and reconciles all opposites. Bluesman Khepa Lee once wrote in a song, "Once your eyes are opened, I know you can trust / That old friend sorrow."

The blues is a contemporary street-wise metaphor for an objective state of awakened perception because true heartbreak is inevitable on the spiritual path. Chögyam Trungpa Rinpoche called this "the genuine heart of sadness"—the vulnerable, softly broken heart of the true warrior. What these wise ones are saying is that heartbreak is our doorway into Reality; it is the pathway of pure *bhava*. For the Baul, we approach to beg at the door of Love with a broken heart.

Impermanence, that peerless heartbreaker, is the first and last teaching that Life has to give us. Heartbreak contains the seeds of our salvation. The only way to realize the sweetness of freedom is to lose everything: every identity, every hope, every shred of that which we think we possess and hold onto as our separate selves. This is the common thread found in all spiritual paths. In the awakened moment, we discover the fatal, fleeting beauty for which we are forever hungering and thirsting—and then it is gone again. Lee leads us to the door of this discovery in his bard poems, written

Death By Music

Some people say you need a heart to survive
And hot blood in your veins, that's what keeps you alive
I have been called heartless, uncaring and cruel
They say I'm cold-blooded, just an unfeeling fool

But how can they judge when they're as blind as can be
When they can't hear the music pulsing inside of me
Well I'm not blue-blooded but I'll give you some clues
My body lives and it breathes cause it's made of the blues

I have known pleasure, I have felt so much pain
I have seen when life's over, there ain't nothing to gain
So I live with a vengeance and my love will not tell
Seen the bright side of heaven, seen the dark side of hell

Walking on the razor's edge, sleeping very light
Hungered by the blazing sun, fed by the night
Satisfied with the joy in the cracks between my sorrows
Not counting on the future of illusory tomorrows

— Lee Lozowick

with the unmistakable touch of one who has intimate knowledge of such a mystery.

Look deeply into any song and the teaching may be found there. In "Death by Music" the poet speaks to every one of us who has felt deeply misunderstood, and yet has been touched by the glance of the Divine and can never forget. This touch, or taste of *rasa*, is how we are lured onto the path. We feel like misfits because we are unable to accept the lies of the world, and we have become aware of our hunger and thirst. We sense the meaninglessness of the social structures around us; we have an acute sensitivity to the prevailing anxieties and precarious reality of our times; we long for sacred culture even as we begin to face our own emptiness and impending death—the truth of impermanence—and we long for a holy sanity with which to embrace it all.

Even revered teachings and past glories can become crystallized to the extent that they are rendered into empty, dead, static forms or constructs of the mind—the sacred cows of the spiritual path. Sooner or later these must be examined in the bright light of nonattachment and then released. If we do not let go, the path itself will arrange life in such a way that we are forced to go beyond our previous insights into the unknown. The way of all Life is change, evolution, growth; nothing lasts forever.

"Death by Music" hooks us immediately into its aching mood of longing. We are identified with the poet, who takes us further into the mystery of opposites until we are woven in and out with nonduality and the sweetness of duality that is objectified. There we may find satisfaction, but only in "the joy in the cracks between my sorrows." The message is that we will get to this joy by "Walking on the razor's edge, sleeping very light / Hungered by the blazing sun, fed by the night." This is an image that hints of the ancient alchemy of sun and moon, dark and light, of the interplay of Krishna and Radha within the human body, as well as in our relationship with the physical cosmos. Divine Alchemy is a powerful path; only spiritual warriors dare to take it as their own.

Lee once made the offhand comment, "The best warriors are aware even when they're sleeping," a teaching that reverberates in the lines of the poem. This is a secret of esoteric practice common to all serious practitioners of mantra, in which the awareness of the *nama* or sacred name reverberates day and night. The Bauls have a practice of observing one's self or remaining aware in sleep—a very advanced practice that is the fruit of years of discipline. In such a practice, we meditate upon the mantra or *nama* while falling asleep, so that the mind is guided toward the sacred sound. Eventually, even the sleeping state is informed by the Divine Name.

Lee's lyrics connect the patterns of life in the mandala of *sadhana*, pointing us toward a seamless whole of many parts that work in harmonious concert to bring us to *bhava*. To find *bhava* is to discover our own broken heart; to find *bhava* is, as Lee said, "to have a wound that only God can heal."

We may well be asking, "Why should I want to have a broken heart? Is that fleeting joy worth the pain?" In poet Lee's *sandhya*

Traveling with Bhava

You can be awake in your dream and observe, knowing that you are dreaming, and you can direct the dream. Shushupti. If you wake up, you start doing japa, mantra, again. In the early morning, we start chanting Sri Krishna names in song or inside. When we first wake up, when we start waking up, our bodies are more fragile, and the mind is weak. We think, "If I can just be in bed for five minutes more." This is the first sign of laziness! In that dozing, you would like to visit the part of your mind that seeks comfort! It's common for most people. For a man, the desire or body becomes active; for a women, it is more in the mind. Even if you don't have sexual fantasies, but you think about your physical lover and how comfortable it is in her embrace, and that happens in that first five minutes, you are filling that space with that.

That is why we get up at three a.m. to practice—to remain awake and to chant. If we are constant with this practice during the day and during sleep—sleep in the body, sleep in the mind—when we are traveling with bhava to reach rasa, then there is a continuous flow of joy, where you are not able to chant anymore! That is not sleep, because we are in rasa.[5]

— Parvathy Baul

---

[5]   Interview by the author with Parvathy Baul, August 2014.

bhasa, having a body that is made of "the blues" is a perfect metaphor for the state of longing for Krishna, the Beloved—a state of being that becomes the highest attainment for a Baul. As twilight language, the blues is about love in separation—*viraha*. It is a working symbol that merges easily with the dark blue of Krishna's skin.

As a metaphor for the spiritual path, "the blues" is another way of saying that one has entered into a sacred and therefore sacrificial relationship to life and death, or Enlightened Duality. What we are seeking is to penetrate the mystery of the statement, "My body lives and it breathes 'cause it's made of the blues."

When we are finally able to *sing* the blues, we have entered into a full embrace of impermanence and the fact that we are hopeless beings, longing for the Eternal in an existence in which all things pass. Ruin and loss become the sweet taste of a refined *bhava*, as we become infused with joy and sorrow in equal measure in an exquisite, excruciating mood that rolls on into eternity.

Such delicate and tender moments arise and subside like everything else, touching the heart and infusing us with the surprise of grace. In such moments we are "satisfied with the joy in the cracks between my sorrows." A serious practitioner could take this one line of wisdom and make it his or her meditation for the next twenty years, the completion of which would be nothing less than the fruition of the path. To engage such a journey of heartbreak and compassion, of beauty and sorrow, of exaltation in love and loss is to submit to the wound that only God can heal … and in this way, we court the Beloved. ❀

On stage in Bourges, France, 2006.

CHAPTER 9

Bhava

Deliverance is not for me in renunciation. I feel the
embrace of freedom in a thousand bonds of delight.

Rabindranath Tagore

THE SANSKRIT WORD BHAVA MEANS BECOMING, state of being, or mood. There are many different flavors of mood that we experience daily, ranging from superficial to sublime, from unpleasant to lovely, beautiful, or inspired. The Bauls are seeking a particular flavor, or *rasa*, of mood—the transcendental mood that cannot be explained or described, which is *maha-bhava*, the great divine mood that leads to the eternal flow of *rasa*. It is a mood that is beyond language, and yet we could say that it is filled with joyful praise and a purity of divine love, or tinged with the bittersweet of longing for the unattainable, uncatchable "man of the heart."

Bhava is a vital element of the path that is shared by Bauls of the East and West. There is no linear access to *bhava*; it does not conform to mental concepts, rules or constructs. While *bhava* mysteriously appears and disappears, arises and subsides by fact of Grace or Divine Influence, it is also true that divine moods can be courted, begged into existence, through the choices we make and the actions of our everyday lives. In fact, the spiritual practices that are given by guru and path are the doorways to sweet and sacred *bhavas*.

SVABHAVA

The Sanskrit term *svabhava* (from the root word *sva* or self and *bhava* or becoming) is the mood that is discovered at the origins of one's self. It is the essential law of one's innate nature, the substratum of which is *sahaja*, and has close links with conscience, basic goodness, Organic Innocence, and the qualities of virtue that guide and inform human existence. *Svabhava* is not one's psychological disposition, although it may gleam like gold through the matrix of personality. *Svabhava* is auspicious and naturally resonant with *sanatana dharma*, or the eternal truth; if we are attuned to *svabhava* we will always turn toward the ultimate good in life's myriad circumstances.

Sahaja and *svabhava* are not reserved for great beings or spiritual authorities while the ordinary person remains bereft and disconnected; these are the original blueprint within every human being, which may be tasted through remembrance, cultivation, and active intention. Underpinning *svabhava* are truth, beauty, love, bliss, which are reflected in the dignity, generosity, kindness, compassion, and nobility of the individual. These qualities have their source in mood, and so the question of how we may actively refine the flavors of mood takes on paramount importance on the spiritual path. Once we begin to cultivate the higher qualities of mood, we are inevitably drawn into a long-term process of examining our attitudes, opinions, assumptions, projections, beliefs, and mental or emotional habits of all kinds—for these can make or break our efforts on the path.

Khepa Lee declared in a song, "It's not over there upon some distant star / It's right inside of you," just as the Baul poet Gosain Gopal wrote, "Forget not that your body contains the whole of existence."[1] Lee's lyrics express the many different moods of *bhava*; they carry us into the heart of being, the place where the doors to the soul may be flung open. Lee's poem-songs resonate at deep levels within us and lure us blinking from our caves of shadows and smoke into the golden sunrays of day or the cooling beams of the moon. They catalyze the potentials of *bhava*, through which we may come to know the primacy of natural ecstasy as the innate state of our own original innocence—and in this way, *rupa* reveals *svarupa*.

VIRAHA

The cultivation of *bhava* is inseparable from the bhakti ideal of *viraha*, or love in

---

Sweet Torture

Millions of bright stars
On a cool clear night
Endless thoughts of love feels so good
It's such sweet torture
Not being in your bed
Sweet torture with you—
Only in my head

Torture, I really don't mind
Pain and pleasure melt into one
Sweet torture don't know what I'll find
Darker than a moonless night
And brighter than the sun

Distant woman, don't think
You'll ever be mine
So I worship you from far away
It's just a fantasy that we will be wed
So I will settle for sweet torture instead

Been a dream for so long
I've lost reality
But I hide it very well so one sees
The pictures on my brain
Are clearer every day
Ah sweet torture, I wouldn't
Have it any other way

— Lee Lozowick

---

[1]   *Songs of the Bauls of Bengal*, translated by Deben Bhattacharya, p. 63.

Oh Yogi Ramsuratkumar, my Krishna!
    Here I lay, Radha, in adoring glance
upon Your Supreme and Sublime Form,
    heart swollen with none but You,
eyes red with tears, for You come
    and go amongst Your infinite
bevy of lovers as Your whim and will
    dictate, always joyous
and ever full of the Passion of
    Only God, no one but He,
the Supreme which You Yourself are.
    My Madhava, I have tasted Your
sweetest nectar, You have suffused
    me with Your touch, melted
me in Your embrace, and now
    left me alone with You,
oh yes, with You, but taken Your body
    to dance another dance with
another gopi as I, one with You,
    joined in eternal union,
pound my soft hands upon the
    tender grass where we played
and call Your Name with
    abandon, surrender and desire.
This play, this paradox, this

maddening Divine Justice!
Of course, I know I must release You
    to delight Yourself with the
infinite Universe of waiting
    and expectant women (some
male and some female) who eagerly
    prepare themselves for the tryst.
I know I must let You go, though
    You will go in any event whether
I free You or not, the call of
    Your destiny and the demand
of Life playing the most captivating
    tunes through Your cosmic flute,
bringing to You those love-crazed
    with the Vision of Your Beauty,
Your irresistibly hypnotizing Radiance.
    Oh Sun, Blue Lord, Black Night,
hear Your Radha's cry and bring
    Yourself home just one more time.
Satisfy this insatiable longing and
    heed her begging appeal.
Yogi Ramsuratkumar, my Krishna,
    I await with breath, body and soul.

— Lee Lozowick

separation, which is a state of inner long-ing. This quality or taste of yearning has its source in *prema* (pure love) and is coveted by many connoisseurs of the path. If one merges with the Beloved, then one is in a state of union in which individuality ceases to exist—only God exists. If one longs for the Beloved, across the spectrum of degrees of longing, then love in separation, or *viraha*, is the mood.

We can discover and relish this mood in the work of many poets, and especially in the poems of the great *bhaktas*—Andal, Chandidas, Jayadeva, Mirabai, Vidyapati, and Tulsidas, to name only a very few. In Lee's *ninda stuti* poems of praise to Yogi

---

2   Lee Lozowick, *Intimate Secrets of a True Heart Son*, Dec 14, 2009, pp. 226–227.

Ramsuratkumar, the mood of *viraha* is transmitted to the reader in the poet's begging for separation, so that he may stay in a state of adoration of his Beloved.

BHAVA AND POETRY

Lee had a great interest in the invocation of divine mood, and one of the primary ways in which he experimented with this possibility was through the power of the word combined with music performed onstage in song. Lee's performances with his bands were known for their mysterious blend of presence and showmanship combined with lyric and melody—a tradition that continues with Lee's bands after his physical departure. There is no substitute for the power of live performance of art—theatre, dance, or song—to invoke a mood with transformational potential in the audience. Lee spent twenty-five years of his teaching work playing in exactly this arena, and it all started with his prolific lyric-writing.

The metaphors for the cultivation of *bhava* are many. We may speak of potent substances such as honey, syrup, nectar, juice, ambrosia, elixir, pollen, sugar, morning dew, wine, sweet liquor, and the bodily essences that are catalyzed by the process of yoga. In the infinite vastness of creation, these are the kisses of God, which we may know and cherish in the inner journey of the spiritual path.

And so, in the world of Baul poet Khepa Lee, we encounter a direct relationship

---

Nabanidas Baul

His voice is not always melodious or pleasant to listen to. During my recording of Nabanidas Baul in his village in Birbhum, Nabanidas had lost his voice owing to an overdose of hemp that he had been smoking before he started singing. There was a small crowd in a sweet shop in Siuri, listening to him. The audience did not care about the quality of his voice, as he was able to communicate to his listeners naturally, effortlessly. Through his songs, Nabanidas directed his questions and answers to himself, and yet he was able to stir every single individual in this village gathering. The audience sat spellbound, listening, asking him to sing over and over again.[3]

— Deben Bhattacharya

What makes you think
you are human?
Having squandered
your heritage of heart,
you are not lost in lust...

— Nabanidas Baul

---

between *sadhana*, sweetness, sensuality, song, and *svarupa*; between *rasa, rupa*, and rock & roll—the Western Baul equivalent of those great Baul poem-songs that transmit the secrets of life. All of this is synthesized

---

[3] *Mirror of the Sky*, Deben Bhattacharya, p. 36.

that Organic Innocence is always present as the divine underpinning of the darkest and brightest facets of human existence.

These poems make the lyrical transition full circle from transcendent to temporal by speaking with frank honesty to all areas of human experience: relationships in general but especially those of a sexual nature; the bondage of social politics at every level of society; war and violence; the ecological demise of our planet and the global decay of sacred culture; the ridiculous and darkly absurd ironies of life; as well as the call of the heart for God and our most ancient longings for the personal Beloved.

Baul songs are sung to audiences in compelling performances that carry a mysterious transformational power. When we live in a state of praise, we are in relationship with the Divine, and our actions communicate the subtle force of a transformed inner state of being. Lee's music combs our minds free of tangles and grit, making way for the essential to move within us and catalyzing an ecstatic communion that flows between musicians and listeners. From the view of *sahaja*, perfection is not the goal; if it can be said that there is a "goal" at all, then it would be the invocation of mood or *bhava* and *rasa*, in praise, adoration and worship.

Praise and worship are true not only of Lee's sublime poems to Yogi Ramsuratkumar; in countless love songs he praises earthly love between human partners.

and blended into the *bhava* of praise—an elixir made of love, devotion, truth, clarity, gratitude, adoration, worship, dedication, and unshakable commitment, which pleases the Divine above all other offerings.

Written in *sandhya bhasa*, the twilight language of the soul, poetry holds the sacred and the profane together in the palm of one hand and lifts them both to higher ground. These are songs that offer a unique doorway into the Real; they can shake us from sleep as easily as Lee's physical presence and actions did during his lifetime. His lyrics reflect an amazing finesse with the red-blooded spirituality of the *sahaja* path, in which we may discover

---

4   Parvathy Baul, *Song of the Great Soul*, pp. 21–22.

Parvathy Baul performing in St. Pierre de Maillé, near Lee's ashram, France, 2011.

On stage with his blues band Shri in France, 2007.

As he often said of himself, "I'm a raging Romantic, with a capital 'R.'" What are the love games of Krishna with the *gopis* if not romantic—the great Romance between human and Divine?

In *Take Me Away*, one of countless *saha-jiya* love poems written by Lee over the years, he invokes a burning, tender love that is both erotic and transcendent; it speaks of the love of man and woman while it simultaneously

---

Take Me Away

Woman, turn me into blood
so I can run through your veins
turn me into freedom
so I can break your chains
let me be the food
that feeds your hungry soul
let me be the fullness
to fill your every hole

Take me away, take me away
I don't want me anymore
take me away, take me away
leave only you, you, you
take me away, take me away
I only want what I adore
take me to the only thing that's true
leave only you, leave only you

Give me the power
to fill you with peace
let me be the force
that grants you sweet release
let me be the perfect rose
to satiate your senses
let me be what's needed, baby
to burn down your fences

Take me away, take me away
I don't want me anymore
take me away, take me away
leave only you, you, you
take me away, take me away
I only want what I adore
take me to the only thing that's true
leave only you, leave only you

Let me be the blood
that pumps through your heart
let me be the inspiration
giving you a start
make me into sugar
sweeten your flesh
turn me into soft skin
to cover your warm breast

Take me away, take me away
I don't want me anymore
take me away, take me away
leave only you, you, you
take me away, take me away
I only want what I adore
take me to the only thing that's true
leave only you, leave only you

— Lee Lozowick

Yours

First thing I feel every morning
When the sunlight greets the day
Is the love I feel for you
Love true, yes – come what may
Now some feel their love varies
Like the moods of the mind
But mine for you is steady, steady,
Steady and I know you'll find

Chorus:
I am yours
I am yours
I am yours alone
Yours alone
Flesh and bone
I am yours alone
I am yours

I go through the motions
Getting done all I need
But never am I separate

From you in word or deed
My interests seem to vary
Yeah but that's just surface waves
On the ocean of my love for you
Love from birth to grave

The last thing every evening
I know before I sleep
Is the love I have for you
Love that's sweet and deep
Well many think I'm crazy
To have no other one
But I don't care what other's say
When all is said and done

I am yours
In every form
Yours throughout all time
And what's more love – You are mine
I am yours

— Lee Lozowick

points directly at the love of human and divine. "Take me away, take me away, I only want what I adore…" Is he speaking to his lover or to his God? The poet's fluid use of metaphor crosses layers and dimensions of meaning, taking us into uncharted oceans of longing for the great intangibles.

The *bhava* of these songs is one of love and longing—of *viraha*, or love in separation—that inevitably calls us to clarity and truth, which is necessary to keep the flame of love burning. It is not possible to have *prema* or love without also having truth; they go hand in hand.

BROKEN HEARTS & BLUE BHAVAS

Lee's poems have a unique way of fearlessly splashing into the onrush of life to navigate the stream, making use of all life has to offer and hiding the transcendent in the raw passionate language of the streets. Regardless of experience or education, everyone can understand the gist of it. There is a correlation between mystical truth in the most cosmic sense and the need for truth at the level of our daily lives. Mystical truth means very little if it is not integrated at all levels of our experience. This requires a common sensical, down-to-earth piercing of the illusions in which we are mired.

"The truth will set you free," are the oft-quoted words of Jesus. It is on every level, from mystic to mundane, that we must pursue and court "the truth." In the teaching poems of Khepa Lee, even the sting of a satirical or sarcastic poem moves us toward a clearer view of reality as it is. Lee's message has tremendous relevance to the heartbreaking concerns of our times, in which we suffer a terrible separation from nature in all forms, including our own bodies—a belief that effectively severs us from the direct experience of life as the Sacred.

At odds with social conformity, Bauls have a bone-deep sensitivity for what is genuine and real. Many artists have tapped this *sahajiya* spirit of the Baul—the *sahaj manush*, or natural man—because it is the human blueprint and is often experienced as the primordial urge to creativity. The difficulties of sustaining the raw force of creative energies in the body are well known; many artists who tap this fire burn out very quickly. For the practitioner on the path, the powerful energies and *bhavas* that are invoked are contained and assimilated through the disciple of spiritual practice.

Too Real

Gimme a joint, gimme a bottle
I'll take the needle, if I gotta
Do anything to help forget
Cause I'm not ready for the real truth yet
Gimme some woman, a sex machine
A real fast car, know what I mean?
Play me some music, dirty and loud
Anything to keep me out of the crowd

Life is full of beauty
But is seems
Like ugliness is winning
It's got the means, so it seems
Life can be so pleasant
And perhaps it only me
But the pain is too much
To smile on, to smile on

Send me to some tropical isle
Let me watch them movies go by
Give me them distractions
Anything will do
I don't need the sympathy
Of those who'll say what's true
Fascinate and thrill me
Take me for a ride

Give me lots of credit
So I can shop all day
Give me lots of liberty
So I can have my way
Fascinate and thrill me
Take me for a ride
I'll be safe and satisfied
Long as I can hide

— Khepa Lee

Once we have caught the fragrance of *sahaja*, we begin to recognize the Baul spirit in many poets, whose gift for sculpting words satisfies our urgent longing for what is real. The bard poet who is a Baul at heart—regardless of nationality, race or sex—reflects the sun-bleached bones of a radical honesty to us. In this sense all true poets are outlaws; to live outside the unspoken agreements and attitudes of the conventional world is to see through a fundamentally false worldview that turns human beings into sleepwalking robots. Bob Dylan once said, "To live outside the law you must be honest."[5]

The credo of honesty—and "ruthless self-honesty," as Lee instructed—guides our natural hunger for an authenticity that Baul poets give to us in full measure. It is the yearning for what is Real that compels us to break free of the prison of social politic and awaken to the greater reality. The poet's great gift is the resounding call to remembrance, to a recognition of inborn glory, to a self-renewing vision of universal virtue.

The guru-as-poet wages a "war of justice," as Sanatan Baba wrote of Khepa Lee—a war of the spirit that potentiates the awakening of the ordinary mind into the magnificent vistas of vast mind. The guru-as-poet conquers the hearts of all as he showers delight and *bhava*, sweetness and nectar, on the souls of those who are hungry and thirsty for truth. The guru-as-poet transmits the joy of renunciation that places

Grip

We all want just what we want
We're unwilling to be free
To drop the chains that bind us
And see reality
We think that the universe
Will follow our rules
We sing our songs of me and mine
While acting like blind fools

Unhappiness and misery
Seems to come from those out there
In fact it's our rigidity
Telling us it's so unfair
Grip, it's got a grip

— Khepa Lee

That enchanting river
Reflects the very form
Of the formless one
Sense the essence of the matter
My undiscerning heart,
And feel the taste
On your tongue

You see only
A little ditch of life
And remain involved in it
In drunken stupor

— Gopal (p. 61)

---

5   "Absolutely Sweet Marie," by Bob Dylan.

In the mood, on stage in Germany, 2006.

our feet firmly on the ground of selflessness, as we discover the joy of simplicity, sacrifice, and the fulfillment of living lightly on the Earth. The guru-as-poet worships the natural way and thus teaches us to discover the inborn wisdom of the body. The guru-as-poet "begs at the door of love" and reveals the lucent path to the Beloved.

As we court the truth and a radical self-honesty, we begin to see and experience the human condition, the plight of our world, and our own place in it. We live with an awareness of the suffering in the world and in the personal sphere of self and loved ones in such a way that our hearts are constantly pummeled with the truth. The suffering of others becomes viscerally real to us, and in bearing this truth with as much heart and dignity as possible, we become someone who has the blues.

> *"In beauty we are one, by beauty we pray, with beauty we conquer."*
> — Nicolas Roerich

BHAVA AND BEAUTY

One of the most powerful ways to cultivate *bhava* is through our active relationship with beauty. One of Lee's key instructions in the last years of his life was "Seek beauty and avoid suffering." In this teaching, he refers to the neurotic suffering of ego's desperate grip on dominance in all things. To avoid suffering is to accept the reality of impermanence and take refuge in the path. In the process, we find ourselves in a confrontation with the dead-end sufferings of the false world of contemporary values.

> Pain is inevitable, but suffering is optional.
> — Khepa Lee

To seek beauty is to cultivate that which is beautiful in our lives. As Dr. Robert Svoboda observed in his book on the science of vastu, "Stendahl maintained that 'Beauty is the promise of happiness,' and suggested that 'There are as many styles of beauty as there are visions of happiness.'"[6] During his lifetime, Lee embraced beauty in many forms, in ways that were sometimes startling and sometimes eliciting a joyful response. In the last eight years of Lee's life in particular, he began to surround himself with sacred art. Taking on the role of sacred merchant, he created what Gilles Farcet, a long-time disciple of Arnaud Desjardins, called "the Sacred Bazaar"—a traveling market of sorts, in which Lee's students and friends could obtain exquisite sacred objects of beauty and antiquity, mostly of Hindu and Buddhist origins but also from the Christian, Muslim, Taoist, and shamanic traditions. Lee believed that, in these troubled times, it is important to create spaces of sanctuary and spiritual beauty, and he encouraged everyone to adorn their homes and offices and living spaces with the gods, goddesses, and symbolic emblems of spiritual power.

Creating a sanctuary that will sustain us through difficult times was a common theme of Lee's teaching in this phase of guru-as-merchant. He often spoke prophetically, saying that he saw hard times ahead as the Earth continues to struggle under the forces of ecological disaster, warfare, and human greed. His advice to us was to create spiritual sanctuaries wherever possible—on ashrams, in small community enclaves, in private homes. To cultivate an environment of beauty and sanctity is one way of invoking *bhava* in our daily lives. We take beauty in through the physical eyes and the eyes of the soul, and the soul is uplifted. Beauty plants the seed for a *bhava* that can take root and flower within us.

BHAVA AND PRAISE

The cultivation of divine mood is both mystical and practical, with a working utility that has transforming effects from the personal to the transpersonal. It may be that our capacity to praise is the key that

---

6   Dr. Robert Svoboda, *Vastu: Breathing Life into Space*, p. 17.

unlocks the doors of the soul to that discovery. Having an intention to cultivate positive mental states and harmonious moods is where we begin.

From the Baul view, cultivating *bhava* is all important in developing the ability to work with suffering—negative emotions, dark mental states, or terrible experiences. Slowly we build the strength and resilience to bounce back quickly when we have fallen into anger, jealousy, greed, or hatred. One important way to cultivate wholesome and uplifting moods is to simply put ourselves aside and serve others. In stepping outside of our self-preoccupation to reach out to another, a stormy mood can be dispelled. By spending time with a child, an elder, a friend in need—or magnanimously cleaning up the kitchen for the others who "should have done it themselves"—we can cultivate humility and generosity, and can literally shift a funky mood into a spacious clarity of being, from which new potentials of *bhava* may arise.

Praising others in a genuine way cultivates a wholesome mood. Everyone is worthy of praise in some way; simply acknowledging a fine quality that we notice in another (and especially one with whom we usually find fault) is a virtuous act that benefits all.

Yogi Ramsuratkumar's instruction to praise as a constant spiritual practice dovetails perfectly with what Lee called "the primacy of natural ecstasy," giving rise to the

> ### *Rasa is the Goal*
>
> *Bhakti, chanting the Name of God, is our technology. We develop bhava, which is the mature emotional state. But bhava is not permanent. The permanent state is rasa. Rasa is everflowing and never stops. Rasa is the goal. For a Baul, we have adopted bhakti as our tool, our practice to overcome negative emotions. All that anger, greed, passion, becomes one-pointed, focused on the Beloved. It's very childlike and innocent. If we have anger, hatred, pride, whatever, we turn it toward Him. Bhava is selfless. If we reach bhava, even if tears flow there is no pain, but there is intense joy. Rasa is not affected by negative states. When there are no tears, no anger—that is rasa.*[7]
>
> — Parvathy Baul

essential *bhava* of the Western Bauls. The practice of praising carries multiple depths of meaning and potential for a practitioner. It is a revelatory practice that reveals itself when we engage it with heart and intention. When praise erupts spontaneously, it carries the many nuances of joy. Ecstatic praise, rich praise, joyous praise, simple and ordinary praise are the fruition of the path and the path itself.

Praise takes many forms. Praise of the beauty and magnificence of Creation and its

---

[7]   Interview with Parvathy Baul by the author, August 14, 2013. Ferme de Jutreau, France.

Lee with his gandharvas.

Blind Devotion

Got a question for you honey
Please forgive my great emotion
Is it dangerous to love you
With such blind devotion?
Yeahh —

Ask me to do anything
Your wish is my command
I will fly up to the sun for you
Bring it to your hand
I will conquer armies
You know what I mean
Allow me to adore you
Be your slave, not your queen

Fingers intertwined, paroxysm of love
That is my idea of praying
Lost in your lover so deeply
You don't even know what you're saying
Don't know much about the subject of holy
But I think I have come pretty near
When I look into his eyes
There I am, transfixed with fear

Blind devotion, what else is left
Nothing that is worth very much
Blind devotion, consume me in your path
Let me feel the heaven and sorrow
Of your touch

— Lee Lozowick

Creator exalts and uplifts the one who praises. Praise can be expressed in solitude or in relationship with others; it can be voiced in conversation, speaking, singing, writing, or thinking. Praise can be utterly silent and empty. It can occur in a fleeting second or permeate the mood of the hour or the day.

Praise is an attitude as well as an ecstatic flight of the soul. Praise is both ordinary and extraordinary. Spiritual practices of all kinds may be engaged as acts of praise. Lee referred to his poetry to his master as "poems and prayers," and in the transmission of these, we may discover the secrets of praise. Praise comes from gratitude, and as Ma Devaki, the personal attendant of Yogi Ramsuratkumar, once said, "Gratitude *is* Grace." Praise is the doorway through which Grace may enter. ✸

---

8   Lee Lozowick, *Intimate Secrets of a True Heart Son*, 1 Dec 2009 Jayanthi Day II, pp. 210–212.

Flooded by memories, overwhelmed
    to tears, heart too small to
contain all of this, and so running over
    and covering vast domains,
solar systems, galaxies, universes,
    filling them all with Praise of You,
golden Praise, honey Praise,
    diamond and ruby Praise,
pearl Praise, opulent, unceasing,
    flowing like Mother Ganga
at Gangotri, spreading like
    a carpet of the softest, finest silk,
nurturing as the holy cow's milk,
    sustaining as Vishnu's Blessings,
tinged, nay radiant with
    the Light of a Thousand Suns,
and in the end, only You.
    Yogi Ramsuratkumar, Holy of Holies,
Ark, Refuge of the poor, the lost,
    the sinner as well as the saint,
how is it that this little sinner lee,
    Your Minister of Praise,
never at a loss for words, feels
    so moved by You as to be
almost struck dumb, stunned
    into silence, mind thick
with the Beacon of Your Benediction,
    body surrendered to You
in Faith and Obedience, Your Name
    echoing in every cell, chanting
Itself, hot as a volcano
    and cool as a glacier,
all and everything all at once?
    How is it, how is it?
And how is it that this bad Poet,
    apprentice madman and even
Your True Heart-Son, lee, has

been the recipient of so
voluminous a quantity of Your
    smiles, Your caresses,
Your mighty slaps on the back,
    Your gifts of artifacts, Your dhoti,
shawls, so much, so much, and
    has been Blessed enough
to hear so much of Your Laughter,
    to absorb so much of Your Love,
to be touched so deeply by Your
    Presence, to have had so many
opportunities to talk with You,
    to hear You sing and expound
the Holy Dharma, "Father is One, All,
    past, present, future, this, that,
anything, everything," to have
    listened to You speak this
wild Heretic's name so many times,
    to have been called to Your Throne
these multitude of times?
    Ah Father, Yogi Ramsuratkumar,
every day, and today on Your Jayanthi,
    these blisses, small and large,
humble Your arrogant Fool,
    throw him to the dust at Your Feet,
stab him again and again with
    the knives of devotion to You,
and with the always and ever true
    Praises and Prayers that
never cease to leave his trembling
    body extolling You, You, and
You again, only You, the Lord.
    With pranams from Your Sacred Path,
tears to wash Your dusty Feet and
    head bowed, this is lee, Yours, all Yours.[8]

— Lee Lozowick

CHAPTER 10

Kaya Sadhana

Sahaja is a yoga for the same reason as all other yogas. It is
a path that leads to the discovery of "That with which one
is born," the pure being living in the temple of the heart.

Sri Anirvan

THE BAUL TERM KAYA SADHANA REFERS TO THE TRANSFORMATIONAL POTENTIALS of the human body and those practices or yogas that may catalyze such potentials. While Lee used this traditional Baul term, he also spoke of "Divine Alchemy" and used the phrase "the body knows" in referring to the transformational process that occurs in the heat of the tantric path. To begin such a consideration, one must have a tremendous commitment and discipline in order to ignite and sustain an inner fire that is hot enough to transform gross amalgams of raw ore into gold—to use a classic metaphor of traditional alchemy. Furthermore, it is important in tantric practice to establish a life of both inner and outer simplicity, which creates spaciousness within (and without) and helps to hone attention in a one-pointed manner toward the goal. Cultivating a life of simplicity alone is a very difficult challenge for most Westerners, and therefore, we should sincerely and genuinely ponder the depth of our commitment before we embark upon a tantric path.

Once we have determined that we are sufficiently committed, healthy, and strong enough to endure the course (it is said among *tantrikas* that you should not begin the practice if you are not going to see it through to fruition), then we should proceed with eyes wide open and with the help of a qualified guide. There are many dimensions of *kaya sadhana* in the teachings and practices of the Western Bauls, and in these Khepa Lee took a more conservative and traditional approach than the historical Bauls. Lee had a deep understanding of the needs of Westerners on the spiritual path; in most cases, he recommended a slow, measured maturation through the building of an inner matrix over long periods of time.

The Western Baul path gives many stabilizing and transformative practices—all of which are aspect of *kaya sadhana*—that establish a firm foundation from which one may delve into deeper aspects of tantric practice. These include a vegetarian diet, daily study, exercise, and meditation, and breath practices that work with the cellular interstices of the body in a powerful alchemy. Detailed instruction for these breath practices have never been published but were openly disseminated by Lee to his students through the oral tradition. The two primary breath practices are the Heart Breath, through which personal, global, and universal energies are purified and harmonized, and the Cyclical Breath, which works with the descending current of energy in the body and encourages a natural movement toward ascension of *prana*, or life force. Both of these practices are essential to the path, providing super fuel to any formal sexual *sadhana* that may be engaged. Other dimensions of *kaya sadhana* include the sun practice and visualization of the *ishta devata* in the form of the guru.

While Lee openly initiated his school (*kula*) at large into specific breath practices, he was much more reticent and conservative with sexual practices. Because of the superficial fixation on sex that permeates culture in the West, he made enormous efforts in his teachings to free us from the spell of our fascinations and addictions in the domain of sex and sexuality. While many may believe they are called, in fact very few are fully equipped—psychologically, emotionally, physically, spiritually—to engage the arduous discipline that is required in sexual *sadhana* with a partner. Often stating that he only gave specific instruction in sexual yoga

to "a handful of my students," Lee encouraged sexual yoga only for those couples who demonstrated a mature and stable overall practice within a monogamous, long-term, committed relationship.

It may be more productive to avoid the lure of so-called "tantric sex" and focus instead on the many other available forms of *sadhana*, all of which lead to the ultimate goal of the path. This is a very sane and simple approach that leaves one open to enjoy a loving, affectionate, fulfilling sexual relationship with a partner. Through this approach of simplicity, we may grow up, become responsible adults, and learn to serve others in a productive and useful way. The true path is practical, savvy about human nature and foibles, promotes peace and sanity in relationships, and always leads one toward liberation from illusion and suffering.

Tantric sex can be the biggest distraction and seduction that we encounter on the path; it can lead to a dead-end in which we are lost in dreams of spiritual glamour or fooling ourselves with ideas of "progress." Tantra unleashes profound power, which will then be channeled in one way or another—we must continually ask ourselves if the polestar we are following is love or power. If we have not taken the maxim "know thyself" seriously, then we can end up in very big trouble.

It is important to dispel the myth that in order to be Baul, one must have tantric sex and sing songs! *Kaya sadhana* is a way of life. It is a unified, inclusive, continuous field in which we live fully, so that our actions, thoughts, and intentions are informed by the context of the spiritual culture—the *sahaj* vision in all its simplicity and complexity.

Perhaps the most important yoga of all is to discipline our personality manifestations so that we are able to interact with each other with kindness, generosity, and compassion. This is a process of Divine Alchemy, for we are *changed* by the accumulated force of our virtuous actions. Because pure tantra cultivates a conscious awareness of continuity—the truth that we are connected to all of Life—we can practice in a powerful way by contemplating the vastness of the sky or the life of trees or the fleeting beauty of the sunrise, or by making pottery or growing a garden, cooking a meal, digging ditches or building houses, or in loving interchanges with friends and children. Honing our capacity to Pay Attention to and in the body through breath, body awareness, speech, movement, gesture, and verbal interactions (a reliable and constant mirror of one's state of being)—these are the daily fare of tantric practice.

The development of a personal spiritual culture, internally and externally, leads to an alchemy that is fully accessible to couples and singles as well as those who have chosen celibacy as a path. Although Lee was not opposed to a natural calling toward celibacy for some, he had faith in the transformational potentials of the human body, which includes a full spectrum of experience in which a sane, grounded, easeful relationship to sexuality is one dimension. He

recommended that couples stay together for a lifetime and have sex, not waiting till one or both are "in the mood" or until one is free of problems or neurotic blocks. He advised couples to engage sex on a regular basis, building trust and communion over time; if there are blocks and neuroses and fears in the way, he instructed partners to keep going until a breakthrough or a moment of the extraordinary arises. This instruction is one of many demonstrations of Lee's faith in the natural wisdom of the body—"the body knows."

Under Lee's wise guidance, we explore the deeper reaches of this phrase, which carries a specific meaning in terms of sexual yoga: the *sadhana* rests upon the amalgam of combined practices (matrix) rather than technical expertise. Some technique is useful, beginning with the breath practices prescribed by the path and the yogic discipline of non-ejaculatory sex for men, along with its counterpart for women (retention and redirection of orgasm and orgasmic fluids). Nonetheless, it is the focused placement of refined attention on our partner and the wisdom of the alchemical body that leads the way. The body is Organically Innocent and revelatory; if we relax and trust the process, the body will reveal its secrets. As one cultivates a rarified mood (*bhava*) through intention and attention, the body opens and guides, so that in a natural, spontaneous, easy way, the inner chambers of bodily worship of the Divine may be discovered.

As *sadhana* matures over the years, sexual practice with a partner also matures. Partners

What Is the Motive?

The psychological motive that drives us toward sex is not the urge for pleasure or beauty; it's the urge for the release of tension, or to control, manipulate, or dominate the other, or just the biological urge to procreate. If we look at our sexual activity and take the last ten times we had sex—with ourselves or with a partner, it doesn't matter—we should consider how many of those ten times we were motivated by pleasure, love, beauty, or by those neurotic needs. Are we motivated by the desire to serve others? For sex to be alchemical or transformational, we have to turn the flow from down and out to up. This is the natural evolution of sexual energy from youth to old age, or sexuality for nuns and monks and practitioners of all traditions.[1]

— Khepa Lee

and moods. As in every aspect of practice, what is organically true and natural for us when we are twenty-five may be quite different at fifty-five or seventy-five. On the "Divine Path of Growing Old," we may even reach a point at which physical sexual union is not necessary—as the adepts tell us, the best sex is entirely subtle, as one's focus shifts from the phenomenal world of form to less tangible dimensions of being.

The Divine Alchemy of *kaya sadhana* is available to all practitioners, whether one is a householder or ashram renunciate, in a couple or a solo practitioner; everyone can embrace spiritual work in the various dimensions of life's activity. Any time sexuality is

will inevitably need to develop patience, spaciousness, endurance, compassion, and tolerance for each other's differences in terms of how fast each one evolves. "The Divine Path of Growing Old," to use another one of Lee's teaching phrases, will result in a process of maturation that changes the sexuality of a couple; the nuances of love play grow into deeper, more sublime and subtle forms

Sweet and Tender Love

Make love, sweet and tender love (not the harsh, abrupt, self-serving coupling that often goes by the name of "love")…. Touch your lover's hand, caress (just a brush, no need to linger when you are "all there") her (his) neck or forearm, hug your child, tight but not too tight, inhale the aroma of that flower, of a moist morning's lawn, of the budding tree. "Watch me, while I touch the sky." "See you in the purple rain."
    'Nuff said.[2]

— Khepa Lee

---

[1]   M. Young, *As It Is*, p. 644.
[2]   Lee Lozowick, *"A Tale Told by an Idiot, Full of Sound and Fury, Signifying…"*, p. 195.

engaged, we must constantly keep the goal in mind for egoic distractions, addictions, and fascinations are seemingly endless. For the Western Bauls the purpose of *sadhana* is to discover and live relationship with God in both personal and impersonal aspects. Through the mutual love of couples in union, the *bhava* of adoration is cultivated, and one's partner becomes a doorway through which the Beloved may be directly experienced in the mood of adoration. At the same time, the practitioner must earnestly cultivate this inner relationship and communion reciprocity with the Beloved, because the inner yoga is essentially an individual process, even though it may be shared in the intimacy of a committed relationship.

The path will always bring us back to the reality that every individual is ultimately

A Baul mela, Kolkata 2008.

alone with the Beloved, and practice is essentially an inner process for every person, no matter how much communion we may share with others. On the spiritual path, sooner or later we must face the cosmic fact of our aloneness; through embracing this truth—like the *gopis* with Krishna in the *ras lila*—we may discover the dawn of peace, beauty, love, wonder and awe in the panoramic view that awaits us.

A MELA IN KOLKATA

In 2008 Lee and his group went to a local *mela* (festival), the Baul-Fakir Utsab, through an invitation received by Lalitha from her friend, Sandip. The event was held in a tiny enclave in the heart of Kolkata and

---

Conserving Energy

The more energy we have, the more energy we conserve, the more energy we are able to generate, which means we can better serve the evolution, harmony, and health of the world. The more energy we have, the powerful our acts of kindness and generosity communicate to others, and the more power our prayers have.[3]

— Khepa Lee

---

[3]   M. Young, *As It Is*, pp. 642–643.

billed as "a festival of wandering minstrels," where Hindu Bauls and Muslim Fakirs (sometimes called Auls) were gathered to play handmade acoustic instruments and celebrate the spirit of their music. Making our way past a large white canvas tent in a small park-like area, we walked a short way down the street and up stone stairs into a makeshift structure built on a porch on the side of a building. This "room" was loosely thrown together from canvas and plastic tarps stretched across bark-covered wooden poles and bamboo lashed together with rope. The floor, covered with scattered straw, reeds and cotton rugs, was littered with cigarette butts, ashes and bits of trash. The smell of marijuana and hashish drifted on the air, mingling with the heavy scent

Gour Khepa.

Durga Dasi (far left) and Gour Khepa (far right)
singing with their daughter and Muslim Auls.

Gour Khepa.

of tobacco. Five musicians were playing in the center of the space.

A very slight, thin man was stretched out directly behind where we sat with Lee. He was lying on his back on top of a helter-skelter collection of bamboo mats, cotton rugs and dirty blankets. He appeared to be asleep. Just beside him was a crude set-up for making tea. A *duggi* and *anandalahari* hung from the wooden supports near his head. He was bare-chested, wearing a dhoti of *sadhu* orange typical of traditional Baul dress. An *ektara* lay nearby. He looked like a wanderer, dust-stained and well-sculpted from living close to the bone.

In the center of the tent were several musicians. One was playing a *dotara*, a five-stringed lute, with passion and dexterity, and the music was working its magic. The small hand drums popped with exclamations of sound in rhythmic counterpoint to the deeper steady beats of the large double-headed drum. The song ended, and the singer relaxed into back-up mode with his *dotara* as the *sarinda* (a handmade violin-like instrument) player took over with a new song in which "Jai guru jai ..." was the hearty refrain. One song flowed into the next until it seemed we were floating along on a river of music.

The man who had been lying on the floor sat up and started speaking in English. His thin chest was bare except for a necklace of stone beads and a *rudraksh mala*. His cotton

dhoti looked like it had seen countless miles. His teeth were darkly stained from years of hard living, and despite his ragged appearance, he was by far the brightest light among the characters in the tent. He gave us a brilliant smile and immediately started talking in broken but clear English.

Introducing himself simply as "Khepa," he said, "I am Baul Hindu."

"Baul Hindu!" He re-stated, pointing to himself and then toward the circle of musicians. "Those guys are all 'Muslim caste.' You know—Muslim?" Pulling out a notebook and pen, I began to take notes as he told us that he had been on a binge, drinking too much alcohol and getting into "a big fight and too much bad boola boola." He pointed proudly to his instruments and said, "*Anandalahari*," and then "*ektara*."

He was smiling and talking fast as he explained, "I play those. I travel, I travel all over, Europe, many places. My name is Khepa. See? Here is my passport. You see, all places I have gone." His passport appeared from somewhere; he opened it and showed

---

[4] Sri Anirvan, *Letters from a Baul*, p. 7.

> The body of man
> Is a land of wish-fulfilling—
> care will produce
> a harvest of jewels.
> Plough it in a propitious time.
> Hopes that ushered you
> to this material world
> will bear fruit...
>
> — Kalachand

it around. In the space that said "Name" the single word, "Khepa" was typed. There were stamps from many countries, and the passport was weathered and old.

"I have a big problem," he continued in a friendly way, as if he has known us for a long time. "I am not so good," he continued, referring to his health. He had been sick for a long time. He had walked a very long way, cold and hungry, to an ashram. Somewhere along the way, he contracted typhoid, but he had no money for medicine. He lamented how expensive medicine had become in Bengal. Even five years ago, he said, people could afford medicine. But now, poor people are sick and they have no medicine.

He spoke about his extensive travels in the West and other details of his life, placing particular emphasis on the fact that his mother was a Khepa Baul, his grandmother was Baul, and all the rest of his family were Bauls.

The music started up again. A woman in a red and yellow sari had come in a few minutes earlier; now she joined the circle of musicians and was playing the *kartals* with skilled ease. A girl, who looked to be about twelve years old, obviously her daughter, sat beside her. Khepa joined the musicians, and as the song began and the unique sounds of his *anandalahari* claimed the space, a radiant smile passed between him and the woman. The mood brightened as they began to jam. Smoke floated on random sunbeams, so rare with the constant blanket of smog in Kolkata. The music was inducing a deep, inexplicable happiness that flowed like nectar through the ambient space. Another musician arrived to join the group and they flowed into a new melody that resounded with names of Krishna: "Madhava, Keshava!"

As we walked out to the main tent with Sandip, I mentioned the idea of an interview with the man named Khepa. Sandip became enthusiastic.

"Oh, that is Gour Khepa!" he said. "He is a very well-known Baul, one of the true Bauls, a real practitioner. He had a *huge* experience! He traveled a lot, all over Europe, with Paban Das Baul, Purna Das Baul and Shubal, who took the

Baul music out to the world. Gour Khepa is an amazing musician. Gour Khepa is *mad*—completely mad! That's why he is Khepa."

Later, back in the small tent, Gour Khepa agreed to an interview with one condition. "*No money!* No money—I not business. Just talk," he stated emphatically. Without any further ado, he picked up his instruments and a small bundle and walked very fast, leading the way back over to the big tent. He jumped up on the low plywood stage and sat in the middle of a big blue cotton rug that had just been placed there. Lee sat down facing him while several other Westerners from his group gathered around along with Sandip, who was translating, and a few other curious Bengalis. After setting up the recorder, with photographers on standby and ready to capture the moment, we began to talk.

Many of Gour Khepa's comments were enigmatic or cryptic because he was speaking in the symbolic language that is typical of Bauls when they talk about dharma and practice. He began by saying that the time would come when the rhythm of the breath would stop, and he would be going to the graveyard.

"I am still alive," he said with a charming smile, "so better you take my interview now—better you hear my words directly than when I am dead from someone else!" He laughed gleefully.

Answering the first question, "What does it mean to be a Baul?" Gour Khepa began in Bengali with Sandip translating into English. "Baul is not a word. Baul is a sense. Baul is to control the air within the ida, pingala, and shushumna."

Changing to English, Gour Khepa said, "Yoga. Baul yoga. *This* is Baul. *This* is Baul!"

> Lust and love
> And the erotic acts
> Are housed in one single place...
>
> — Haude Gosain

His knees struck the ground forcefully as he went into one hatha yoga *asana* after another. "*This* is Baul. I don't want to talk. It is better that I show you." He moved his body into another *asana*. Coming out of the pose, Khepa spoke again.

"What we get from our sadhana, we try to teach the same thing to other people through our music. Baul sadhana!" Gour Khepa said with a broad smile, his sense of humor captivating us as his body moved into another *asana*. His joy was infectious as he continued in English, "Blah blah, no good. Many people blah, blah, blah, blah. No good! Sadhana no blah blah!" He smiled and laughed again, "Sadhana is *sadhana*! Again, and *again*!"

Donning his patchwork robe, which he tied deftly around his waist, Gour Khepa took his seat, the demonstration of asana clearly over. He paused for a moment then he said, "I am not eating for the last seven days and not eating again for seven days. Only milk and medicine. Problem something, now very good." He was quick to explain to us that he eats very little. "I don't like heavy food. Heavy food, no good. Light food, very good. Like milk, ghee, subji (vegetables), potatoes, things like that. I am giving up eating rice."

NO YOGA, NO BAUL

Gour Khepa continued to make a point about performers who dress up like Bauls but don't follow the spiritual culture or inner yoga. "They are facing terrible problems in their lives," he said. This poignant criticism of the growing trend of entertainers who don the traditional Baul dress as a costume—wearing the iconic Baul orange, pink, or saffron-colored clothes and *alkhalla*, or patchwork robe—without actually doing the *sadhana* was a theme he had begun earlier.

Almost twenty years before, during his stay in Arizona, Sanatan Baba had commented similarly that only Baul

of celibacy. He began to make an important distinction between "inner puja" and "outer puja," the latter of which he reproached as merely a way of making money.

"I have no money puja," he stated. "This is my upper-stair puja. Like flowers are used in puja, every laughing face is like a flower for me," he said with a brilliant smile. "That is what I use for my puja." He explained that the inner *puja* occurs "upperstairs, not downstairs."

His spontaneous responses were permeated with the Baul view: the ceremonies performed in temples are a money-making business that separates people from their own hearts. In some places the old custom of barring temple worship to women, low caste people, and Westerners still prevails; temple worship is too often caught up in the tangle of money, greed, dogma, and prejudice against gender and caste, which taints the ritual worship from the Baul point of view. When the context is authentic and pure, the disposition of daily life can be suffused with inner worship, which shines from the face as a radiance which blesses all. That very radiance was shining from the beautiful face of Gour Khepa as we sat and talked.

yogis of a certain level of accomplishment in *sadhana* could wear the *alkhalla* (patchwork jacket). This was clearly a big concern for Gour Khepa, as were Bauls with cell phones, which he seemed to consider symbolic of an inauthentic life and lack of practice. Now he was saying that he had given his cell phone away. He passionately lamented the negative influences of the "modern world" that have impinged so completely upon his world.

In response to a question about daily *puja* to an *ista devata*, he answered in English, "I worship myself, my *brahmacharya*. *This* is my worship," he said, touching his chest, again referring to his yogic practice—the all-encompassing way of life of Baul spiritual culture. It was clear that he used the term *brahmacharya* in reference to his discipline of sexual continence—non-ejaculatory sex—as opposed to the common translation

> The essence of love
> Lies in carnal lust
> Bearing a deep secret.
> Only lovers can unravel it....
>
> — Chandidas Gosain

Khepa continued to share his view of the path, telling us that it was very important to be careful what we put in our two mouths (mouth and genitals). Then he chidingly poked fun again at "business pujas," corporate business people and those who have no real feeling, who donate large amounts of money to build big temples.

Speaking passionately about his guru, Horipada Goshai, who was still alive but very old, in his nineties, Khepa explained that his first gurus were his mother and father. His second guru was Shashan Bashgiri, and his last guru was Horipada Goshai.

When we are born, he said, we have "everything" locked away in *manipura chakra*. "What I have here is a key," he said, "is Krishna, Krishna." In the stream of Bengali that was rapidly tumbling out of Gour Khepa, the word "khepi" stood out. Sandip translated, "He says, 'My Khepi is like a partner, a thief who came to steal all my things I have inside.'"

In perfect English Gour Khepa explained, "My Khepi, partner. Wife. Durga Dasi. She stole the key. She opened the manipura and stole everything." His smiling face was animated and triumphant. He said, "Khepi. Durga Dasi. Durga Dasi!" He continued in Bengali.

Sandip translated, "That's why we need the guru, to keep this thing intact, in the same place, to lock it again. The guru locks it again."

Gour Khepa found this absolutely delightful, and in between his joyous laughter and chuckles, he said, "Partner. Wife. Durga Dasi. Khepi is a *thief!*" He smiled broadly, enjoying the metaphor and interplay. "Durga Dasi terrorist! Smuggler!" He laughed some more. As Gour Khepa explained further in Bengali, Sandip relayed, "He is saying that the Khepi is like a terrorist who came to steal all his things, and the guru is the key to hold it, to lock it again." One of the Bengali men standing behind Gour Khepa commented sagely, "It's a very deep philosophy."

In the interplay between partners, the delicate balance between power and love at the levels of psychology and personality, and between self and other, have correlates in the sexual dimensions of relationship—truly a deep philosophy. The guru, who instructs in the teaching and the practice or yoga, gives us the key to resolve the problem of losing ourselves in another person, so that the interplay of two can feed spiritual growth for the mutual benefit of both partners. In the example of sexual interplay, the female partner can help or hinder the male partner in his efforts at the discipline of sexual continence, while the male partner can callously use the female partner and her mystical essences for his own advancement.

Sandip translated further, "He says if the Khepi doesn't steal the soul… they can live together. If they know the trick—both of them—they can live together for a long time. But if they don't know the trick, one of them will have a lot of problems, and one of them will die or something. If both of them know the trick, they will have a saint's life."

Making sure we had understood correctly, Gour Khepa broke in again in English, saying, "If they do the same sadhana. *Same sadhana.* Same stay. If one stay and other one goes, this is no good. The same completely—then they can stay together. *Together,*" he emphasized. He said that one other very important *sadhana* for them was to serve people who are in their sphere of life. Then he added, speaking of Durga Dasi, "She's a mother."

DURGA DASI

We soon learned that Khepi was the woman in the red and yellow sari whom we had seen at the beginning, when Gour Khepa played music with the other Bauls in the tent. Several people who had gathered around to hear Khepi talk with the Westerners ran to get her.

While we waited, Sandip explained that Gour Khepa has a very big life traveling and playing music. Like many if not most Bauls, he has a penchant for intoxicants. "He doesn't have much discipline, because he's a completely *crazy* person. If he wanted to, he would travel a lot. You heard the name of Paban? In the seventies, Gour Khepa and Paban Das had many gigs in Europe. All the money Gour Khepa gave away. I saw him—he gives things to everyone. He doesn't want anything. He is still alive because of Khepi, because he drinks a lot, because he is something *crazy*! She keeps him really strong because he's completely crazy, and he's been drinking the last couple of weeks."

Gour Khepa is considered one of the last of the older generation of Bauls, and although he has traveled extensively, he lives in a very modest, one-story house in Bolpur, near Shanti Niketan. Turning away from the glitz and glamour of fame and fortune, like Sanatan Das, he had continuously lived a simple earthy life. The newspapers had reported that, at the Kenduli *mela* a few years ago, Gour Khepa and Durga Dasi avoided the crowds and high-profile *akhras*, set up camp in a bamboo grove and cooked over an open fire for the visitors and students who came around them.

When Durga Dasi arrived a few minutes later, Gour Khepa spoke in English, saying, "This is my wife. This is my Khepi. She is my nitric acid. I am not silver, I am *gold!* This is nitric acid. I am gold. I am gold, no silver. I am not silver. I am pure gold! This is nitric acid. You understand?"

In response to some perplexed looks on the faces of the Westerners, Lee clarified easily, "Nitric acid is the chemical used to test gold to see if it is real." Gour Khepa seemed anxious to get across the point that this idea is found in the Bible and Koran as well as in the *puranas*—the great, vast collections of sacred myths and stories, relating the qualities and teachings of major Hindu deities. It was not his idea, he said, but it was his scripture, his *dharma*.

Indeed, their way of life seemed to be working very well for this Baul couple, whose committed relationship has endured for twenty-five years. They told me that they met at the Kali (Kamakhya) temple, a famed *shakti pitha* and favorite place of Bauls in Assam, and decided to stay together; now they have a twelve-year-old daughter named Loki, who joined them a few minutes later.

Khepi did not speak any English, which made the conversation more chaotic as she answered questions and the bystanders all translated at once, along with Sandip and Gour Khepa.

"What it is for a woman to serve? What does Khepi say?" She answered, then turned to Gour Khepa, who talked very fast in Bengali for what seemed like a long time.

"They are saying they live together," Sandip said, "so the best way is to help each other emotionally and physically. She is saying, 'I go to people, I beg and I cook. I try to help Khepa with whatever I have.'"

Speaking firmly and forcefully, Gour Khepa said in English, "She *stay*. She is not leaving me. *Very* important."

His communication implied that this was not an easy choice at times, as Khepa has had a wild life with many excesses. Just as his name, Khepa, implied, Gour was one who lived far beyond the safe boundaries of custom and convention. Living with such a one is a *tapasya* (arduous spiritual discipline) of a certain kind, requiring great love, commitment, and inner strength. It was obvious that Khepi had a depth of character as a *sadhika* that kept her beside Khepa, no matter how difficult it may have been. It was equally clear that Durga Dasi was able to provide a kind of sanctuary for Gour Khepa that is very rarely found in today's Western relationships.

That Khepi placed a premium importance upon the fact that she begged as an aspect of her relationship with Gour Khepa placed her in a very traditional, old-time stream of Baul *sadhana*, as begging is an essential element of Baul life and practice.

Gour Khepa continued, "It's a very happy day. It's a really good day for me that I can talk and give information." He smiled. Speaking about his relationship with Khepi, he used an earthy metaphor, saying, "She is the land, and I am the farmer!" When Sandip translated this in English, Gour Khepa started laughing ecstatically. Khepi's broad smile and twinkling eyes said that she was enjoying the metaphor as well.

Khepi's presence brought an important new element into our exchange. For many years researchers have been uncertain about the role that women play among the Bauls. Some have asserted that women do not engage *sadhana* at all but are servants and exchangeable sexual partners to the men who perform yogic practice with them—conclusions drawn largely because Baul women would not talk, or confide, in researchers who came among them. Without question, traditional female Bauls face many hardships, but Gour Khepa and Durga Dasi were painting a much bigger picture; their message was a fresh wind blowing in the oppressive gloom of projections made by scholars and anthropologists.

Sitting before us was a woman of impressive presence—a woman immersed in *sadhana*, who exemplified the Baul ideal. Exuding equanimity and wisdom, Durga Dasi's eyes radiated a depth of maturity and sparkled with a quick sense of humor. I remembered a quote from Parvathy Baul's

book, in which she speaks about the life of the female Baul:

Struggling hard, the female Baul attains the qualities of extraordinary compassion and stability of heart; so they can smile even at obstacles. As one [Baul poet] has aptly put it:

> Oh Beloved!
> Burn me
> Burn me hopelessly
> Burn the incense of my heart
> For the incense
> Does not give out its perfume
> Until it is burned [5]

KHEPA AND KHEPI

The question "Who is *ista devata* for Durga Dasi?" elicited an unhesitating response from Durga Dasi, who looked at Khepa and gestured toward him, saying, "For me, my Khepa."

Gour Khepa gave us another one of his jubilant smiles and said, "Once you feel the real relating, it will *change* you inside." The beauty, simplicity and power of this quintessential Baul understanding of the alchemy of woman and man in relationship, alive in the potential of *kaya sadhana*, was made all the more poignant by the music that drifted on the air as soaring melodic voices, drums and *ektaras* deepened the communion that we had entered into together. Time seemed to flow past us like warm honey.

---

[5]   Parvathy Baul. *Song of the Great Soul*, p. 24.

After a few moments Gour Khepa explained further, then Sandip translated: "He is saying the reason why she sees him and considers him as God is because on the opposite, he also considers her as goddess, and they worship each other. He said, 'We are like the father and mother of Jesus. We see each other like this. I was alone, and I found a partner. We found each other, and we have an understanding and balance, and that is why we are so happy.'"

Gour Khepa generously gave us a glimpse into the *sadhana* of relationship between women and men in the Baul way. This exchange contained many key principles of the quintessential Baul message: the path is about earthy practice in the body—not about intellectualizing, grandstanding, and proselytizing: "No blah blah!" Radha and Krishna are found within the individual, and the quickest way to discover and cultivate this innate potential is in and through relationship. For man, woman is the key to this relationship, just as Gour Khepa gave his Khepi the highest compliment: she is the one who determines whether or not he is "gold." And most importantly, the fruition of relationship *sadhana* is found in the fact of their mutual adoration of each other as *ista devata*, because the nature of the human being is ultimately divine.

ADORATION

Many of Gour Khepa's statements seemed to have multiple levels of meaning. On one level, his humorous, tongue-in-cheek reference to Durga Dasi as a "thief, terrorist, and smuggler" may have been an affectionate reference to the yogic practice of male continence in sexual intercourse. If a couple chooses to practice sexual yoga, no progress can be made without this discipline; in Bengal, Baul gurus have been known to refuse to see their disciples for twenty-five years after they had "slipped" and had unplanned children! Among the serious Baul practitioners, it is the guru who advises the couple when to have a child, and this is engaged with conscious intention.

It is not an easy yoga in which to achieve mastery, particularly since the Bauls—both East and West—understand the importance of a passionate, earthy sexual chemistry between partners. It's important to love one's partner if adoration is to be achieved, and for most people it is easier to feel and know this kind of love if it is personal rather than impersonal. However, when love and body chemistry are both involved, it's also easier to get carried away and forget one's purpose in the heat of the moment, which puts a strain on yogic practice. At the same time, a passionate bodily love yields the prized *bhavas* and ultimately the divine elixir of *rasa*, which may be called adoration.

True love and blazing sexual chemistry make an excellent recipe for invoking the mood of adoration, or *mahabhava*, which may lead to the divine *rasa* that eternally flows. At the end of our brief but rich time with Gour Khepa and Khepi, light shone from their open faces as he spoke of their mutual happiness together.

"They worship each other," Sandip translated as Khepa spoke in Bengali.

Gour Khepa concluded, "That is why we are so happy."

The Bauls have discovered a great secret: it is through the human love of man and woman, in the body, in sexuality, in everyday life, that the Beloved may be discovered. In order to know this hidden potential, man and woman must worship each other. The truth of this declaration came across loud and clear from Gour Khepa and Durga Dasi—in their radiant, shining eyes and their exuberant joy in the total simplicity of their way of life. It was the inspiring key note of their message; it was the melody and rhythm of their song.

Gour Khepa died in January 2013 in a car accident in Shanti Niketan, Bengal; Durga Dasi and their daughter continue to live in their small dwelling in Shanti Niketan. Gour Khepa's life was a moving, vivid, wild demonstration of authentic Baul *sadhana*. 🏵

The Transformation of Sexual Energy

The intelligent use of sexual energy may or may not have sex as its starting point. Many in both Eastern and Western traditions are celibate and are tremendously vital and juicy individuals. That results from the intelligent use of sexual energy. There are two domains of sex itself: physical sex, which is almost always debilitating, believe it or not, and sex that is energetically creative, or subtle sex. That's where the alchemy comes in.

Every individual human being could be considered an energy generator. There is life as we know it, in which there is a certain amount of energy—money, resources, or subtle energy. We feel alive or feel exhausted. But there tends to be a limited amount of energy, so the alchemy of sex and love is geared toward generating more energy.

Human begins can serve many functions on Earth. We can actually help create a world of greater peace, harmony, health, and beauty—not that we can make war stop, but if enough people were using energy creatively, the result would be the end of war and violence and cruelty. Personally, I'm cynical—I think human beings are unwilling to do anything that doesn't serve themselves, so I don't think we'll see that in our lifetimes. However, every little bit helps.

This energy can be used completely selfishly or more generously, more selflessly. Most of the occult, metaphysics, and of course black magic are all about using this energy selfishly. If someone is giving a fancy lecture on love but is thinking about how the success of this lecture is going to make them famous, then it is done for selfish reasons. So sexual energy is a doorway to extraordinarily subtle, refined, and higher forms of energy, but we have to use it properly.

The metaphysical journey of the human being is a constant cycle from the most refined and subtle realms to the grossest realms [Lee gestured to his body]. There are two options: we can continue to function in that cyclical pattern over and over but nothing ever changes, or we can enter into a cyclical pattern that is like a spiral, so every time we enter the cycle at a different or higher level. That's what the path is about.

We're already as gross as we are going to get, physically. When our attitude is self-centered rather than other-centered, that's as gross as our attitude gets. Some people are more inhuman in their behavior than others, but the psychology is the same. The difference between a killer and a healer, or a professor, is our childhood psychology, but the context is no different. We are manipulated by unconscious forces in the psyche; we have no choice in anything. Doctors and nurses have chosen their profession because of childhood experiences,

---

6   M. Young, *As It Is*, pp. 642–643.

not out of conscience. If you want more about this, I suggest you read Alice Miller, but read with an open mind because what she has to say is shattering.

Human beings are essentially at the bottom of a cycle: energy had descended, become matter and ego, and we are stabilized in this position. From here we have the opportunity to begin the process of ascension. Sex happens at the base of the trunk of the body. In the Eastern tradition there is the concept of the chakras—seven of them—with the highest at the peak of the head and the lowest at the base of the spine. The way the subtle energy is blueprinted in the subtle body follows the physiological system of brain and spinal cord. It starts in the head, goes down the front of the body to the base of the spine, turns around and goes back up the spinal line to the head. There are a lot of technical specifics to this, but I'm being very brief this morning.

Physical sex happens with the genitals, down at the bottom of the cycle, so the descending energy flows down. When energy comes to rest at the bottom of the body, we have two choices: to let it run out of the body, because that's the momentum and direction in which it is going, or to turn it around and encourage it to ascend. All forms of yoga—hatha yoga, kriya yoga—are designed to take the current of descending energy and turn it around,

allowing it to be used in subtle domains of energy we could call ascent.

There are three primary forms of energy leakage in the body: 1) Serious physical illness. When we get sick, we just get sick—there is not much we can do about it but take care of ourselves and heal. 2) Negativity, like gossip, criticisms of others, focusing on violence, or passionate discussions of war and cruelty. Emotional outbursts—anger, rage, vindictiveness. All these are forms of energy leakage in the body that lead to weakness and degeneration. And, 3) the usual forms of sex.

Sooner or later what we want to do is to begin to work with alchemical sexuality, or the transformation of sexual energy. There are two ways in which that can happen: unconsciously and consciously. My work could be called transformational work or tantric work. In my work this energy is worked with consciously, technically. But there are many spiritual schools in which the practices—if engaged properly and practices with integrity—alter one's relationship to sex, and this process happens unconsciously. If we are working with principles of kindness, generosity, and integrity in relationship without dealing specifically with sex, then sex—as one of the most intense aspects of relationship—will automatically begin to enter into transformational possibility.[6]

— Khepa Lee

CHAPTER 11

Synthesis

The discipline of sahaja begins with the acceptance of the whole of life just as it is. The heart opens up to receive it and to live it.

Sri Anirvan

IN THEIR MAD FLIGHT THROUGH THE NATURAL WORLD OF FLOWERS, bees seek nectar that will be transmuted into honey for the queen bee, which insures the ongoing life of the hive. In the process of their search, honeybees pollinate plants and trees that depend upon this delicate exchange to become fertile and eventually bear flower and fruit. Life depends upon the reciprocity of these complex relationships and their ongoing interconnected exchange. This is a useful metaphor for the vital importance of an open-minded, unifying relationship between religious and spiritual traditions. Without this healthy and wholesome exchange between the many different paths (which are ultimately One), religious traditions can become authoritarian, stagnant, dangerously fundamentalist, and even fascist. Lee sometimes cautioned his students about the dangers of this kind of "churchification."

Every church, temple, synagogue, mosque, or *sampradaya* is a carrier of human qualities, some bright and some dark. Pride, arrogance, and self-righteousness can be the dominant tone of a group—or humility, receptivity, willingness to grow and accept new ideas, loving acceptance, generosity, and kindness. When any group, religion, or organization becomes "churchified," a stultifying rigidity sets in, resulting in the kind of religious oppression that the Sahajiyas and Bauls rebelled against hundreds of years ago. Even a commitment to the ordinary, down-to-earth, simple, here and now spontaneous path can become a staunch, unyielding position and a rigid, deadening philosophy—and so every individual must work to remain self-honest and flexible with regard to a chosen path, personal disposition, or inclination.

A living tradition that has the power to transform its constituents must stay alive—fluid, radiant, transparent and open to the flow of sacred energies. One of the ways to insure this is to interact and share openly with other traditions in a way that does not sacrifice or compromise the integrity of the distinct path that is embodied in the vessel of temple, church, mosque, or *kiva*. Like Yogi Ramsuratkumar and Swami Ramdas, Khepa Lee had a highly creative, universal view of the spiritual path. During his life, Lee often made visits to friends and peers in other traditions around the world; he actively cultivated very close relationships with teachers of diverse paths such as Arnaud Desjardins, Llewellyn Vaughan Lee, E.J. Gold, Traktung Rinpoche, Yvan Amar, Dr. Robert Svoboda, and many others—a tradition that is carried on today by senior students of the Hohm Community.

Lee tasted the many flavors of the teaching while keeping the integrity of his own lineage and unique approach to the traditional path. He specifically used his love of study to fuel the practice of his students by sharing his many forays into the great traditions, and in this sharing of nectar from many flowers, what was already sweet became sweeter. He emphasized the interdependent nature of study and practice, commenting during a talk given in February 2006 that study alone yields knowledge without experience, while practice alone yields experience without knowledge. When we have experience without knowledge, we cannot actually work with and integrate the meaning of our experience on the path. Without knowledge, we lack the necessary container for our experience, which leaves experience unconnected to the whole and meaningless in a very practical sense.

THE WORK

Lee frequently commented on teachings from other schools and traditions, and at the same time, he insisted upon a respectful acknowledgement of his sources. There were many ways in which Lee extracted useful teachings from other streams of the path; the use of specific terms coined by other teachers is one of the chief ways that syncretism showed up in his teaching style. Similar to his utilization of the term "chamber," amicably borrowed from his friend, E.J. Gold (referring to a space in which a transformational invocation of the Sacred may occur), Lee freely adapted the Fourth Way term "the Work" from the Russian mystic G.I. Gurdjieff. Over the years "the Work" was liberally peppered throughout his discourses; he employed this handy term as a shorthand version of his more formal phrases, Divine Alchemy, Enlightened Duality and the Great Process of Divine Evolution and as a synonym for the universal term, "the path."

Wherever Lee found a genuine, living stream of the Work, he gave a certain homage, whether it was in the teachings of Gurdjieff, tantric Buddhism, or the work of Werner Erhard, which Lee respected and participated in at different points in his life, beginning as early as 1975. He participated in Sufi *dzikrs* and in the Sixteenth Karmapa's Black Hat ceremony, or traveled to hear speakers from the Fourth Way, with as much respect and honor as he chanted the name of Yogi Ramsuratkumar or gave teachings at the ashram of his closest friend, Arnaud Desjardins. None of this ever replaced his

relationship with his master, which remained
enshrined at the center of his heart and life.
Similarly, Yogi Ramsuratkumar was known
to travel long distances to see J. Krishnamurti
and Swami Nityananda, as well as his three
spiritual fathers: Ramana Maharshi, Sri
Aurobindo, and Swami Ramdas.

It could be said in universal terms that
the Work is the vast potential for the realization of Just This or the raw perception of
naked awareness—Reality as it is—through
engaging a life of practice which aligns one
to the Great Process of Divine Evolution.
"The Work" is an all-inclusive term that is
big enough to contain the spectrum of *sadhana* on the path, from teaching, dharma, or
philosophy, to practice, yoga, and *tapasya*.
The Work includes all practices that pro-
mote refined inner culture—the tantric and
devotional practices of Baul *sadhana*.

TANTRIC BUDDHISM

Lee also had a particular love for tantric Buddhism, a tradition in which he was well-versed
and widely read. He sometimes said that his
master, Yogi Ramsuratkumar, must have kept
him away from the Sixteenth Karmapa (who
Lee met in the mid-1970s in New York)
and Chögyam Trungpa Rinpoche, because
he would have become a student of a tantric
Buddhist lineage if he had met them prior to
his own awakening in 1975. Lee had a particular resonance with these two great Buddhist
teachers; the published works of Chögyam
Trungpa Rinpoche in particular have been
and continue to be an important source of
inspiration for Lee and his students.

Lee frequently used the Buddhist
descriptions of the three vehicles of the
path—Hinayana, Mahayana, and Vajrayana
—as source material in his talks, in which he

---

[1]   Khepa Lee, Lee Lozowick, "A Tale Told by an Idiot, Full of Sound and Fury, Signifying...", p. 114.
[2]   Sri Anirvan, *Letters from a Baul*, p. 6.

commented upon the phases of *sadhana*. He also often used the term "basic goodness," which was originally coined by Chögyam Trungpa Rinpoche. Lee once said that he wanted to be remembered for two things: as an advocate for children and an advocate for genuine crazy-wisdom teachers like Chögyam Trungpa Rinpoche.

THE HINDU TRADITION

Connections between Lee's original revelatory teachings and the great classical teachings of Hinduism are easily traced, for it is the Hindu tradition that is found at the roots of the Hohm Community, both in *parampara* (in the lineage of Swami Ramdas and Yogi Ramsuratkumar) and in *sampradaya* (in the connection of spiritual clan to the Bauls of Bengal). Lee named three systems in particular as the most vital links with the heritage of his master: the Hindu philosophical tradition of Samkhya (250–325 BCE); the teachings of Jnaneswar Maharaj (1275 CE); and most of all, the commentaries of the great *bhakti* preceptor, Vallabhacharya (1400 CE) on the *ras lila*, or Krishna's love play with the *gopis* as described in the tenth canto of the *Srimad Bhagavatam*. What follows is a brief sketch of these important classical teachings.

SAMKHYA

In the Hindu system there are six *darsanas* (ways of seeing or points of view) through which one may perceive and understand reality: 1) Samkhya, which takes the view of ontology, or the science of being; 2) Nyaya, or logic and epistemology; 3) Vaisheshika, or physics and atomic theory; 4) Yoga, or spiritual practice and meditation; 5) Purva Mimamsa, or hermeneutics and ritual worship; and 6) Vedanta or metaphysics. The study of these are immense undertakings; even in the field of yoga alone, one could spend a lifetime, for there is not only academic study but also practice to be mastered.

Chronologically speaking, Samkhya came into play between 250–325 BCE, two or three hundred years after the arrival of Buddha. Originally expounded by Kapila, who authored the *Samkhya Sutra*, Samkhya is attributed to the school of Isvarakrishna.

Samkhya is a dualistic system which states that Reality is not singular but plural, beginning with the two great polarities of *purusha* (consciousness or the transcendental Self, of which there may be endless numbers) and *prakriti* (Nature). Isvarakrishna declared that *prakriti* is a multidimensional creation ruled by three primary forces, the *gunas*, which are described in the *Samkhya Karika* as "joy, joylessness and dejection" having the purpose of "illuminating, activating and restricting. "They overpower each other, are interdependent, productive and cooperative in their activities."[3] This ancient text further states:

---

[3] Georg Feuerstein, *The Yogi Tradition*, p. 102.

On Samkhya and Sahaja

Sahaja can be defined as follows: "That which is born in you, that which is born with you," a state of pure essence. The body, the spirit, the impulse of life and intelligence are all there. Nothing must be rejected or mutilated, so that "one and the same thing" can be consciously established.

That is why Samkhya, which is the path by which the state of sahaja is attained, speaks a great deal of the waking state that is the normal level of all activity. It also speaks of the state of consciousness interiorized in dreams, which later becomes the state of deep sleep. Shankaracharya instructs us about these four different states in his philosophy.

In sahaja, there is a fifth state, that of a totally awakened consciousness; it contains in itself the four states of wakefulness, dreaming, deep sleep, and the state in which deep sleep exists along with the other four states. There is no longer any differentiation between the various states, all of them being unified at a single point.

From that moment on, everything becomes your food. Everything is one and the same thing in you. Then you are faced with a new task in the realm of sensation and relaxation. It becomes a question of forgetting oneself….a letting go in a region that is very subtle and hard to discover. Voluntary forgetting is a task that is just as difficult…. as self-observation. It is only approached much later, when memory has become submissive and fulfills its true role….

In practice, Samkhya is a technique to realize the expansion of sahaja. Neither the one nor the other takes into account gods, demons, paradises, hells, or formalism of any kind, in the course of inner effort. The point where Samkhya and sahaja converge is in the whole of life, which becomes in itself the object of meditation. Therefore serenity within oneself and a right relationship with life and one's fellow beings becomes a way of being.

He who practices a spiritual discipline will use Samkhya to learn how to look at the movements of Great Nature in all its manifestations without interfering with its movements, to recognize its imprint on everything and to observe the ability of prakriti to pass imperceptibly from one plane of conscious to another. Not to react to any of its movements would, in fact, mean to live in the very heart of life without being affected by it. But at the beginning, this state cannot be taken for granted, for it is not merely by observing the movements of prakriti that one becomes its master.

The disciple will turn his gaze upon himself and discover, although he had never before seen it, the countless inner disturbances created by everything in him that says: "I like and I do not like; I want and I do not want; it's right and it's wrong," and so forth, which prevent him from noticing that in himself there is a stormy prakriti identical to the one that exists around him. This is a slow work and a true discipline in itself. [4]

— Sri Anirvan

---

[4]   Sri Anirvan, *Letters from a Baul*, pp. 5-6.

Sattva is regarded as buoyant and illuminating. Rajas is stimulating and mobile. Tamas is inert and concealing. The activity [of the gunas] is purposive like a lamp [made up of various parts that together produce the single phenomenon of light.][5]

This teaching provides a glimpse of the large and small cycles of cosmic and terrestrial life and the ups and downs of one's daily experience as well, because everything is informed by the three *gunas*. Samkhya teaching contains much more detail, which is best left to the study and research of the reader.

It is interesting that Gurdjieff also spoke of three forces that rule the Universe: the denying, the affirming and the reconciling. These qualities could be said to correspond to the three *gunas* of Samkhya, which characterize existence: *tamas* (darkness or torpor: the denying force), *rajas* (excitement: the affirming force), and *sattva* (light: the reconciling force). These may also be translated as passivity (*tamas*), activity (*rajas*) and consciousness or harmony (*sattva*). By the power of our own capacity to know and experience these forces underlying life, we come to wisdom, of which awakened faith is one of the grand apotheoses.

JNANESWAR

Jnaneswar, the *siddha* sage of eleventh century India, wrote *Jnaneswari*, a classic commentary on the *Bhagavad Gita*, and his poetic sutras *Amritanubhava: The Nectar of Self Awareness*, a paean in praise of both nondual and dual (Enlightened Duality) dimensions of existence.

While his teachings reflect a resonance with the philosophy of Samkhya, Jnaneswar was above all a great lover of the guru, who taught radical reliance on guru as God. He further posited that nothing is false or illusory; rather, everything is the play of consciousness. Not only does the world have its existence in God; the world is God.[6] This perspective is entirely resonant with the natural *sahaja* theism of Lee's teaching of Enlightened Duality that finds its expression in the interrelatedness

---

From the Amritanubhava

I offer obeisance to the God and Goddess,
The limitless primal parents of the Universe.
The Lover, out of boundless love,
Has become the Beloved.
Both are made of the same substance
And share the same food.
Out of love for each other, they merge.
And again they separate
for the pleasure of being two.
They are not entirely the same...
Nor are they not the same.
We cannot say what they really are.[7]

---

[5] Georg Feuerstein, *The Yogi Tradition*, p. 102.

[6] Jnaneshwar Maharaj, *The Nectar of Self Awareness*, Syda Foundation, 1979, p. i.

[7] Ibid, p. 5.

of Organic Innocence and the Primacy of Natural Ecstasy.

An intimate knowledge of these truths was stated time and again by Swami Papa Ramdas and Yogi Ramsuratkumar, as they extolled the guru's grace and praised the sacredness of life in its manifest diversity as well as its underlying unity.[8] Ma Devaki, the attendant of Yogi Ramsuratkumar who resides at his ashram in Tiruvannamalai, remembered that Yogi Ramsuratkumar demonstrated his love for the teachings of Jnaneswar by often quoting him, especially in the early years with his devotees. Yogi Ramsuratkumar was known to say: 'Those who read Jnaneswar will not remain the same!'"[9] Such is the transformational potential when we study objective scriptures.

THE LOVE GAMES OF KRISHNA

When we consider the deep interconnections and synergies that are so natural to the Bauls of the West, we soon encounter the love games of Sri Krishna with the *gopis*, which Lee often commented on as the closest description of his work with students that he had encountered in all his years of study. At the guru's instruction, the Western Bauls have delved deeply into the text of *Vallabhacharya's Commentaries on the Love Games of Krishna*, translated by Father James Reddington, a Jesuit priest who lived in India for many years and developed a profound passion for the Krishna myth. Father Reddington became a close personal friend of Lee, visiting the Arizona ashram twice in the early 1990s to give teachings on the love games of Sri Krishna.

The Bauls of Bengal have used this poetic metaphor for centuries to portray the process of devotional *sadhana*, in which the *sadhika* moves from obsessive self-reference to pure God-reference, and in the process, both male and female alike become Radha in relationship to Krishna. The tenth canto, or Book Ten, of the *Srimad Bhagavatam*, recounts the story of Krishna and his love play with the *gopis* in Vraja, culminating in their sublime moment of epiphany in the *ras lila*. It is a metaphorical story of the soul's total love for the Supreme Lord, attained through an arduous struggle with pride, anger, jealousy, and all the many passions of human nature. Through the *bhava* of complete and total attention (*sarvatmabhava*) on the Lord, the *gopis* realize ultimate surrender and union with Krishna as their own true nature.

As Krishna departs to serve humankind, the *gopis* are left love-maddened, bereft, and alone. In the loss of Krishna's loving companionship, which cannot be duplicated by anyone else, they suffer extreme, inescapable, unmitigated heartbreak, which

---

[8] See *Enlightened Duality: Essays on Art, Beauty, Life and Reality As It Is*, Lee Lozowick and M. Young, Hohm Press 2009, for more about Swami Papa Ramdas on Enlightened Duality.

[9] Cited in *Samarpanam: Life and Teachings of Yogi Ramsuratkumar* (p. 86) quoting *Waves of Love* by Mother Vijayalakshmi.

includes the realization of the many errors of their own ways when he was with them. As they reflect upon their pride, anger, jealousy, competitiveness, and grief—and their utter aloneness—they come to the only solution: their obsession with Krishna must become divinized. The only way out of grief and sorrow is to realize Krishna within their own hearts, which they do. It is important to note that in the original scriptures, it is not a single *gopi* but a group of *gopis* together who enter into and fulfill the direct experience of the living Lord.

This occurs after Krishna leaves them, as he goes on to his many other *lilas* that are described in the great spiritual epic, the *Mahabharata*, which recounts Krishna's play as counselor to the Pandavas in their war with the Kauravas. At the beginning of this war, Krishna serves as the chariot driver (Parthasarathy) for Arjuna. In a crucial moment of sublime generosity, Krishna expounds his yoga of devotion in a luminous outpouring known as "the song of the Lord"—passed down to seekers today as the *Bhagavad Gita*. Yogi Ramsuratkumar had a special love for chapter twelve of that sacred scripture.

While Lee dipped into the sweet flowers of Vallabhacharya's commentaries on the love games of Krishna, he had his own unique contribution to make.

SACRED ART

Another important field that Lee entered into in his taste for nectar, and which he pollinated with great enjoyment during the last

---

The Eternal Lovers

In certain branches of the Bhakti tradition of India, where Radha/Krishna, the eternal lovers, are worshipped, the ideal Realization, the ultimate manifestation is to become the embodiment of Radha/Krishna in one's own singular form, to find the lover/Beloved dynamic not between two discrete forms but here, in this body, in this nervous system, right here, right now. Typically in this path, Krishna is seen as the ishta devata, the object of one-pointed devotion, attention, concentration, even fixation we could say, [and] the devotee enters into the position, the viewpoint of Radha, the adoring one, lost in her obsession, in her complete surrender to Krishna, whatever His mood, whatever His expression, whatever His movement, even if those do not consider the devotee personally.

.... One could say, if one wanted to take a very superficial view of things, that this framework, this principle, is simply the perfect relationship between the anima and the animus, the masculine and feminine aspects of our biological system. This, of course, suits the scientific community and the Western psychological model, but this simplistic overview is no more than the opinion of ignorant, exoterically focused bigots, unwilling to dig deeper, unwilling to investigate their own being profoundly enough to discover the Objective Esoteric nature of human essential Unity with all that is, the continuity with the Universe in all its infinitude. In fact, this model is a literal image

(continued on next page)

of the interplay and co-dependent (not in the neurotic, pathological sense, in the healthy holistic sense) intertwining of the nondual and the dual, Enlightened Duality as I call it—the literal Union of Krishna as Divine and Radha as incarnate, or of the pure Abstract and the distinct existence. In a very real way, in fact, Krishna and Radha are not mere symbols or archetypes, but are actually what, who, they appear as. Dangerous ideas here, yes it is no wonder so many people, even highly educated scholars and researchers diminish this truth by putting it in a palatable philosophy that not only skirts the real issue but satisfies all but the most intrepid adventurer....

Being the True Heart Son of Yogi Ramsuratkumar....I must stand for the Real, even if ridiculed by the vast majority of contemporary post-modern seekers, including, sadly, the vast majority of adherents to the Radha/Krishna field of spiritual work. This Embrace, the embrace of Radha/Krishna within the human form, the two within one, the eternal non-separate lovers here—literally and physically as well as subtly, as well as pure emptiness—in the human body of the worshipper. This is the acme of the practice, the Awakening to the life of Adoration within a context of already present, intrinsic Faith, Surrender, Obedience, Wisdom, knowledge. This is the pristine Radiance of Radha/Krishna as One,

even as they play as two—even as their Union is the highest aim of Love, unidentifiable as anything but what it is, impossible to define in language, concept, or mind, the experience, indescribable and yet alive in manifestation.

This, I must make precise, is not the modern popular tantric illusion of a couple worshipping one another as God and Goddess, the man playing the role of Krishna (or Shiva), the woman playing the role of Radha (Shakti, Parvati, etc..), no, no, no, no. The dynamic explained, well at least alluded to, in this essay is the interiorization of the ostensible paradox of Creation/Creator, God/man, Abstract/concrete.... This is Radha and Krishna as RadhaKrishna living not in some mystic heaven but here, now, as-it-is and as can only be known, never understood. So don't try to "understand" this essay. Let it sink in, let it seep in, let it seed itself in the rich furrows of a heart and soul, of actual cells, longing for this knowledge, pining away for the lack of it. Let this provoke, disturb or comfort. In any case it is, and will not be discouraged by the self-centered and neurotically narcissistic viewpoints of contemporary spirituality. It is, has always been, always will be, because it is not other than True, than Truth.[10]

— Khepa Lee

---

[10]   Khepa Lee, Lee Lozowick, *A Tale Told by an Idiot, Full of Sound and Fury, Signifying...*", pp. 37–39.

seven years of his lifetime, was sacred art, and specifically antiquities of the East. The introduction of divine images through the tremendous influx of sacred art that Lee has made available within his sphere of influence vitally reflects the stream of the *pushti marga* (path of grace) of Vallabhacharya in particular and in the tantric and *sahajiya* dimensions of the *bhakti* tradition. It is one of the many ways Lee's lifetime passion for the love games of Krishna found a wide range of expression. In this Lee enacted the playful connoisseur who sought to share his joy of the sacred image with everyone he met.

It is a natural human tendency to express beauty in paintings, sculpture and words; art itself is traditionally the expression of a sacred culture. Historically, Vallabhacharya's teachings were manifested in every field of the arts, making the personal God all the more alive and accessible. The importance of divine images as *svarupa* cannot be over-estimated, as they confer great blessings and transmission of Reality upon the devotee.

Revelry in the beauty and wonder of Creation marks the pleasure-as-prayer of the connoisseur of life, whose context is enjoyment as a way of celebrating the Divine. It is the *jivan mukta*—one who lives fully in the state of liberation—who may engage full enjoyment through the senses to develop a subtle body of enjoyment. Lee's example in this is one of the many great teachings demonstrated by his life. But, without this context, any form of revelry may quickly become the self-aggrandizing activity of the libertine, the rebel without a cause who generates suffering and karmic entanglements as he or she careens through the world, seeking nothing more than the gratification of personal desires. In other words, wherever the true *bhakta* experiences *bhoga* (enjoyment), it springs from love of the Lord.

NOTHING NEW UNDER THE SUN

The eclectic blending of teachings from many different traditions runs true to the open-minded Baul way, in which the strict adherence to nonduality resides easily alongside adoration of Krishna and Radha, all of which co-exist in a harmonious symmetry with the Sufi ideal of a personal Beloved. Lee has sometimes used the truism, "There is nothing new under the sun," and in this sense, the dharma has existed from the beginning of time and endures in many forms and expressions, coming through wise men and women of universal realization over the eons of human life on Earth. Great realizers often have their own particular way of revealing the secrets of the Universe; they express a unique window into truth, which may appear to be shaped differently than others.

Nonetheless, the truth is the truth, and it is recognizable in many different forms. Just as there are many paths up the mountain, each path has its secrets byways and inner passages which, when revealed, help the trekker to climb the mountain's sharp and steep grades. At the same time, the mountain, its peak, and the sky above it remain essentially the same, although the climbers on the eastern summit might describe the terrain and view differently than climbers on the western summit. Like Jnaneswar, who clearly states that he has not revealed something new but has shone a light on what has always been, Khepa Lee has always given this basic truth its due.

The Bauls and Sahajiyas, with their creative amalgams that blended the timeless way of *sahaja* with ancient Buddhist and Hindu tantra merged with the devotional passion of classical bhakti, have known and lived this truth for hundreds of years. Those who follow in their footsteps are grateful to these peerless pioneers, and to their Western counterpart, Khepa Lee, who fearlessly forged ahead to manifest new expressions of the eternal path. And so, with *pranams* to the eternally-present Yogi Ramsuratkumar and his true heart son Lee, this small book is offered in service to all who walk the path.

The Guru's Blessing

May we, all beings, be happy and fulfilled in Dharma, Buddha, Sangha, and Guru (even the Guru!), and may the joy and power of the Blessings of Yogi Ramsuratkumar flow unimpeded like the Ganges in monsoon, and may the opulence, the pushti of our service to Krishna, and therefore to Self, never wane, never waver, never be in doubt or conflict. May we abandon ourselves to ourselves, Realizing only God, the other, and "Just This," and may all Divine beings celebrate our Guru Yoga and pour their Benediction upon us and ours like honey gushing from an overfull hive. May we live lives of fulfillment, creativity, deep satisfaction and profound value and profit to the Work. And may every child, adult, and elder smile at you, knowing and seeing your transcendental and your immanent beauty, delight, and perfection. In fact, may delight and joy plague you unavoidably, and may you never suffer unnecessarily, having embodied fully all of this, my wishes for you. I bow to you with hands folded, forehead to the ground and eternity before us.

— Lee Lozowick, July 2010

Sangeetha Lyrics
(a companion CD)

Yogi Ramsuratkumar with Ma Devaki listening to Lee's band—liars, gods, & beggars— at Sudama House, 1994.

Anonde Bawlo

Anonde bawlo, jai guru jai, Anonde bawlo, jai guru jai	*say with joy, hail to the guru, hail*
Anonde bawlo, jai guru jai, Anonde bawlo, jai guru jai	*Say with joy, hail to the guru, hail*
Jaiyo bhakoto Jaiyo bhagawan, Jaiyo janardano jagojanopran	*hail to the devotee, hail to God*
Jaiyo bhakoto Jaiyo bhagawan, Jaiyo janardano jagojanopran	*hail to the devotee, hail to God*
Jaiyo gopibalabho madonogopal	*hail to the darling of the gopies – Madanagopal*
Jaiyo gopibalabho madonogopal	*hail to the darling of the gopies – Madanagopal*
Jaiyo, jaiyo khepa sadguru jai	*hail, hail to the Khepa, hail to the true Teacher*
Jaiyo, jaiyo khepa sadguru jai	*hail, hail to the Khepa, hail to the true Teacher*
Jaiyo Jagobondhu jaiyo gopinath, jaiyo dinobondhu janokinath	*hail to the Lord of the world, hail to the Lord of the gopis*
Jaiyo Jagobondhu jaiyo gopinath, jaiyo dinobondhu janokinath	*hail to the Lord of the world, hail to the Lord of the gopis*
Jaiyo brojokishoro jaiyo srinath	*hail to the Adolescent of Braja, hail to Srinath*
Jaiyo brojokishoro jaiyo srinath	*hail to the Adolescent of Braja, hail to Srinath*
Guru govinda jaiyo, jaiyo oki jai	*hail to Govinda the teacher, hail o hail*
Guru govinda jaiyo, jaiyo oki jai	*hail to Govinda the teacher, hail o hail*
Anonde bawlo, jai guru jai, Anonde bawlo, jai guru jai	*say with joy, hail to the guru, hail*
Anonde bawlo, jai guru jai, Anonde bawlo, jai guru jai	*say with joy, hail to the guru, hail*
Jai, jai, jai, name jom parajai	*hail, hail, the saying of his name defeats Jam (Yama - the god of Death)*
Jai, jai, jai, name jom parajai	*hail, hail, the saying of his name defeats Jam (Yama - the god of Death)*
Jaiyo Jagannatho jai oki jai	*hail to lord Jagannath, hail, hail*
Jaiyo Jagannatho jai oki jai	*hail to lord Jagannath, hail, hail*

Yes My Lord

Oh Lord, You brought me to my knees
Lord You humbled me
Taught me all the hard things
I once refused to see
At first I fought with everything
You wanted to provide
Now I see your love is deep
You brought me to your side

Yes my Lord
I'm walking next to you
Right beside of you
walking straight and true

Yes my Lord
You cut me to the core
You led me through your door
Yes my Lord

I told myself that the little lies
Were really fine in fact
Ain't no harm I said
Everyone's like that
Yes You helped me realize
Everyone was my excuse
My salvation and my soul
They all belong to You

Lee Lozowick Project performing on tour in Sezanne, France, 2007.

Yours Alone

First thing I feel every morning
When the sunlight greets the day
Is the love I feel for you
Love true, yes – come what may
Now some feel their love varies
Like the moods of the mind
But mine for you is steady, steady,
Steady and I know you'll find

I am yours
I am yours
I am yours alone
Yours alone
Flesh and bone
I am yours alone
I am yours

I go through the motions
Getting done all I need
But never am I separate

From you in word or deed
My interests seem to vary
Yeah but that's just surface waves
On the ocean of my love for you
Love from birth to grave

The last thing every evening
I know before I sleep
Is the love I have for you
Love that's sweet and deep
Well many think I'm crazy
To have no other one
But I don't care what other's say
When all is said and done

I am yours
In every form
Yours throughout all time
And what's more love – You are mine
I am yours

Lee and Shri with Purna Das and Bauls, Kolkata, 2008.

Can You Trust

The streets are stayin' dirty
Feels like the sky will fall
The airwaves filled with mindless trash
Can't get no peace at all
And we complain so easily
But what is it we will do?
Good words fall on deaf ears
They're just not gettin' through

Can you trust your mother?
Can you trust your chief?
Can you trust your brother?
The one who killed the thief
Can you trust the scientists?
Can you trust a friend?
Can you trust the holy laws
Reinterpreted by men?

Rome had nothing on us
And that so long ago
What is it we are doing?
We're just lost amidst the show

Now fire it will claim us
And take us back again
It's grinnin' through its death mask
No, no respecter of men

Well governments are crooked
The jails are all too full
And do we even notice?
So driven by the pull
Well, life is just now hangin'
By a real thin thread
If we're to stop the avalanche
We must, must get out of our head

liars, gods & beggars, 1993.

Grip

We all want just what we want
We're unwilling to be free
To drop the chains that bind us
And see reality
We think that the universe
Will follow our rules
We sing our songs of me and mine
While acting like blind fools

Unhappiness and misery
Seem to come from those out there
In fact it's our rigidity
Telling us it's so unfair
Grip
It's got a grip

It's not that things are always peaceful, nice and neat
Life can be a struggle yeah, it ain't all pure and sweet
But we can complicate it by thinking we dictate
Each and every outcome / we don't control our fate

Hey relax, it's not so bad.
Stop the desperation.
We can never guarantee.
The way it is is the way it is.

Unhappiness and misery
Seem to come from those out there
In fact it's our rigidity
Telling us it's so unfair
We are not the victims
We petulantly claim
Open up your eyes and see
It's only love that's calling our names.
Grip
It's got a grip

Lee Lozowick Project in France, 2007.

Too Real

Gimme a joint, gimme a bottle
I'll take the needle, if I gotta
Do anything to help forget
Cause I'm not ready for the real truth yet
Gimme some woman, a sex machine
A real fast car, know what I mean?
Play me some music, dirty and loud
Anything to keep me out of the crowd

Life is full of beauty
But is seems
Like ugliness is winning
It's got the means, so it seems
Life can be so pleasant
And perhaps it only me
But the pain is too much
To smile on, to smile on

Send me to some tropical isle
Let me watch them movies go by
Give me them distractions
Anything will do
I don't need the sympathy
Of those who'll say what's true
Fascinate and thrill me
Take me for a ride

Give me lots of credit
So I can shop all day
Give me lots of liberty
So I can have my way
Fascinate and thrill me
Take me for a ride
I'll be safe and satisfied
Long as I can hide

Attila the Hunza playing at the Festival du Rock, Flamel, France, 2003.

Take A Chance

It might seem a little risky baby
No you ain't been here before
This chance you could be takin'
It'll open up the door, yeah
You can't even start to see it
Cause right now you're livin' blind
Come on and take a try…
I think you'll like what you will find

Come on take a chance with me
Come on take a chance yeah!

Hey, I've got an invitation
Take a chance – take a chance on me, yeah
To an endless possibility
For a heavenly romance, baby
Hey I've got an invitation

Take a chance – take a chance on me, yeah
Come on and see – come on take a chance

I can feel your knees a knockin'
I can feel your poundin' heart
You been under wraps too long
I think it's time for you to start
Hey boy it's not too risky
I know it will blow your mind
I can't say that's a bad thing
You can give it back sometime

It might feel kinda dangerous
And there ain't no one left to blame
But if you get this simple clue
Your life won't ever be the same

The Denise Allen Band on tour in Europe, 2013.

Hooked By Your Eyes

It's not that I believed in
Every word you said
It's just that I was blinded by
The life that you had led
It's not that I got trapped by
Your pretense and your lies
I saw them all quite clearly
But I got hooked by your eyes

Your body shouted stay away
But your eyes said come on in
Some say the soul is mirrored there
I guess it must have been
I thought it was such good fortune
That led me here to you
I never would have figured on
The hoops you'd put me through

I trusted you and what did I get
A broken heart I can never forget
I got hooked by your eyes
I trusted you and where am I now
All alone and wonderin' how
I got hooked by your eyes

I sure would have been glad, baby
To be your circus clown
But that's not what you wanted
I could see as you put me down
I know you figured that you had
The perfect little slave
But that's a role that didn't fit me
So I chose this grave

I trusted you and what did I get
A burnin' pain I can never forget
I got hooked by your eyes
I trusted you and where am I now
Down and out and wonderin' how
I got hooked by your eyes

Love's Fools

Honey, let's throw caution to the wind
Let's forget the rules
Don't you know you're drivin' me crazy
Let's be love's fools
Just you and me without no limits
Let the flesh be our only guide
Don't let the past dictate the future
Take freedom for a ride

Oh, what is it about us?
Ah, who can really say?
Oh, I feel the wave rising
Ah, carry me away

Let's explore the unknown, darlin'
Try things we never tried
Won't it be almost too much
With heaven on our side
Oooh this feelin' such a wonder
Words cannot express
How I'm feelin' about you, honey
When you're sayin' yes

liars, gods & beggars, 1997.

Death By Music

Some people say you need a heart to survive
And hot blood in your veins, that's what keeps you alive
But I been called heartless, uncaring and cruel
And they say I'm cold-blooded, just an unfeeling fool

But how can they judge when they're as blind as can be
When they can't hear the music pulsing inside of me
Well I'm not blue-blooded but I'll give you some clues
My body lives and it breathes cause it's made of the blues

I have known lots of pleasure, I have felt so much pain
I have seen when life's over there ain't nothing to gain
So I live with a vengeance and my love will not tell
I have seen the bright side of heaven, seen the dark side of hell

Walking on the razor's edge, sleeping very light
Hungered by the blazing sun, fed by the night
Satisfied with the joy in the cracks between my sorrows
Not counting on the future of illusory tomorrows

Kate Parker singing with the Shri Blues Band, France, 2013

POEM TO YOGI RAMSURATKUMAR

So many birds here,
   chirping and trilling
their beautiful songs,
   each one pure, pristine, unique.
I could swear that
   although each song is different
they are all singing
   Your Sweet Name.
Yes, I am sure of it.
   The more closely I listen,
the clearer it is —
   Yogi Ramsuratkumar, Yogi Ramsuratkumar.
But then doesn't every created thing
   sing Your Name?
What else would any creature
   desire but Your Name?
Once we have heard Your Name;
   the delicacy, the joy of it
overwhelms us totally,
   until all we need is that Name.
So we, each of us, sing Your Name
   in our own way,
yet all sing the same Name,

Yogi Ramsuratkumar, Yogi Ramsuratkumar.
This is Your Blessing,
   dearer than life itself.
You are the Essence of existence,
   You are All, dear Father.
This mad Heretic of Yours
   sings Your Name
in countless ways, infinite ways,
   and it soothes the suffering
of the many worlds with the sound
   of Yogi Ramsuratkumar, Yogi Ramsuratkumar.
Living in awe at Your Compassionate Love
   for Your struggling but faithful children
to whom You have made a gift
   of Your glorious Name,
Your true heart-son lee lozowick
   becomes the dust at Your Feet
and Praises You endlessly
   for this Merciful Benediction.*

---

*   Lee Lozowick, *Death of a Dishonest Man,* June 25, 1996, 779–780

To Me

Come to me, when you are lonely
Come to me, when you are down
Come to me, for I am comfort
Come to me, turn it around

Oh come to me, come to me darlin'
Come to me, yes come to me
Come to me, I'll be your answer
When the question's too hard to see

Oh when the night is dark and scary
When the day is hard and long
I am here to hold you closely
Come to me, I am your song

When a smile just seems too painful
And when laughter is far away
I am joy, come let me hold you
Come to me, I'll let you stay

Denise Allen singing with her band on tour, 2013.

Pare Loye Jao Amay
(Take Me Across)

Take me across, my Beloved
I am waiting, I am sitting here still
I am waiting to go
Oh, the merciful One!

Alone, I remained
At the ghat in loneliness
Watching the setting sun
Now I see no one to hold on to
Except you, my Beloved

I have neither meditation nor prayers,
My Beloved, I have nothing to offer
I roamed in vain, I heard that
You are a savior of broken hearts,
So I call you again and again

It you don't show the right path to the wanderer
It will be a shame to your name!
Lalan says, who would name you again
As "the King of Boundlessness"?

— Lalan Fakir

Biswanath and Parvathy singing in Kolkata, 2008.

Keep On Lovin' You

If there were only one thing
left in life to do
I wouldn't do another thing
but keep on lovin' you

Lovin' you,
my darling
Loving you
I wouldn't do
another thing
but keep on
loving you.

If I had one single wish
to keep from being blue
don't you know what I'd wish for —
to keep on lovin' you

If I had but just one dream
guess what I'd dream too
even while I sleep at night
I'd keep on lovin' you

The Shri Blues Band in Europe, 2013.

Take Me Away

Woman, turn me into blood
so I can run through your veins
turn me into freedom
so I can break your chains
let me be the food
that feeds your hungry soul
let me be the fullness
to fill your every hole

Take me away, take me away
I don't want me anymore
Take me away, take me away
leave only you, you, you
Take me away, take me away
I only want what I adore
take me to the only thing that's true
leave only you, leave only you

Give me the power
to fill you with peace
let me be the force
that grants you sweet release
let me be the perfect rose
to satiate your senses
let me be what's needed, baby
to burn down your fences

Let me be the blood
that pumps through your heart
let me be the inspiration
giving you a start
make me into sugar
sweeten your flesh
turn me into soft skin
to cover your warm breast

Take me away, take me away
I don't want me anymore
Take me away, take me away
leave only you, you, you
Take me away, take me away
I only want what I adore
take me to the only thing that's true
leave only you, leave only you

Take me away, take me away
I don't want me anymore
Take me away, take me away
leave only you, you, you
Take me away, take me away
I only want what I adore
take me to the only thing that's true
leave only you, leave only you

Blind Devotion

Ask me to do anything
Your wish is my command
I will fly up to the sun for you
Bring it to your hand
I will conquer armies
You know what I mean
Allow me to adore you
Be your slave, not your queen

Got a question for you honey
Please forgive my great emotion
Is it dangerous to love you
With such blind devotion?
Yeahh —

Fingers intertwined, paroxysm of love
That is my idea of praying
Lost in your lover so deeply
You don't even know what you're saying
Don't know much about the subject of holy
But I think I have come pretty near
When I look into his eyes
There I am transfixed with fear

Blind devotion, what else is left
Nothing that is worth very much
Blind devotion, consume me in your path
Let me feel the heaven and sorrow
Of your touch

Deborah Auletta singing with Shri, 2007.

Pranams to the Lineage

Om saha naavavatu
Saha nau bhunaktu
Saha veeryam karavaa–vahai
Teja–svi naa–vadheeta–mastu
Maa vidvishaa–vahai

Om. May we, Guru and disciple, be protected together.
May we enjoy the fruits of our actions together.
May we achieve strength together.
May our knowledge be full of light.
May we never have enmity for one another.

Om Swami Papa Ramdas Maharaj Ki Jai
Om Yogi Ramsuratkumar Maharaj Ki Jai
Om Anjaneya Khepa Lee Maharaj Ki Jai

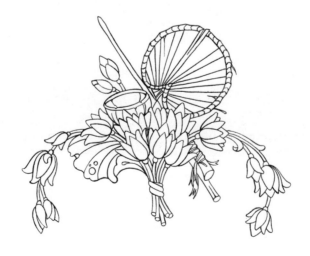

Hohm Sahaj Mandir Discography

Compiled by Karuna Fedorschak

The Hohm Discography is a catalog of the recorded songs of Lee Lozowick and has appeared in the back of each of the three poetry books—*Death of a Dishonest Man, Gasping for Air in a Vacuum,* and *Intimate Secrets of a True Heart Son*—complete up to the date of each of those publications.

The songs are listed in a timeline by band and cassette or CD recording, beginning with liars, gods & beggars, Shri, Attila the Hunza, Denise Allen Band, and the Lee Lozowick Project. The catalog contains over five hundred songs, including about fifty songs from Lee's two rock operas, *John T* and *The Nine Houses of Mila.* Besides the two operas, in the "also available" category at the end, is a country cassette called *Gold Ring* and a new age instrumental offering, *Angelic Symphony.*

Not represented here, are the many songs that were composed and even performed, but never recorded, as well as numerous extant notebooks of uncomposed lyrics currently in safekeeping with several of the composers. Lee was a prolific lyricist and poet who often remarked on the unending flow of songs that arose constantly, and described holding back this floodtide of lyrics simply because there were other priorities for his attention.

For the Western Baul practitioner these songs are a map of the many shades of human experience, a guide to *sadhana,* a rich source of material for self-observation, and not least, a testament to the possibility of transcendence. Although historically each band has performed their own repertoire of Lee's songs, there is the possibility for any Baul band or practitioner-musician to access the full catalog for study and performance. From this perspective, the discography is a sumptuous menu of songs to be "eaten."

We present the discography here as an archival record and an invitation to the reader to explore this vast catalog for enjoyment and edification.

liars, gods & beggars
DISCOGRAPHY

ACCUSED
1989—Recorded at Indian Hills Studios, Claremont, CA

Cassette includes:

Lady	Spite
Front Door Man	Fever
It's Not Fair	Deep Love
Good Intentions	You Don't Understand
Accused	Free Ride

LIKE MERCURY
1991—Recorded at Circe Studios, Prescott, AZ

Cassette includes:

Double Trouble	Don't Think
Petty Tyrant	Don't Lock Your Love Away
Virgin	Beggar's Blues
Those Old Blues	First Things First

OUT OF OUR HANDS
1991—Recorded at Circe Studios, Prescott, AZ

Cassette includes:

Divide And Conquer	Pale Face
Pay You Back	The Man
Prove It	Anger Or Sorrow
Out Of Our Hands	Miss Erotic
Woman in This World	Modern Man

LILITH
1991—Recorded at Circe Studios, Prescott, AZ

CD/Cassette includes:

Fix Your Face	No Shame Lady
Bad Dream	Moist
Just A Woman	Lady Stop My Mind
You Never Know	Lilith
Sugar Shock	

JUST SMOKE
1992—Recorded at Chaton Studios, Scottsdale, AZ

CD includes:

You Love	I Know You
Just Smoke	Little Red Rooster
Refused To Die	The Way It Always Is
All Night Long	Love Ain't Enough
Righteous	When A Man
The Thrill Is Back (I Don't Want)	

ECCENTRICITIES, IDIOSYNCRASIES, & INDISCRETIONS
1992—Recorded at Chaton Studios, Scottsdale, AZ

CD includes:

Make The Right Choice	Twisted
Where We Are	Licking At Our Doorstep
Who Am I	How's Alice
Turn On The Lights	I'm Busy
Anything But Tame	Time Makes No Difference
The Face Of Your Denial	Standing
Very Fine Line	

LOVE IN HELL
1993—Compilation Album
Released on The Nice Music label (Germany)
Published by Warner/Chappell

CD includes:

I Know You	Anything But Tame
You Don't Understand	When A Man
You Love	Gimme, Gimme
Divide And Conquer	Lady Stop My Mind
Licking At Our Doorstep	Make The Right Choice
Just Smoke	Even Love Has Its Price
Very Fine Line	You Never Know

CHTHONIC BOOM
1994—Recorded live in Arizona

Double Cassette includes:

Volume 1
Lady
Through It All
Slaughter
Time Enough
They Say
Are We Having Fun

Volume 2
She Was A Fine Girl
Confess
These Days
Angel Still
When It's Me
No Hidden Meanings
Just A Moment
These Boots Are Made
    For Walking

MAÑANA, INANNA
1995—Recorded at Phase 4 Studios, Phoenix, AZ

CD includes:

What Is It About You
Delivering My Heart
Working Girl

Through It All
Shakin'

VUJA DÉ
1996—Recorded at Luna Recordings, Prescott, AZ

CD includes:

Vision Of You
Hunger Of Love
The Magic You Are
    Working
Love's Fools
He's A Good Man
You
I Have Seen The Future

Can You Trust
Breaking Through
Ain't No God
Can You See
G-Thang
What Good Does It Do
I Just Seen You Uptown

STEAVIE BEAVER
1998—Recorded at Luna Recordings & Circe Studios, Prescott, AZ

CD includes:

Make A Little Room
    For Grace
Dream Of Freedom
Endless Highway
May The Morning
    Come Slowly
Trouble-Oh
Work With It (Cold Slab)

If You Want It
The Way She Blushes
Beneath The Strain
Insane
Fury Of The Storm
Happy Dick

TRANSFESTITE
1999—Recorded at Luna Studio, Prescott, AZ

CD includes:

All There Is To Say
The Place I Haunt
Why Do You
If This Is Love
Big Girl
Love's Fools
All There Is To Say

Don't Know How
I Love You
It Ain't Love
The Sleep Of No Return
Little
The Magic You Are Working

VIF ET MORDANT (ALIVE & KICKING)
LIARS, GODS & BEGGARS
FEATURING LEE LOZOWICK
2011—Retrospective CD
Tracks remastered at The Aspen Grove, Bozeman, Montana

CD includes:

You Don't Understand
Shakin'
Gimme, Gimme
You
Fix Your Face
Spite
Sugar Shock

Righteous
Just Smoke
Can You Trust
Licking at our Doorstep
Where We Are
Work With It

* All albums except *Love In Hell* and *Vif et Mordant* released by:
LGB Music
PO Box 31
Prescott, AZ 86302
928-717-1783   FAX 928-717-1779

Shri

DISCOGRAPHY

GOOD THING
1995—Recorded at The Salt Mine, Phoenix, AZ

Cassette includes:

Those Old Blues	Good Thing
Show Me Where You Stand	Had Your Chance
You Can Have My Husband	Keep On Lovin' You
Put Your Body On The Line	Blind Devotion
Sunnyland	

MIZ BLUES SHOES
1995—Recorded at Luna Studios, Prescott, AZ

CD/Cassette includes:

The Score	Mission
Don't Need You	All Along
Ball & Chain	All Along The Highway
Don't Make Promises	No Fantasy
Blues School	Look Out
Goin' To Brownsville	

HOOKED
1996—Recorded at Luna Studios, Prescott, AZ.

CD/Cassette includes:

Play	Tell Me
Born Under A Bad Sign	Can't Find My Way
Hooked By Your Eyes	Home
If You'd Like It	Ain't No Mystery
As Long As You Love Me	Earthly Love
	Man So Healthy

SHRISON IN HELL
1998—Recorded Live at Lyzzards Lounge, Prescott, AZ

CD/Cassette includes:

Woman with My Class	Course Of Action
Time to Face	Driftin'
Action	Lapidary Blues
Wearin' Thin	Off Limits
Good	My Bleeding Heart
Left My Baby Standin'	G-Thang
Blind Devotion	

SEE SHRI PLAY THE BLUES
1999—Recorded at Luna Recording Studios, Prescott, AZ

CD/Cassette includes:

Volume 1	Volume 2
Turn Around	Fame
Medley: 2 Hands	Girl Of Action
I Learned My Lesson Good	Spite
Loser Blues	All Of Your Love
Wasn't Workin'	Ain't Left Me Yet
Silken Cross Blues	18 Wheeler Truck
A Woman With My Class	It's Not Fair
I'm A Man	Blues Is Alright
Smokestack Lightning	I Love You
Voodoo Chile	
Sweet Little Angel	
Course Of Action	
Dreamin' 'Bout Dreamin'	
The Great Equalizer	

FLOWERS OF SHRIVIL
2000—Recorded at Living Head Studios, Phoenix, AZ

CD/Cassette includes:

Done Me Wrong	You Got To Move
Sugar	I Seen
Crime	Natural Healer
Holy	Treats
Beggar's Blues	Get Back
Things	Used To Be
Rise Up	State Of Mind
Cheatin'	

SHRINO ELEGIES
2001—Recorded at Living Head Studios, Phoenix, AZ

CD includes:

Slippery	Shooter
Death Don't Have No Mercy	Last Thing
Don't Hedge Your Bet	My Obsession
Preachin' Blues	Married To The
Fishin'	Blues
Lunch	Labyrinth Of Love
Angel Of Mercy	Sharp Tooth Woman
	Mighty Tight
Woman	

CORNER ON THE RAIN
2002—Recorded at Living Head Studios, Phoenix, AZ

CD includes:

Million Miles	Gone
What You Need Me For	Cadillac
Have You	Better Off Single
Ache	You Almost Got
Texas Flood	Me That Time
Cannot Hide From The Blues	Over
Corner On The Rain	Service
	When The Levee
	Breaks

LIVIN' ON THE STREETS
2003—Recorded at Living Head Studios, Phoenix, AZ

CD includes:

I Don't Know	Can't Get No Credit Blues
Telephone	Ready
My Pond	Weather
Masters Of War	Engineer
Lord Your Burden	Busy All Night
My Dream	Ben Franklin Blues
Had	

TIME TO GET REAL
2004—Recorded at Double Wide Studios, Paulden, AZ

CD includes:

Help Me	Possible
Something On My Mind	Trial
The Thrill Is Back	Learned To Cry
Since I Fell For You	After Dark
How Could I	Doin' Time
Operator	Drive
3 Legged Dog Blues	Invite The Lord To Stay

SHRI: LIVE IN EUROPE 2004
2004—Recorded on tour

CD includes:

DISC ONE	DISC TWO
Service	Help Me
Over Your Head	What You Need Me For
Walkin' Blues	Done Me Wrong
I'm Worried	Voodoo Chile
Angel Of Mercy	Operator
I Don't Know	Cannot Hide From
One Way Out	The Blues
Crossroads	Trial
Left My Baby Standin'	First Time I Met The Blues
Summertime	All Along The Watchtower
Summertime	Two Hands
	I Learned My Lesson
	Good
	Smokestack Lightnin'

DOGS OF DEVOTION
2007—Recorded at Cat Door Studios, Prescott Valley, AZ

CD includes:

Tryin'	Where My Heart Used
Trouble	To Be
Time To	Got To Do
Small Change	For Me
On Your Way Down	Fact
News	Don't Work
Motherless Child	Dock Of The Bay
Magic	Dark Angel

LUCKY THIRTEEN
2009—Recorded at Circe Sound Studio, Prescott, AZ

CD includes:

Bring Your Sister	What's Love (Again)
Sold Me Out	Closet Klepto
Scales	Rock 'n Roll Star
Why	Silence
I Been Lovin' You	Jesus Gonna Make Up My
Talk About Love	Dying Bed
Depraved	Baby's Talkin' Bullshit
Cryin'	Again Blues
	I Shot Her On A Full Moon
	Night

AIN'T LOOKING FOR A CURE
2012—Recorded at Circe Studios, Paulden, AZ

CD includes:

Death By Music	For Your Own Good
As Long As You Love Me	Everybody Knows
Let It Go	Gonna Rock
Dark	Don't Think
Going Down	My Dream
Take Me	Full Moon Night

SHRI BLUES BAND: DEMO CD
2011

CD includes:

Talk About Love
Dark Angel (live)
Depraved
All Along The Watchtower (live)
Piece Of Ass (live)

SHRI BLUES BAND: LIVE IN LEIPZIG!
July 30, 2012—Recorded live at Reihe am Bachdenkmal
in Leipzig, Germany

CD includes:

Crossroads Blues	The Prodigal Son
Philosophize	Whistlin' Past The
Dark	Graveyard
Going Down	Roadhouse Blues
Get Me On That Train	Gonna Rock
Walkin' Blues	House Of The Rising Sun
I'm Worried	All Along The
	Watchtower

SHRI BLUES BAND
2014—Recorded at Circe Studios, Paulden, AZ

CD includes:

Yes My Lord	Keep On Lovin' You
Good Times	Down To The Heart
Telegram	Talk About Love
When The Levee Breaks	Operator
I Put A Spell On You	Fact Of Life (AKA
Hey Heartbreaker	Tina's Blues)
Ask Me	Weather
There Goes The	Like A Fire
Neighborhood	Beggar's Blues

All albums released by:
Bad Poet Productions, LLC
890 Staley Lane
Chino Valley, AZ 86323
928-848-9291   FAX 928-717-1779
visit: www.shriblues.com for more information

Attila the Hunza
DISCOGRAPHY

THE FIRST OF MANY AMAZING ALBUMS BY ... ATTILA THE HUNZA
2001—Recorded at Circe Studios, Prescott, AZ

CD includes:

Everywhere You Turn
A Few More Hours
She Was A Fine Girl
Mine
It's A Shame
Catch It On The Run
Real
Calcutta Nights
Going Down
Old Friend Sorrow
Too Real
They Say
Cost
Ditty
Death By Music
Amazing Grace

TIME WILL TELL
2002—Recorded at Circe Studios, Prescott, AZ

CD includes:

I Only Think About You
Lost
Surprise
Sweet Torture
Time Will Tell
Memories Can't Last
Chemistry Of Flesh
Lonely
You Don't Believe
Forbidden Fruit
Dancing Barefoot
A Very Fine Line
Old Time's Sake
Stand Up

CAUGHT IN THE MIDDLE
2004—Recorded at Circe Studios, Prescott, AZ

CD includes:

Inside Out
My Dream
Deep Love
Don't Hold Back
Two And Two
Goddess
Caught In The Middle
Monsters
What About
One Thing
Good Times
No Choice

LAST LOVELY GASP
2006—Recorded at Dondi Music Studios, Prescott, AZ

CD includes:

Oh Loneliness
Wet Kiss
If This Is Love
Mind
Please
Corner On The Rain
For Better Or Worse
Whistlin'
How Else
As Ye Sow

All albums originally released by:
Attila the Hunza, LLC
P.O. Box 31
Prescott, AZ 86302
928-717-1783   FAX 928-717-1779

Denise Allen Band
DISCOGRAPHY

NOT JUST ANOTHER DIVA
2003—Recorded at Circe Studios, Prescott, AZ
(originally released as *Denise Lisenby*)

CD includes:

Get You Down	Never Satisfied
Love Me Now Or Love Me Later	To Me
	You Rescued Me
Everybody	Get Me On That Train
Driftin'	Adventure
The Lord Is Real	Mercy Of The Lord
How'd You Like	Where Did The Dream Go
Why Didn't You Tell Me	Trouble In Mind
Practice What You Preach	

HE TAKES MY SOUL
2004—Recorded at Circe Studios, Prescott, AZ
(originally released as *Denise Lisenby*)

CD includes:

Gonna Have to Fight	Fine
His	Back Together
He Fills Me Up	Reward
Undream You	Winner Take All
He Takes My Soul	Under The Influence
True Lie	Kid Gloves
Freedom	To The Core
Thought I Knew	There Goes The Neighborhood

DIAMONDS & SILK
2007—Recorded at Evolution Sound Lab, Prescott, AZ

CD includes:

Turn Around	I Heard
What Can You Do	Flaming Red
You Can Weep	Envy
Alone in Heaven	Live With It
Grown Up	She Knows
If	All Along
Make A Little Room	He

TRUE
2008—Recorded at Circe Sound Lab, Prescott, AZ

CD includes:

Ain't No Sin	Memory
Recreated	Pity
Greed	Welcome to Denial
Who Will	Love
Three Times	The Man
When I Grow Up	Whether You Love Me Or Not
Yes to No	

YOU/ME/US
2010—Recorded at Evolution Sound Lab, Prescott, AZ

CD includes:

Don't Say No	How Love Is
Own You	Too Far
When	Get On It
You're Gone	Why Should Love Be Torture
You Bought It	Leavin'
All	Probably Will
Winds Of Fate	

THIS HEARTBREAK
2012—Recorded at Circe Studios, Paulden, AZ

CD includes:

Enough's Enough	Can't Prove It By Me
I Don't Mind	Out Of Touch
Me	What Do You Want
Take A Chance	I Will Forget You
Lookin' Pretty Good	Better Not
Ain't It Funny	Lust for You
Hey You	Listen Closely
Promises	

All albums released by:
Bad Poet Productions, LLC
890 Staley Lane
Chino Valley, AZ 86323
928-848-9291   FAX 928-717-1779
visit: www.deniseallenband.com

Lee Lozowick Project
DISCOGRAPHY

ECRASE PAR L'AMOUR (CRUSHED BY LOVE)
Lee Lozowick
2004—Recorded at Cake or Death Studios, Bozeman, Montana
Originally released as *DOG'S DAY IN THE SUN*

CD includes:

Yes My Lord	She Said
What's Love	Listen
What Do I Do	Yours
Monsters	Grip
Another Side	Survival
Untitled	

L'ANGE BRISE (BROKEN ANGEL)
Lee Lozowick
2006—Recorded at The Aspen Grove, Bozeman, Montana

CD includes:

Pretty	Philosophize
Brought To Life	My Child
Brave	Look Ahead
This Morning	Take Me
It's You	Past Is Past
Please	Changing Of The Guard

LEE LOZOWICK PROJECT: LIVE IN EUROPE
2007—Recorded on tour

CDs include:

DISC ONE	DISC TWO
Take Me	Philosophize
Grip	Isis
Changing Of The Guard	Honky Tonk Woman
Elisa	You
Survival	The Way She Blushes
I'm Your Man	Look Ahead
Dance To The Music	The Future
Love Never Dies	You Can Leave Your Hat On
I Put A Spell On You	Please
Hey Joe	Too Real
Unchain My Heart	Little Red Rooster
You Give Love A Bad Name	

UNE LANGUE DE VENIN, UNE AME D'AMOUR (A TONGUE OF VENOM, A SOUL OF LOVE)
Lee Lozowick
2008—Recorded at The Aspen Grove, Bozeman, Montana

CD includes:

Eyes On You	In Love All Right
Stay In Love	Diamonds
Is It True	Damned If You Do
Would You	Piece Of Ass
Take Me Away	Madhouse
Get Off	Gilded Cage

THE OTHER LEE LOZOWICK PROJECT: LIVE IN INDIA
2008—Recorded live at the Calcutta South Club, Kolkata, India

CDs include:

DISC ONE	DISC TWO
Beggar's Blues	Love Never Dies
Brought to Life	Take Me
Help Me	Trouble
Grip	Yes My Lord
Death Don't Have No Mercy	Motherless Child
All Along The Watchtower	Isis (reprise)
Isis	

All albums released by:
Bad Poet Productions, LLC
890 Staley Lane
Chino Valley, AZ 86323
928-848-9291   FAX 928-717-1779

Also Available

GOLD RING

Country Crossover by Lee Reid
1991—Recorded at Circe Studios, Prescott, AZ

Cassette includes:

Tired Of Being Mine	Wishful Thinking
Right Hand Man,	Endlessly
Left Hand Woman	It Was A
How I Am	Hard For Her
Sorry	Look Out
Gold Ring	

ANGELIC SYMPHONY

New Age Instrumental Music by Temenos
1991—Recorded at Circe Studios, Prescott, AZ

CD/Cassette includes:

Nine X Twelve	Apprentice's Hope
Future Dream	This Moment Forever

IRSHAD

An instrumental collection of traditional Middle Eastern music
2001—Recorded at Circe Studios, Prescott, AZ

CD includes:

Mwashah
Dkhul Barwal "Ala Ya Mudir Al-Rah"
Murakkaz "Ah Ya Muddasin"

JOHN T

An Original Rock Opera based on the life of John the Baptist
1996—Recorded at Luna Studios, Prescott, AZ

Cassette/CD includes:

Tell Me John	John's Song To God
Flame Startin' Pill	The Banquet
Should We Make	Disciple's Lament
The Move	We Have Come To You
Well Lookee Here	Tell Me, Tell Me
You're Our Lord	Almost Forgotten
Quiet Children	It's A Tragedy
Compromise	Did You Hear The News
Final Days	Hello Old Friends
Maniac	
The Bedroom	
Herodius & Salome	

NINE HOUSES OF MILA

An Original Rock Opera based on the lives of Marpa and Milarepa
2003—Recorded at Tangent Recording Studio, Paulden, AZ

CDs include:

DISC ONE	DISC TWO
What Will We Do	The Only Thing
As Your Husband's	Oh, Dear
Brother	Just One More
Mila's Promise	This Is It
Dear Friend	Mother Cares For You
Sit Down	Here You Have It
I'm Back	My Son, My Son
Done	Sit
No One Else	This I Will Assure You
Marpa	Mila's Song
Here I Come	Enlightenment
Can You Tell Me	Homecoming
Luck's With You Today	The Last Time
I Need A Building	Finale

SMALL CHANGE

Seven Songs
2013—Recorded at Smash Studios, New York City

EP includes:

Little
Just A Moment
One Thing
Hooked
Yours Alone
Surprise
Good Deal

Glossary of Sanskrit Terms

Abisheka—Offering made to a deity during a formal ritual; a liquid oblation or offering such as milk, honey water, ghee, and other precious substances.

Advaita—Doctrine of nonduality.

Akhra—Place where tantrika Bauls live.

Alkhalla—Patchwork robe, jacket, or wrap worn by initiated Bauls.

Ananda—Bliss.

Anandalahari—A one-stringed instrument made of a gourd, the string being made of gut and strummed rhythmically with a plectrum.

Anuman—Baul teaching on spiritual "hearsay, gossip," meaning spiritual ideas and attitudes not gleaned or apprehended through direct individual experience. See *bartaman*.

Arati—Ritual waving of lights, usually a cotton wick burning in ghee, or clarified butter, before a deity as a way of honoring and invoking blessings.

Asana—Posture, usually in hatha yoga.

Ashram—The sanctuary where devotees and practitioners of a lineage live; an often somewhat secluded place where a guru and devotees live.

Atman—The essential individual self, known after enlightenment to be identical with Brahman.

Avadhuta—A saint or mystic who has gone beyond all egoic self-concern and lives in a childlike state of spontaneous innocence and purity, naturally renouncing all social restrictions and norms. They have no worldly obligation and often live "sky clad" and wander or roam freely.

Avatara—Incarnation of a god on Earth.

Bartaman—Baul teaching of direct experience of the Divine.

Baul or Bauls—A sect of wandering *tantrikas*, minstrels and mystics of Bengal who follow the *sahaja* path, in which the transcendent reality co-exists with earthly existence in the doctrine of *svarupa* and *rupa*. Placing a great emphasis on the divinity within the human being, they consider the relationship between man and woman to be a metaphor for the relationship between Radha and Krishna. It is generally accepted that the Bauls evolved out of the Vaishnava Sahajiyas, claiming Chaitanya and his disciple, Nityananda, as their original gurus.

Baul gan—Spontaneous events of song and dance in which the teaching may be communicated or transmitted.

Bhajans—Spiritual songs sung in kirtan.

Bhakta—One who is a devotee.

Bhakti—Devotion.

Bharat—An ancient name of India.

Bhava—A divine mood.

Bhiksha—Alms.

Bhikshu—Mendicant, sadhu or beggar who receives alms.

Bhoga—Enjoyment.

Bindu—Mystic point or dot, compared to a pearl or seed, as the place where energies converge and diverge, as in meditation.

Bodhicitta—Buddhist term referring to the enlightened mind/heart that wishes to free all beings from illusion.

Brahmacharya—Spiritual purity, discipline, or celibacy, chastity, or control of the senses. Also the phase of life of a young student.

Brahman—The Supreme Reality of the Upanishads.

Brahmanas—Those of the Brahmin caste.

Brahmin—The priest-caste, the highest of the four castes delineated in the Vedas.

Caryapadas—Buddhist dharma poem-songs.

Caste—The Vedas elucidate a cultural and spiritual order to human society based on four "estates" or castes: Brahmin (priesthood), Kshatriya (warrior), Vaishya (merchants, farmers, and artisans) and Shudras (servants).

Chakras—(Wheel.) Psycho-energetic centers in the body. Most systems of tantric yoga teach that there are seven located along the spine: *muladhara; svadhishthana; manipura, anahata; vishuddha; ajna*, and *sahasrara*.

Chelas—Spiritual students of a guru.

Deva Dasi—The female partner of a Baul practicing sexual *sadhana*.

Dhoti—Length of cloth used as a wrap for Indian men that covers waist to ankles.

Dhuni—A sacred fire used by tantrikas, generally shaped like a yoni and symbolic of the Divine Feminine principle.

Dhyana—Meditation.

Diksha—Spiritual initiation received from a master.

Dohas—Buddhist tantric songs.

Dotara—A two-stringed lute.

Duggis—A small hand drum.

Duhkha—Suffering, pain.

Dvaita—Dualism, dual.

Dzikr—Sufi or Muslim group prayer or worship.

Ektara—A handmade, one-string lute like instrument; played with one hand, it creates a one-note drone tot accompany a simple or complex vocal melody.

Fakir—A Sufi or Muslim practitioner, sadhu or yogin.

Gandharva—Celestial musicians.

Ganja—Marijuana.

Ghee—Clarified butter, used in cooking and as a ritual offering.

Gita Govinda—A poem written in the 1200s CE by the mahakavi, Jayadeva, about the love of Radha and Krishna, symbolizing the relationship between human and Divine Beloved.

Gopis—The cowherd girls of antiquity who loved Krishna and dance the *ras lila* with him in the mythic forests of Vraja.

Gunas—The three primordial forces of nature, according to Samkhya philosophy, that bind and organize material life at all levels. See *rajas, sattvas*, and *tamas*.

Guru—Spiritual teacher, master, mentor, or preceptor.

Guruvada—The path or way of following the guru.

Homa—Sacred fire ritual.

Ida—The nadi or subtle nerve channel (lunar) that runs down the left side of the spine.

Ishta Devata—Chosen deity. *Ishta:* Object of desire; the chosen ideal; the particular form of God that one is devoted to. *Devata:* God.

Japa—Mantra practice using a necklace or rosary of beads.

Jiva—The individual soul.

Jivanmukti—A liberated soul. One who has attained freedom from illusion, or *maya*.

Kamandalu—Water pot, carried by holy mendicants and sadhus.

Kavi—Poet.

Kaya sadhana—Baul term for alchemy of the body; spiritual practice of the body, such as breath practices, which are distinct from practices that are purely mental.

Khepa—Baul term for a man of divine madness; feminine *khepi*.

Kirtan—Adoration or praising the Divine by singing of spiritual songs or *bhajans*. Chanting as a means of *bhakti*.

Kula—Family, spiritual clan.

Kurta—A tunic or shirt.

Lila—Game, sport, dance.

Lingam—Phallus.

Madhukari—Baul term for begging.

Mahakavi—A great poet. Maha (great); kavi (poet).

Mahasamadhi—"The great bliss," a term used to describe the physical passing away of the body of a great saint, guru, or *siddha*.

Mala—A necklace of 108 beads used to tell a mantra, often made of rudraksh seeds.

Mandala—Literally, a "circle." A circle with symbolic geometric contents designed for meditation or transmission of a particular spiritual reality.

Mandapam—An open air shelter with a roof held up by columns or poles.

Manipura Chakra—The third chakra located at the navel or solar plexus, "the city of jewels," which is the seat of personal will power, energy, assertive action.

Mantra—A sacred sound (Sanskrit sacred syllable such as Om, Ram, or a phrase such as Om Namo Narayanaya or Om Nama Shivaya) that is used to focus the mind on the Supreme Reality.

Manur Manush—the Baul term meaing "the man of the heart."

Maya—The manifest world of dual realities, often used to refer to the illusory manifestation of the phenomenal world.

Mela—Festival.

Moha—Delusion.

Mohatsabs—Baul feasts. Also Mahatsabs.

Murti—Divine image.

Nama—The Name of God, i.e., Ram, Krishna, Shiva; Yogi Ramsuratkumar.

Namaskar—Salutations.

Namaste—"I honor the light that shines within you."

Nath Siddhas—A sect of ascetic tantric yogins who worship Shiva.

Nawab—The viceroy or local governor of the Mogul Empire who serves under the shah, or king. Historically, the nawabs of India were persons of great wealth, power, and influence.

Ninda Stuti—A particular form of Indian poetry called ironical praise.

Nirguna—The Supreme Reality without attributes; the impersonal God.

Padavalis—Poem songs.

Parakiya—An intimate female partner, married to another man but in sexual relationship with a Sahajiya practitioner.

Parampara—Spiritual lineage.

Pingala—The *nadi* or subtle nerve channel (solar) that runs down the right side of the spine.

Pithas—"Seats" of spiritual power, often temples, mountains, rivers, or shrines.

Prakriti—Nature, Shakti, or the feminine principle.

Pranam—Respectful greeting of an honored person, usually with hands folded before the heart.

Prema—Pure love.

Puja—Ritual worship.

Puranas—Collections of legend and mythologies about the gods and goddesses.

Purnima—Full moon.

Purusha—The divine masculine principle. Consciousness.

Pushti—As a name, Pushti refers to abundant wealth--the Goddess Lakshmi, while the Pushtimarg of Vallabhacharya is translated as the "Path of Grace." Lee used the term "pushti" to refer to the opulent and beautiful expressions of worship through many forms in the field of Grace.

Rajas—One of the three *gunas* of Samkhya that refers to the quality of action, friction, and heat.

Ramnam—Chanting the sacred name of Ram, the Beautiful One or Supreme Reality.

Rasa—Taste, liquid, nectar.

Ras Lila—Literally "sweet games or acts" and often translated as "dance of divine love," enacted by Krishna with the gopis under a full moon in the metaphorical forest of the village Vraja. The ras lila is depicted as a circle of gopis, each one dancing in mystical communion with her own Krishna.

Rishis—Ancient Vedic sages; "seers" or "beings of light."

Rupa—Physical form of things.

Sadhana—Spiritual practice.

Sadhu—One who has renounced all aspects worldly life to practice *sadhana*.

Saguna—The Supreme Reality with attributes; the personal form of God.

Sahaj Manush—The natural man who has realized the innate *sahaja*.

Sahaj Samadhi—A state of consciousness in which one is identified with the totality or oneness of all life while remaining conscious in the dualistic reality; often referred to as open-eyed ecstatic union with the Divine.

Sahaja—The primordial, innate essence of Life; the easy, spontaneous, natural way, which springs from the deep origins of being.

Sahajiya—Those who follow the path of *sahaja*.

Sakhi—Friend, specifically the gopi friends of Radha.

Samadhi—A state of union or absorption in the Ultimate Reality.

Samarasa—A state of sublime composure in which every action or event in the outer world, however pleasurable or painful, generates the same internal bliss. *Samarasa* represents the flavor of *samabhava*, the state of mental, emotional, and spiritual equanimity; they interact in a reciprocity in which each nourishes the other.

Sampradaya—Spiritual clan or school.

Sandhya Bhasa—Twilight language; the symbolic, highly metaphorical speech of poetry, myth, and dreams.

Sangeetha—Music, divine music.

Sangha—Company; community; companions.

Sarvatmabhava—The *bhava* of one pointed focus of attention of the *gopis* on Lord Krishna.

Satsang—Good Company. Companions of the truth; a gathering of companions on the path.

Sattvas—One of the three *gunas* that relates to being; the reconciling or harmonizing aspect.

Seva—Service.

Siddha—A term for an adept who has realized the Supreme Reality.

Siddhi—spiritual power that occurs in *sadhana* or is developed through *tapasya*.

Shabd—The yoga of sound and vibration.

Shaktas—Worshipppers of Divine Mother, or Devi, in her various forms: Kali, Durga, Lakshmi.

Shakti Pithas—"Seats" or sacred places of the goddess.

Shaivites—Worshippers of Lord Shiva.

Shiva Lingam—Iconographic phallus that symbolizes the Absolute or masculine principle of divinity.

Shunya—**or sunya**. Emptiness.

Sushumna—The *nadi* or subtle nerve channel that runs down the center of the spine.

Svabhava—The mood or *bhava* that is innate to one's individual being.

Svarupa—The divine subtle form or archetype that is underlying the *rupa*, or physical form, of manifest things, such as the human body.

Tamas—One of the three *gunas* of Samkhya that refers to the quality of inertia or darkness.

Tantra—A set of ancient texts and practices that expound a path and practice that includes all dimensions of life experience and usually centers around the worship of the feminine principle, or Shakti.

Tantrikas—Those who follow the tantric path.

Tapasya—Extreme effort or spiritual discipline.

Tejas—Spiritual radiance.

Triveni—The convergence of the three rivers—Saraswati, Yamuna, and Ganga; the symbolic meeting point of the three "rivers" of the human body—*ida, sushumna,* and *pingala*. An important Baul teaching of the meeting place where Krishna and Radha converge and play in the human body.

Vaikuntha—Vishnu's heaven.

Vaishnava—A sect of worshippers of Lord Vishnu in his various avataras, most specifically Krishna or Rama.

Vaishnava Sahajiyas—Followers of the *sahaja* way who are also worshippers of Lord Vishnu.

Vidya—Knowledge.

Viraha—A state or mood on the sahaja path known as love in separation

Yoga—Any practice or aspect of life that links one to God.

Yogin—One who practices yoga.

Yoni—Symbol of the feminine divinity; vulva.

Bibliography &
Suggested Reading

Ambalal, Amit. *Krishna as Srinathji*, Mapin International Inc, New York, 1987.

Anirvan, Sri. *Letters from a Baul, Life Within Life* (original in English), Sri Aurobindo Patha-mandir, Kolkata, 1983.

Bhattacharya, Deben. *Love Songs of Chandidas: The Rebel Priest of Bengal,* UNESCO, *1967.*

———. *Mirror of the Sky*, Hohm Press, Prescott, Arizona, 200?

——— *Songs of the Bauls of Bengal,* Grove Press, New York, 1969.

Bose, Manindra Mohan. *The Post-Chaitanya Sahajia Cult of Bengal*, Gian Publishing House, Delhi, India, 1986.

Das Gupta, *Obscure Religious Cults*, Mukhopadhyay Publishers, Calcutta, 1969.

Divine Message to Humanity —H.H. Yogi Ramsuratkumar, the God Child, Chennai, 1988.

Dunham, Bandhu Scott. "Black and White," *Tawagoto*, Hohm Press, Prescott, Arizona, 1988.

Fedorschak, Vijay. *Father and Son*, Hohm Press, 2009.

Feuerstein, Georg. *The Yoga Tradition*, Hohm Press, Arizona, 1998.

Hayes, Glen A. *Tantra in Practice* (edited by David Gordon White), "The Necklace of Immortality: A Seventeenth Century Vaisnava Sahajiya Text," Princeton University Press, New Jersey, 2000.

Hudson, Dennis D. *The Body of God: An Emperor's Palace for Krishna in Eighth-Century Kanchipuran*, Oxford press, New York, 2008.

———. *Tantra in Practice* (edited by David Gordon White), "Tantric Rites in Andal's Poetry," Princeton University Press, New Jersey, 2000.

Jnaneshwar Maharaj, *The Nectar of Self Awareness,* SYDA Foundation, 1979.

Kinsley, David. *The Divine Player: A Study of the Krsna Lila,* Motilal Benarsidass, Delhi, 1997.

Lozowick, Lee. *Chasing Your Tail....* Hohm Press, Arizona, 2009.

———. *Living God Blues*, Hohm Press, Arizona 1985.

————. *In the Fire*, Hohm Press, New Jersey, 1978.

————. *A Tale Told by an Idiot, Full of Sound and Fury, Signifying...* Hohm Press, Arizona, 2009.

————. *Acting God*, Hohm Press, 1980.

————. *The Cheating Buddha*, Hohm Press, 1977.

————. *The Only Grace Is Loving God*, Hohm Press, Arizona, 1982.

————. *Words of Fire and Faith*, Hohm Press, Arizona, 2013.

McDaniel, June. *The Madness of the Saints: Ecstatic Religion in Bengal*, University of Chicago Press, Chicago, 1989.

Miller, Barbara Stoler. *The Gita Govinda of Jayadeva*, Motilal Banarsidas, Delhi, 1984.

Mother Vijayalakshmi. *Waves of Love*, The Yogi Ramsuratkumar Ashram.

Mukerjee, Prabhat. *History of the Chaitanya Faith in Orissa*, Manohar Publications, New Delhi, 1979.

Openshaw, Jeanne. *Seeking Bauls of Bengal*, Cambridge University Press, New Delhi, 2004.

————. *Writing the Self: The Life and Philosophy of a Dissenting Bengali Baul Guru.* Oxford University Press, USA, 2010.

Parvathy Baul. *Song of the Great Soul: An Introduction to the Baul Path*, Ekathara Baul Sangeetha Kalari, Keralam, India.

Rajneesh, Bhagwan Shri. *The Beloved*, Volume I.

Ryan, Regina Sara. *Only God*, Hohm Press, 2004.

Sarkar, R.M. *The Bauls of Bengal*, Gian Publishing House, New Delhi, 1990.

Svoboda, Robert E. *Vastu: Breathing Life into Space*, Namarupa Publishing, NYC, 2013.

Tapasyananda, Swami. *Sri Chaitanya Mahaprabhu: His Life, Religion & Philosophy*, Sri Ramakrishna Math, Chennai, India.

Ramdas, Swami. *The Essential Ramdas*, Anandashram, Kerala, India, 2008.

The Upanishads, translation and commentary by Alistair Shearer et al, Mandala, Unwin Paperbacks, London, 1978.

White, Bose, M.M. *The Post-Chaitanya Sahajiya Bult of Bengal*, Gian Publishing House, Delhi, 1986.

White, David Gordon. "Introduction," *Tantra in Practice*, Princeton University Press, New Jersey, 2000.

Young, M. *As It Is—A Year on the Road with a Tantric Teacher*, Hohm Press, Arizona, 2000.

———— *Spiritual Slavery: A Biography of Lee Lozowick*, Hohm Press, Arizona, 2011.

———— *Yogi Ramsuratkumar—Under the Punnai Tree*, Hohm Press, Arizona, 2003.

Books By and About Lee Lozowick

Capellini, Farcet and Young. *Facets of the Diamond.* Prescott, AZ: Hohm Press, 1995.

Farcet, Gilles. *L'Homme se lève à L'Ouest: Les nouveaux sages de l'Occident.* Paris, France: Albin Michel, 1992.

Fedorschak, VJ. *Father and Son: The Indian Beggar King and the American Master and Bad Poet Lee Lozowick.* Prescott, AZ: Hohm Press, 2009.

Lozowick, Lee. *A Small Collection of Feuilletons by one of the Rasnochintsy.* Prescott, AZ: Hohm Press, 2008.

_____. *"A Tale Told by an Idiot, Full of Sound and Furn, Signifying..."Something Far Too Important To Be Disregarded (In Spite of Shameful Syntax, Misspellings and Sentences Almost As Long as the Mississippi River).* Prescott, AZ: Hohm Press, 2009.

_____. *Acting God.* Prescott Valley, AZ: Hohm Press, 1980.

_____. *Alchemy of Love and Sex.* Prescott, AZ: Hohm Press, 1996.

_____. *Alchemy of Transformation.* Prescott, AZ: Hohm Press, 1995.

_____. *Beyond Release.* Mt. Tabor, NJ: Hohm Press, 1976.

_____. *Chasing Your Tail: Notes That May Be Difficult To Follow On Subjects That May Be Difficult To Grasp.* Prescott, AZ: Hohm Press, 2009.

_____. *The Cheating Buddha.* Prescott Valley, AZ: Hohm Press, 1980.

_____. *Conscious Parenting.* Prescott, AZ: Hohm Press, First edition 1987, revised and expanded 2010.

_____. *Cranky Rants and Bitter Wisdom from One Considered Wise in Some Quarters.* Prescott, AZ: Hohm Press, 2002.

_____. *Death of a Dishonest Man: Poems and Prayers to Yogi Ramsuratkumar.* Prescott, AZ: Hohm Press, 1998.

_____. *Derisive Laughter.* Prescott, AZ: Hohm Press, 1993.

_____. *Eccentricities, Idiosyncrasies, And Sacred Utterances of A Contemporary Western Baul.* Prescott, AZ: Hohm Press, 1991.

_____. *Feast or Famine—Teachings on Mind and Emotions.* Prescott, AZ: Hohm Press, 2008.

_____. *Gasping for Air in a Vacuum: Poems and Prayers to Yogi Ramsuratkumar.* Prescott, AZ: Hohm Press, 2004.

_____. *Getting Real.* Prescott, AZ: Hohm Press, 2004.

_____. *In The Fire.* Mt. Tabor, NJ: Hohm Press, 1978.

_____. *In the Mood of "In the Style of the Eccentricities, Idiosyncracies And Sacred Utterances of A Contemporary Western Baul".* Prescott, AZ: Hohm Press, 1994.

_____. *In the Style of Eccentricities, Idiosyncracies And Sacred Utternaces of A Contemporary Western Baul.* Prescott, AZ: Hohm Press, 1992.

————. *Intimate Secrets of a True Heart Son: Poems and Prayers to Yogi Ramsuratkumar.* Chino Valley, AZ: Hohm Press, 2012.

_____. *Laughter of the Stones.* Prescott Valley, AZ: Hohm Press, 1979.

_____. *Living God Blues.* Prescott Valley, AZ: Hohm Press, 1984.

_____. *Poems of a Broken Heart.* Chennai, India: Sister Nivedita Academy Publication, 1993.

_____. *Spiritual Slavery.* Mt. Tabor, NJ: Hohm Press, 1975.

_____. *The Little Book of Lies and Other Myths.* Prescott, AZ: Hohm Press, 2006.

_____. *The Only Grace is Loving God.* Prescott Valley, AZ: Hohm Press, 1982.

————. *The Other Life: Sketches, Cameos and Photographs* [*Counterpoint to* Spiritual Slavery, *the extensive biography of the years of my Teaching Work under the Auspices of my King and Lord, Yogi Ramsuratkumar*] Prescott, AZ: Hohm Press, 2011.

_____. *Yoga of Enlightenment/The Book of Unenlightenment.* Prescott Valley, AZ: Hohm Press, 1980.

_____. *Zen Gamesmanship: The Art of Bridge.* Prescott Valley, AZ: Hohm Press, 1980.

Lozowick, Lee and M. Young. *Enlightened Duality: Essays on Art, Beauty, Life and Reality As It Is.* Prescott, AZ: Hohm Press, 2009. Available in French and English.

Young, M. *Agony & Alchemy: Sacred Art and Tattoos,* Prescott, AZ: Hohm Press, 2005.

————. *As It Is—A Year on the Road with a Tantric Teacher,* Prescott, AZ: Hohm Press, 2000.

_____. *Caught in the Beloved's Petticoats.* Prescott, AZ: Hohm Press, 2006.

_____. "Introduction to the Lyrics" in *Gasping For Air in a Vacuum.* Prescott, AZ: Hohm Press, 2004.

———— *Spiritual Slavery: A Biography of Lee Lozowick,* Hohm Press, Arizona, 2011.

———— *Yogi Ramsuratkumar—Under the Punnai Tree,* Hohm Press, Arizona, 2003.

Hohm Sahaj Mandir Study Manual, Volumes I and II. Prescott, AZ: Hohm Press, 1996.

Hohm Sahaj Mandir Study Manual, Volumes III and IV. Prescott, AZ: Hohm Press, 2002.

Ashrams

Triveni Ashram (Hohm Sahaj Mandir). Originally established in 1980 in Prescott, Arizona by Lee Lozowick, this ashram sanctuary is now located in the high desert mountains of Arizona near Chino Valley. Triveni Ashram is the location of the samadhi shrine or abode of Lee's body—a sacred place of tremendous spiritual presence, blessing, and peace and the center of the mandala of the Western Baul Sampradaya. Daily *puja, arati,* and chanting the *nama* of Yogi Ramsuratkumar, meditation, *seva* and other traditional rituals are observed along with a weekly Sunday *kirtan* and Darshan program with videos of Lee Lozowick. Formal teachings are given by Lee's core group and other senior students four times a week as well as at other gatherings. Formal celebrations occur several times a year, including the Jayanthi (birthday) of Yogi Ramsuratkumar on December 1 and the birthday and *mahasamadhi* day of Lee Lozowick on November 16 and 18 respectively. For more information, call 928-778-9189.

Triveni Retreat Center. Located in the desert hills adjacent to Triveni Ashram, this retreat center was established by Lee Lozowick in 2000. The tradition of spiritually empowered solitary retreat initiated by Lee is carried on today by his students; the retreat center provides excellent vegetarian meals, an atmosphere of profound sanctuary, and the peace and power of a pristine natural environment in the high desert of central Arizona. Serious retreatants of all spiritual paths are welcome. For more information, call 928-499-0290 or 928-636-4627.

To contact Triveni Ashram or Triveni Retreat by mail:

Hohm Sahaj Mandir
P.O. Box 4410
Chino Valley, Arizona 86323

Ramji Association, France. Called "Ferme de Jutreau," this ashram in the countryside of central France was established by Lee Lozowick in 1995. Daily puja, arati, and chanting the *nama* of Yogi Ramsuratkumar, meditation, seva and other traditional rituals are observed along with a weekly Sunday Darshan program with videos of Lee Lozowick. Formal celebrations occur several times a year, including the Jayanthi (birthday) of Yogi Ramsuratkumar on December 1 and of Lee Lozowick on November 18. The summer schedule at Ferme de Jutreau includes monthly seminars, Guru Purnima, and other times of formal teachings given by Lee's core group and other senior practitioners of the Hohm Community. For the annual schedule of events, contact:

> Ferme de Jutreau
> 86260 Saint Pierre de Maille
> France
> 011 33 5 49 84 57 28
> 011 33 5 49 91 01 43

Triveni II, Hohm Sahaj Trust, Tamil Nadu, India. Established by Lee Lozowick in 1999 at the request of his master, Yogi Ramsuratkumar, this ashram is located one block from the gate of the Yogi Ramsuratkumar Ashram in Tiruvannamalai. A regular schedule of puja, kirtan, meditation, seva, celebrations, charitable activities, and many other events can be obtained by contacting Volker and Ute Augustyniak.

> Hohm Sahaj Trust
> Triveni II
> 95 Chengam Road
> Ramana Nagar
> Tiruvannamalai, India 606603

Trimurti's Sat Loka Ashram. This ashram was established in 2000 near Bozeman, Montana by Purna Steinitz, a long-time student of Lee Lozowick. Daily meditation, arati puja, chanting, community and seva are observed. Regular satsang and teachings are given by Purna as well as weekly Darshan and kirtan programs.

> Trimurti
> P.O. Box 1952
> Bozeman, Montana 59771

Kripa Mandir/Rasa Creek Sanctuary, British Columbia. This sanctuary was established in 2008 by Lalitha, a long-time student of Lee Lozowick. The daily schedule includes meditation, arati puja, chanting, and seva as well as a Sunday evening Darshan program. To contact Kripa Mandir:

Rasa Creek Sanctuary
1871 Trinity Valley Rd
Lumby, BC V0E 2G4